THE
EMAIL
REVOLUTION

Praise for *The Email Revolution*

"V. A. Shiva Ayyadurai is the inventor of email, and his journey reveals a much larger story, one that should be evident by now: innovation can happen anywhere, anytime, by anyone. The sooner we embrace this truth, the sooner our lives will be enriched by the thousands of other 'Shivas' that do not have the luxury of working in the established bastions of innovation, but nevertheless have the intellect and the drive to make big contributions."

—Dr. Leslie P. Michelson, Ph.D.,
Director of High Performance Computing,
UMDNJ, Newark, NJ

"I remember vividly my conversations with Shiva in the early stages of his initiative when he was working hard on the creation and development of email. Knowing the basic concept of what he was creating and the fact that it was so innovative, I and another teacher in our science department recommended that Shiva apply for the Westinghouse Talent Search Award for high school students. Email was to be the electronic version of interoffice mail systems. I specifically remember looking at our school district's Interoffice Mail Envelope and thinking about Shiva's having told me that all the intricacies of this labor intensive system, with its creation, delivery, receipt, and distribution aspects, would one day not be necessary. He had an objective/goal to replace it and other things with his electronic mail. He worked diligently at both his schoolwork and the creation of what we now know as email. Shiva was obviously very successful at both."

—Gerald E. Walker, Shiva's Honors and Advanced Placement
Chemistry Teacher, New Jersey State Teacher of the Year and
Livingston High School Principal (retired).

THE
EMAIL
REVOLUTION

Unleashing the Power to Connect

Dr. V. A. SHIVA AYYADURAI
THE INVENTOR OF EMAIL

ALLWORTH PRESS
NEW YORK

Allworth Press books may be purchased in bulk at special discounts for sales promotion, corporate gifts, fund-raising, or educational purposes. Special editions can also be created to specifications. For details, contact the Special Sales Department, Allworth Press, 307 West 36th Street, 11th Floor, New York, NY 10018 or info@skyhorsepublishing.com.

17 16 15 14 13   5 4 3 2 1

Published by Allworth Press, an imprint of Skyhorse Publishing, Inc.
307 West 36th Street, 11th Floor, New York, NY 10018.
Allworth Press® is a registered trademark of Skyhorse Publishing, Inc.®,
a Delaware corporation.

www.allworth.com

Cover design by Mary Belibasakis
Page composition/typography by SR Desktop Services, Ridge, NY

Library of Congress Cataloging-in-Publication Data is available on file.

ISBN: 978-1-62153-263-7

Printed in the United States of America

————————————

To Amma, God's Angel, who opened the doors of Heaven so I could create

•

To Appa, a Genius and one of the most benevolent people I know,
who taught me to solve incredibly complex problems with creativity
and tenacity

•

To Leslie P. Michelson, who believed and changed my life forever

•

To the Great Unsung Heroes of History, who fought uncompromisingly, with
no guile or cleverness, with pure heart and spirit to unleash freedom, and
whose labors we now enjoy

————————————

Statement of Donation

All of the author's proceeds from this book are donated to Innovation Corps, a project dedicated to unleashing innovation among high school youth in inner cities and villages across the globe.[1]

Statement from a young V. A. Shiva Ayyadurai, in 1981, predicting the future of email

"When Thomas Alva Edison invented the light bulb, he never perceived that his invention would have worldwide attention and acclaim; however, it has. The light bulb is an integral part of our daily living. One day electronic mail, like Edison's light bulb, may also permeate and pervade our daily lives. Its practical applications are unlimited. Not only is mail sent electronically, but it offers a computational service that automates a secretary's or file clerk's work of writing a memorandum, document or letter, editing, filing and retrieving."

```
When Thomas Alva Edison invented the light bulb, he never perceived that his
invention would have such world-wide acceptance and acclaim; however, it has.  The
light bulb is an integral part of our daily living.  One day, electronic mail, like
Edison's bulb, may also permeate and pervade our daily lives.  Its practical appli-
cations are unlimited.  Not only is mail sent electronically, as many telexes and
teletypes are capable of doing, but it offers a computational service that automates
a secretary's or file clerk's work of writing a memorandum, document or letter,
editing, filing, and retrieving.  If electronic mail systems become a reality,
they will surely create different patterns of communication, attitudes, and styles.
Volumes of written work, for example, shall become obsolete.
```

From V. A. Shiva Ayyadurai's Westinghouse Science
Talent Awards application submitted in 1981.

V. A. Shiva Ayyadurai
Writing in 1981 as a High School Teenager
in his Westinghouse Science Awards Application

Contents

> "The United States Postal Service (USPS) forgot their brand,
> a trusted provider of mail, be it print or be it electronic."

PART ONE: WHAT IS EMAIL?

> "Email is the full-scale electronic emulation of the interoffice,
> interorganizational paper-based mail system, a system of
> interlocked parts by which all offices in the world were run by."

> "Hearing those two words 'electronic' and 'mail' juxtaposed in
> 1978 evoked *Star Trek's* transporter dematerializing paper and
> beaming it across the ether."

> "Clinton got email as early as 1993 and used it to build his brand.
> Toyota learned the hard way in 2010 after losing $30 billion in
> market value and 16 percent in sales."

> These ten "commandments" will ensure that you use email
> the right way. They will save you time, money, and a lot of
> heartaches.

PART TWO: THE POWER OF EMAIL

> "By integrating email with broadcast advertising, Nike and
> Calvin Klein created a new type of brand intimacy with
> millions overnight. That was revolutionary!"

> "The Bush campaign was smarter than the Gore campaign.
> They knew what they didn't know. They wanted to use email
> to add muscle to their grassroots tactics."

> "P&G did a brilliant take on email. They used email to
> build participatory and neighborly relations, one at a time,
> pioneering brand understanding in a completely new way."

> "Skin and email are both personal. Email allowed Unilever
> to distinguish their brand as being highly personalized—
> delivering the right product for the right skin."

> "Most of the Senate were afraid of email. It now forced a new
> accountability and transparency they were not ready for.
> Kennedy and Frist embraced it as a part of their brand."

> "Citibank, financial institution, and Cookie Jar, a children's
> entertainment company, both recognized the value of making it safe
> for customers. Their extra efforts created a feeling of trust and care."

> "Hilton and QVC knew one thing: handle email complaints
> right the first time around. They saved money, and ended up
> getting more business from complaining customers."

> "With email, unlike phone calls, making false promises can be dev-
> astating. By using email monitoring, American Express and Allstate
> protected their brands and stopped problems way ahead of time."

> "The Guggenheim mastered email to build membership and
> relationships that serve as a model for arts and nonprofits."

> "The lessons from large organizations using email, nearly a
> decade ago, are now relevant and valuable for any business,
> small, medium, or large."

Foreword

Inventor of Email

*"The facts are black and white.
A fourteen-year-old kid working in Newark, NJ
invented email in 1978."*

I n the summer of 1978, I hired a brilliant young fourteen-year-old teenager, by the name of V. A. Shiva Ayyadurai, to be a Research Fellow in my Laboratory for Computer Science at the University of Medicine and Dentistry of New Jersey (UMDNJ), located in the heart of Newark, New Jersey Shiva was given a challenge: create a computer program that would be the electronic version of UMDNJ's interoffice, interorganizational paper-based mail system. Shiva took on this challenge and created a program of nearly 50,000 lines of computer code, which he called "email." In 1982, he was awarded the first US Copyright for "email," the "computer program for electronic mail system."

Shiva defined email as we all know and use it today, as a system of interlocking parts, consisting of the now-familiar components: Inbox, Outbox, Folders, the Memo ("To:," "From:," "Date:," "Subject:," "Body:," "Cc:," and "Bcc:"), Forwarding, Composing, Drafts, Edit, Reply, Delete, Priorities, Archive, Attachments, Return Receipt, Carbon Copies (including Blind Carbon Copies), Sorting, Address Book, Groups, Bulk Distribution, and hundreds of other components and features, which he implemented based on his direct observations of the office environment at UMDNJ.

The facts are black and white. A fourteen-year-old kid working in Newark, New Jersey, in 1978 invented email. Nearly thirty-four years later, on February 16, 2012, a donation ceremony was held at the Smithsonian Institution in Washington, DC, at the National Museum of American History (NMAH), where Shiva was honored. The Smithsonian Institution accepted into their archives his papers, code samples, and other artifacts, documenting the invention of email.

Immediately following this event, a cabal of "computer historians" and industry insiders unleashed a vicious attack on Shiva. The acceptance of his artifacts into the Smithsonian had thrown a wrench into a revisionist history they had been writing for years about the invention of email.

This cabal of insiders was a fraternity with close ties to Bolt, Beranek and Newman (BBN), a subsidiary of Raytheon, a multibillion dollar military contractor, which had positioned itself as an innovator in the lucrative cyber-security and cyber-warfare industry. BBN had built its entire brand image juxtaposing three elements: the word "innovation"; its logo, the "@" symbol; and its mascot, Ray Tomlinson, who they proclaimed to be the "inventor of email." Ray Tomlinson, however, *did not* invent email. At best, Mr. Tomlinson updated a few lines of code in a pre-existing program or protocol called SNDMSG, admitting that it was "a no brainer—just a minor addition to the protocol." All this did was to enable the exchange of electronic text messages across two computers, while using the "@" symbol as the mnemonic for distinguishing between the two computers.

The simple exchange of electronic text messages, however, *is not* email, just as Twitter, another medium for exchanging electronic text messages, which also uses the "@" symbol, is not email. The simple exchange of electronic text messages dates all the way back to the Morse code telegraph of the 1800s, or the 1939 World's Fair where IBM sent a message of congratulations from San Francisco to New York on an IBM radio-type. If we applied BBN's revisionist definition of "email," then Morse code would also be classified "email." What's even more absurd is that, from an etymological standpoint, the word "email" did not even exist until 1978, when Shiva was the first to coin the term. This fact is substantiated by the Oxford English and the Merriam-Webster dictionaries, which place the modern origin of the word "email" *after* 1978. Moreover, M. A. Padlipsky, a pioneer of electronic messaging in the 1960s and 1970s and a contemporary of Mr. Tomlinson, exposed Ray Tomlinson and BBN's conflated claim in the famous essay,

Shiva's rightful claim threatened BBN at its core. The true history of email could have likely hurt BBN's branding as "innovators," in a market where their brand positioning with Tomlinson as the "inventor of email" had given BBN a potential advantage in the highly competitive cyber-security industry.

What should have been an occasion for celebration turned into a wave of unwarranted, bigoted, and highly coordinated attacks on Shiva. These insiders contacted MIT, Shiva's home institution, and asked for his dismissal. I had followed Shiva's career and achievements over the past three decades. After inventing email, Shiva went on to receive four degrees from MIT, started six different multimillion dollar companies, providing hundreds of jobs to people in the Boston area as well as overseas; he has published numerous academic conference and journal papers, received multiple US patents, and has been a good citizen throughout, fighting for the causes and rights of the underprivileged.

Now, a vocal minority committed to protecting the vested interests of a multimillion dollar brand, was trashing Shiva. This was wrong and unconscionable. This cabal began publishing articles overnight in "peer-reviewed" journals, spreading "scholarly" disinformation on email's true history. It was easy for them to do this as their "old boy" network included editors of these journals. They coordinated with BBN's PR machine to feed the press inaccurate sound bites, and attacked any reporter who wrote favorably about Shiva, dismissing them as ignorant and misinformed. They worked together to remove facts on Wikipedia favorable to Shiva, and even went to the extent of creating the InternetHallOfFame.Org website, one week after the Smithsonian event, where they bestowed Ray Tomlinson with the moniker "inventor of email," while local press deemed him the "king of email."

All of this reaction was within weeks of Shiva's donation ceremony at the Smithsonian. It is quite a process to watch how those in power react when their positions are threatened.

As someone who wanted to share the truth and correct a wrong, I knew we could not compete with these industry insiders. We made a decision to share the truth of that fourteen-year-old boy in 1978, who worked in my lab and *did* in fact invent email, by creating a website called www.inventorofemail.com to publish the facts, along with primary sources, to reach the public directly. We spent many months developing the site, referencing those primary sources, and ensuring the accuracy of all the information. And we were successful. Thousands of people began visiting the site. People who visited the site stayed on and read our content, spending an average of seven minutes, compared to a view time of thirty seconds, which the average Internet site receives.

The insiders responded by calling Shiva self-promotional. How ironic, when here was a multibillion dollar company that had spent millions on creating a false brand image! Our website was built entirely by volunteers. Devon Sparks was one such volunteer who spent many sleepless nights in the MIT library, scouring hundreds of documents dating back to the 1950s. His sincere work would put to shame the so-called scholarly work of "computer historians" who were clearly there to perpetuate a false history and ensure BBN's brand image.

In the midst of this controversy, Devon discovered an important document in an old dusty microfiche in the bowels of MIT's library system, dating back to 1977. The discovery of this document would demonstrate how this cabal was purposefully not revealing historical facts.

What Devon found was a seminal RAND Corporation report entitled *"Framework and Function of the 'MS' Personal Message System,"* authored in December of 1977 by Mr. David Crocker, a former BBN employee, and a part of the cabal waging attacks on Shiva. Mr. Crocker, at the time the document was written, was considered an electronic messaging pioneer. In this report, he summarized the state-of-the-art electronic messaging research. The concluding statements made by Mr. Crocker are perhaps the most revealing. He stated with emphasis:

> At this time (December 1977), no attempt is being made to emulate the full-scale, inter-organization mail system. To construct a fully-detailed and monolithic message-processing environment requires a much larger effort than has been possible. . . . In addition, the fact that the system is intended for use in various organizational contexts and by users of differing expertise, makes it almost impossible to build a system which responds to all users' needs. Consequently, important segments of a full message environment have received little or no attention. . . .

In December of 1977, Mr. Crocker unequivocally stated that electronic messaging researchers had made "no attempt" to emulate the inter-organizational mail system. He further admitted that the creation of such a system was "almost impossible."

However, in 1978, the creation of such a system was precisely Shiva's intention when he joined my laboratory at UMDNJ. In 1978, Shiva did that "impossible" feat, which Mr. Crocker referred to in his RAND report, by attempting to and successfully building a system "which could respond to all users' needs." He did this by becoming the first to create an electronic system which was the full-scale emulation of the interoffice, interorganizational paper-based mail system, with the clear intention "to construct a fully detailed and monolithic message-processing environment" that could be used "in various organizational contexts and by users of differing expertise."

Shiva coined the term "email," which was not so obvious in 1978, and associated that term "email" with the system he built. This is why I say the facts are "black and white."

In the midst of these overwhelming facts, Shiva's detractors resorted to the old strategy epitomized by Harry S. Truman's quote, "If you can't convince them, then confuse them." They attempted to spread confusion by arguing that upper case "EMAIL" is different than lower case "email." The only reason upper case was used by Shiva in referencing "email" was because in 1978, in the FORTRAN language, the programming language in which he created email, all variables and program names had to be in upper case. Noam Chomsky, the great linguist and MIT professor, expressed the absurdity of this argument, in a *Wired* magazine interview on June 16, 2012, entitled "Who Invented Email? Just Ask Noam Chomsky":

> What continue[s] to be deplorable are the childish tantrums of industry insiders who now believe that by creating confusion on the case of 'email,' they can distract attention from the facts. Email, upper case, lower case, any case, is the electronic version of the interoffice, interorganizational mail system, the email we all experience today—and email was invented in 1978 by a 14-year-old working in Newark, NJ. The facts are indisputable.

Moreover, email, Shiva's invention, was not a "no brainer" composed of just a few lines of code, but a system of nearly 50,000 lines of complex software that he wrote single-handedly, which converted the entire paper-based system of creating, delivering, receiving, and processing typewritten interoffice paper memos across UMDNJ's three campuses, into a sophisticated, easy-to-use, highly reliable electronic platform, accessible to hundreds of doctors and secretaries.

Shiva's story is eerily similar to the story of Philo Farnsworth, the thirteen-year-old farm boy who created Television. It took Philo many years of fighting vested interests and industry insiders to ensure that the broad public became aware of the truth of the invention of TV. Thirteen-year-old farm boys and fourteen-year-olds working in inner cities are not supposed to invent anything of signficance, based on the "history" of certain "scholars" who want to perpetuate a narrative that innovation can only take place in big companies, large universities, and the military.

This book, appropriately entitled *The Email Revolution*, will provide you with a firsthand account of Shiva's journey from 1978, when he invented email, to modern times, where he helps the largest brands in the world to understand what email truly is, and how to use it in incredibly creative ways. Once we realize that email is a system that directly emulates the interoffice, interorganizational paper-based mail system, Shiva's contribution becomes crystal clear. There is no gray area in this controversy except the one created by those who wish to profit from misinformation.

V. A. Shiva Ayyadurai is the inventor of email, and his journey reveals a much larger story, one that should be evident by now: innovation can happen anywhere, anytime, by anyone. The sooner we embrace this truth, the sooner our lives will be enriched by the thousands of other "Shivas" that do not have the luxury of working in the established bastions of innovation, but nevertheless have the intellect and the drive to make big contributions.

Dr. Leslie P. Michelson
Director of High Performance Computing Lab
University of Medicine and Dentisty of New Jersey (UMDNJ)
Newark, NJ

Statement from Noam Chomsky

"The efforts to belittle the innovation of a fourteen-year-old child should lead to reflection on the larger story of how power is gained, maintained, and expanded. . . ."

The angry reaction to the news of Shiva's invention of email and the steps taken to belittle the achievement are most unfortunate. They suggest an effort to dismiss the fact that innovation can take place by anyone, in any place, at any time. And they highlight the need to ensure that innovation must not be monopolized by those with power—power which, incidentally, is substantially a public gift.

The efforts to belittle the innovation of a fourteen-year-old child should lead to reflection on the larger story of how power is gained, maintained, and expanded, and the need to encourage, not undermine, the capacities for creative inquiry that are widely shared and could flourish, if recognized and given the support they deserve.

Prof. Noam Chomsky
Massachusetts Institute of Technology
Department of Linguistics and Philosophy
Cambridge, MA

Personal Note

In 1978, I was fourteen years old. I loved the New York Yankees. Chris Chambliss and Graig Nettles were my heroes. Baseball and soccer were two of my loves, and I was good enough to make the high school varsity teams in both sports. My other love was mathematics. My parents' home was filled with math books ranging from number theory to topology to calculus. Next to my baseball cards on my dresser were the latest set of math books I was reading. In math, I found a way to structure numbers and find beauty, very much as I suppose how a musician finds beauty in providing order to sets of musical notes.

In the spring of 1978, my mother, Meenakshi Ayyadurai, had a coworker, a mathematician, by the name of Martin Feuerman, who informed her about a special educational program being offered at the Courant Institute of Mathematical Sciences at New York University (NYU). The program was organized by a visionary, Professor Henry Mullish, who wanted to provide high school students with an opportunity to learn computer programming. I was fortunate enough to be one of the forty students who got accepted to this program. The excitement was beyond words—attending the Courant Institute and being in New York City, at the same time. I felt as though I was the luckiest person in the world.

After I finished the intensive course at NYU, where I learned seven different programming languages, my mother was excited to see that I had an aptitude for the new technology, and introduced me to Dr. Leslie P. Michelson, who taught at the University of Medicine and Dentistry of New Jersey (UMDNJ), in Newark, New Jersey, where she worked.

Dr. Michelson challenged me to find a solution to an office technology problem. The doctors in the medical school were starting to use computers, but they were still isolated from each other—so much so that they still used a hand-delivered interoffice paper mail system. He wanted to know if I could invent a computer program that would be an electronic version of the paper-based mail system. This challenge became my obsession. For three years, I dedicated all of my free time to working on this problem.

Dr. Michelson provided me with access to their three HP 1000 minicomputers, a network connection called DS1000 IV, the FORTRAN IV programming language, a CRT terminal, and the RTE-IV relational database. But he did more than that. Because my family had emigrated from India to Paterson, New Jersey, I saw America from the viewpoint of the disadvantaged. After we arrived, my mother started work in a factory. All around me, I saw impoverishment, racism, and social barriers. But Dr. Michelson and his colleagues, though decades older, treated me with respect, collegiality, and kindness. I was given the chance to innovate, and I was successful.

First, I studied how the existing system processed and transported paper mail between offices dispersed across the three separate locations of UMDNJ's campus. Then I set out to duplicate these features in a computer program. What resulted was that UMDNJ, a small school in an impoverished city, had an electronic version of its entire interoffice, paper-based mail system. My creation provided them with the first, easy-to-use user interface with an onboard Word Processor and Editor to view and edit the To:, From:, Date:, Subject:, Body:, Cc:, and Bcc: fields and the ability to link with attachments. I used a modular architecture to ensure reliable and secure transfer, and provided all of the other interoffice mail features, such as Inbox, Outbox, and Drafts folders, as well as an Address Book for managing one's directory of contacts, among a host of nearly one hundred other features that today we take for granted in email programs such as Gmail and Hotmail.

I called my program "email." I selected this name for the very idiosyncratic reason that in 1978 FORTRAN IV only allowed for a six-character maximum variable and five-character subroutine naming convention. On January 21, 1981, I received a Westinghouse Science Talent Search Honors Award for creating email.

In the fall of 1981, I was accepted to MIT. When I arrived on campus in September of 1981, I recall the front page of MIT's official newspaper *Tech Talk*, highlighting three achievements of the 1,040 incoming students. One of those was mine, referring to the email system I had created at UMDNJ. A few days later, I was elected Freshman body student President, and one evening I was invited to MIT President Dr. Paul E. Gray's house for dinner. In conversation, Dr. Gray shared with me how unfortunate it was that the Supreme Court had not understood what software patents were. However, he encouraged me to file Copyrights to protect my invention of email, as Copyright was the only vehicle at that time to protect software authorship. Dr. Gray's advice would prove to be important in the many years to come.

On August 30, 1982, I was awarded the first US Copyright for creating "email," the "computer program for electronic mail system." The issuance of that Copyright was the culmination of my "first life" with email, as its inventor in 1978.

CERTIFICATE OF COPYRIGHT REGISTRATION

FORM TX
UNITED STATES COPYRIGHT OFFICE

This certificate, issued under the seal of the Copyright Office in accordance with the provisions of section 410(a) of title 17, United States Code. attests that copyright registration has been made for the work identified below. The information in this certificate has been made a part of the Copyright Office records.

REGISTRATION NUMBER
TXu **111-775**

TX   TXU
EFFECTIVE DATE OF REGISTRATION

David Ladd

REGISTER OF COPYRIGHTS
United States of America

8   30   82
Month   Day   Year

OFFICIAL SEAL

DO NOT WRITE ABOVE THIS LINE. IF YOU NEED MORE SPACE, USE A SEPARATE CONTINUATION SHEET.

1

TITLE OF THIS WORK ▼

EMAIL

PREVIOUS OR ALTERNATIVE TITLES ▼

COMPUTER PROGRAM FOR Electronic Mail System

PUBLICATION AS A CONTRIBUTION If this work was published as a contribution to a periodical, serial, or collection, give information about the collective work in which the contribution appeared.   Title of Collective Work ▼

If published in a periodical or serial give: Volume ▼   Number ▼   Issue Date ▼   On Pages ▼

2

NOTE

Under the law, the "author" of a "work made for hire" is generally the employer, not the employee (see instructions). For any part of this work that was "made for hire" check "Yes" in the space provided, give the employer (or other person for whom the work was prepared) as "Author" of that part, and leave the space for dates of birth and death blank.

a NAME OF AUTHOR ▼

MR. SHIVA AYYADURAI

DATES OF BIRTH AND DEATH
Year Born ▼   Year Died ▼
1963

Was this contribution to the work a "work made for hire"?
☐ Yes
☐ No

AUTHOR'S NATIONALITY OR DOMICILE
Name of Country
OR { Citizen of ▶
Domiciled in ▶ UNITED STATES

WAS THIS AUTHOR'S CONTRIBUTION TO THE WORK
Anonymous?   ☐ Yes ☒ No
Pseudonymous?   ☐ Yes ☒ No
If the answer to either of these questions is "Yes," see detailed instructions.

NATURE OF AUTHORSHIP Briefly describe nature of the material created by this author in which copyright is claimed. ▼

Created and Wrote entire text of the computer program:

b NAME OF AUTHOR ▼

DATES OF BIRTH AND DEATH
Year Born ▼   Year Died ▼

Was this contribution to the work a "work made for hire"?
☐ Yes
☐ No

AUTHOR'S NATIONALITY OR DOMICILE
Name of Country
OR { Citizen of ▶
Domiciled in ▶

WAS THIS AUTHOR'S CONTRIBUTION TO THE WORK
Anonymous?   ☐ Yes ☐ No
Pseudonymous?   ☐ Yes ☐ No

NATURE OF AUTHORSHIP Briefly describe nature of the material created by this author in which copyright is claimed. ▼

c NAME OF AUTHOR ▼

DATES OF BIRTH AND DEATH
Year Born ▼   Year Died ▼

Was this contribution to the work a "work made for hire"?
☐ Yes
☐ No

AUTHOR'S NATIONALITY OR DOMICILE
Name of Country
OR { Citizen of ▶
Domiciled in ▶

WAS THIS AUTHOR'S CONTRIBUTION TO THE WORK
Anonymous?   ☐ Yes ☐ No
Pseudonymous?   ☐ Yes ☐ No

NATURE OF AUTHORSHIP Briefly describe nature of the material created by this author in which copyright is claimed. ▼

3

YEAR IN WHICH CREATION OF THIS WORK WAS COMPLETED This information must be given in all cases.
1981 ◀ Year

DATE AND NATION OF FIRST PUBLICATION OF THIS PARTICULAR WORK
Complete this information ONLY if this work has been published.
Month ▶   Day ▶   Year ▶   ◀ Nation

4

COPYRIGHT CLAIMANT(S) Name and address must be given even if the claimant is the same as the author given in space 2.▼

Mr. SHIVA AYYADURAI
7 BAKER ROAD
LIVINGSTON, NJ 07039

APPLICATION RECEIVED
01 DEC 1982   8/30/82
ONE DEPOSIT RECEIVED   8/30/82
TWO DEPOSITS RECEIVED

TRANSFER If the claimant(s) named here in space 4 are different from the author(s) named in space 2, give a brief statement of how the claimant(s) obtained ownership of the copyright.▼

NONE

REMITTANCE NUMBER AND DATE
353381 - 8/30/82

MORE ON BACK ▶

My second life with email, a bit more serendipitous, started in 1993, nearly fifteen years later, when I was asked to participate in a competition sponsored by the Executive Office of the United States White House to automatically analyze and sort email messages being received by then President Clinton. In 1993, I was in the midst of my PhD program at MIT. I was the only graduate student to participate in this competition; the other competitors were established companies. I won the contest and subsequently created EchoMail, ironically, a software system to manage a problem that my earlier invention had caused: the growing volume of inbound email messages.

EchoMail became the leading provider of email management and email marketing services to Global 2000 companies. As Chairman and CEO of EchoMail, Inc., I kept detailed notes on my experiences of helping some of the largest brands in the world leverage email in unique ways appropriate to their business. However, it was not until 2011, following news of the potential demise of the United States Postal Service (USPS), that I decided to write and complete this book. It became clear to me that the USPS, which should have embraced email as a way to generate revenue when I had advised them in 1997, did not, because there was a fundamental confusion concerning the definition of "email."

My intention in writing this book was to provide clarity on many things related to email: clarity on the history of email, clarity on what email is, clarity on how it differs from social media, and clarity on the fact that email is here to stay with us for a long time. I hope that this clarity will enable you to use email in very practical and yet creative ways to build one-on-one relationships, be it with your partners, friends, customers, prospects, constituents, or voters.

Email is very personal. When someone gives you their email address, they are inviting you into their lives. This invitation is very different than becoming their "Friend" or "Follower" on a social media page. It is far more personal. The email address can be stored in your contact list or database, and to that email address you can add other personal information, such as their birthdate, personal information, and their likes or dislikes. The data can be used to continue ongoing interactions with them in a more personalized manner. The nature of these interactions can either enhance or diminish the relationship between you and that individual. In this book, my goal was to provide you with a diverse range of case studies to demonstrate how versatile email is, and the many ways in which brands have used email to connect and develop relationships.

In sharing the personal story of inventing email, my goal is to convey the real origin and nature of email so you can see how it is different from other media. Another goal is to inspire young people with the larger truth, that innovation can take place anywhere, anytime, by anybody.

On February 16, 2012, a month after my mom had passed away, my papers, computer code, and artifacts documenting the invention of email were accepted into the Smithsonian Institution. I wish my mom had been there, because without her neither email nor this book would have been possible.

For me, email is very personal. I hope this book allows you to find how personal email can be, and realize its unique nature in building brand and creating real connections.

V. A. Shiva Ayyadurai
Belmont, Massachusetts

Introduction

Email Is Dead?

"The United States Postal Service (USPS) forgot their brand, a trusted provider of mail, be it print or electronic."

"**M**ark [Zuckerberg] is full of $#&*!"

That was my response to Lora Kolodny, technology editor at *Fast Company*, in an August 2011 interview, to the CEO of Facebook Mark Zuckerberg's comment that "Email is Dead." That month, news on email was everywhere. Zuckerberg was predicting email's death, while the twenty-ninth anniversary of email's birth was around the corner on August 30th. And, the United States Postal Service (USPS) was blaming email for its potential demise.

Amidst all of this confusion, Lora was writing an article on the future of the USPS and Email, and wanted my perspective as the inventor of email. News had come out that the USPS was in dire straits, almost bankrupt, and about to lay off 100,000 workers. My blog in 2011 had expressed a critique of such lay-offs and also shared concerns that the USPS should have embraced email far earlier. In 1997, nearly twenty years before, my advice to USPS senior officials that they offer USPS branded email services to small and mid-market companies had fallen on deaf ears. And, I still felt strongly the USPS could provide those email services and rebuild itself in the innovative spirit of one of its founders, Benjamin Franklin, versus being self-destructive by simply firing postal workers and closing post offices, which in my opinion are the most valuable assets of the USPS. The 500,000 workers of the USPS are an incredible door-to-door, customer-facing sales force, which has direct access to nearly every American. Zuckerberg's public relations blitz for his new offering @Facebook, meanwhile, was sending shock waves, with headlines that the new Facebook would kill email. Such comments were adding to the confusion and raising a fundamental question. Was email dead . . . or alive?

USPS and Facebook Both Hate Email

The rise of social media was making email seem "uncool," which Zuckerberg liked. His goal was to reframe Facebook as the new platform for communication, better than email, to gain mind share over his rival, Google's Gmail and the emerging Google+ platforms. Hundreds of articles and books were being published promoting the idea that social media helped to build friendships and establish branding. As that noise grew, email, the elder child of digital text-based communications, was being put in the back seat, a successful strategy for the champions of social media. However, the reality of social media was also beginning to emerge. How could a Facebook user, who perhaps was a social misfit or recluse in the offline world, suddenly develop 3,000 "friends" overnight in the online world of social media on Facebook? What was the nature of those relationships? New research from the realms of social psychology revealed an alarming and growing rate of disconnection, loneliness, narcissism, and voyeurism among users of social media platforms. Data seemed to indicate those connections were ones with minimal intimacy, at best. Major brands, primarily reliant on this new media, appeared *not* to be grounded in any deep value exchange. Social media did however seem to serve the important purpose of building networks of like-minded individuals. These "social networks" were valuable for more collective activities (e.g., organizing the Arab Spring uprisings, group purchasing) not easily afforded by the intimacy of email. Email had its place and so did social media. When one took an objective look, it was clear that one was not going to replace the other. However, in the midst of all the contradictory news on email, it was hard to be objective. The differences between email and social media would need to be understood in order to overcome the confusion and to learn the appropriate use of each medium.

One thing common between Zuckerberg and the management at USPS was this: they both hated email. Email was problematic. Zuckerberg and the USPS took different approaches to deal with this problem. Facebook took the approach of "if you can't beat them, join them," though publicly they presented a different face. Zuckerberg cleverly absorbed email's features into his new @Facebook, while simultaneously claiming that email was dead, as a public relations ploy to distinguish Facebook from Gmail and Google+, whose mainstay was email. The USPS, on the other hand, was neither clever nor strategic. They simply chose to ignore email. In 1997, I was asked to present an educational lecture to senior USPS officials on the implications of email, something that I had routinely done for other senior executives in large companies. That year, email volume had just over-taken snail mail volume. I offered a strategy along with a scenario in which the USPS could create a suite of email services, which they could distribute to small and mid-market businesses. My view was that the USPS was fundamentally in the broader *mail* business, not just the print postal letter business. Their 200-plus-year history of delivering mail, along with a wonderfully well-known and trusted brand—"Neither rain, nor heat, nor snow, nor gloom of night shall stay these couriers from the swift completion of their appointed rounds"—would have made the sale of email services relatively easy to their already existing customer base of small and mid-market businesses. What better organization to bring *electronic* mail services to their tens of millions of *print* mail business customers?

However, the attitude of senior officials at the USPS was one of recalcitrance. The party line of the USPS bosses in 1997 was that they were a $50 billion organi-zation, bigger than Walmart, and did not need to venture into something so risky as email. Fifteen years later, in 2012, the effects of that recalcitrance were clear. Snail mail volume had declined by more than 43 billion pieces five years prior to 2012 and was continuing to decline. Letters bearing postage stamps had declined 36 percent in the same time frame, and nearly 50 percent in the ten years prior to 2012. The USPS bosses' response to this decline was classic: downsize. Nearly 250 processing facilities were closed or consolidated as a part of this "bold" and "innovative" strategy (as they had branded it). In addition, they reduced mail processing equipment by as much as 50 percent, as well as dramatically reducing the USPS's nationwide transportation network. All of this resulted in their fiscal solution: the firing of 35,000 workers.

What was going to be their next bold and innovative move? Fire another 70,000 to 80,000 workers and shut down more facilities and reduce more delivery services?

Innovation Is the Key

Benjamin Franklin would not have been happy. He would likely have done some firings of his own, starting with the USPS bosses for their ineptitude. The USPS forgot their branding as a *trusted* provider of mail, be it print or electronic. This memory loss was the management's biggest failure, leading to the situation in 2012, where the entire future of the USPS was now in question. No one would ever have thought such a future was even in the realm of possibility—America's oldest institution was on the path to being wiped out. A failure to change and innovate, to live up to its true brand promise, had caused this fiasco. The irony of this was that Franklin, who helped to envision and implement the USPS, was one of the world's greatest innovators. His visionary leadership was a far cry from the leadership of the current USPS bean counters, committed to maintaining their turf in a declining world of postal print mail. The writing was on the wall as early as 1997. The world had transformed from print to electronic, and these highly paid executives, with teams of research analysts paid to watch future trends, simply and consciously chose to ignore email—for fifteen years!

Though my frustration with the USPS bosses was significant, I did have a solution. It was obvious: *the USPS should own email.* Such ownership would enable the USPS to offer a suite of services not only to protect the public's interest in private email transactions, but also to create a whole new set of job opportunities for the postal workers.

This solution may initially appear dissonant when compared to the current postal worker's job of handling print mail; however, when one really understands what email is (as we will do in part 1 of this book), and when one looks at what the USPS is, this solution is obvious. For me, as the inventor of email and as the founder of EchoMail, I not only knew what email was but also knew that there was a massive need for managing the growing volumes of inbound email to companies of all sizes. At EchoMail, we had built a large multimillion dollar business addressing this need for large Global 2000 customers. I had worked with some of the largest brands in the world including Nike, Citigroup, Calvin Klein, Procter & Gamble, and others to help them define their brands in the digital world using email. They used email as a medium to build one-on-one relationships; that was not possible with social media (as we will show in the detailed case studies in part 2 of this book). It was clear to me that millions of smaller companies could also benefit from the power of email to build and sustain their brands. This was in the realm of the USPS, which had access to those tens of millions of small, mid- and large-size companies. In my 1997 educational lecture to the USPS, I had shared with them how they could provide email services with minimal changes to their existing USPS infrastructure, and with relatively minimal retraining of their postal workers.

USPS Can Provide an Email Service, Truly Secure and Private

There are many ways in which the USPS can provide email services. There are two that are important to discuss.

First, the USPS can offer email, much the same way Google and Hotmail offer it today, as a public service. However, the USPS's offering of email, if implemented through the body of existing laws which ensure privacy in the transaction of postal mail, could provide an email service that doesn't compromise privacy as it happens currently when we use commercial services such as Google, Hotmail, and others. When I invented email in 1978, there was never any intention of creating a commercial company to offer email as a software platform. At that time, it was all about innovation and creating something new, and getting users to use the system—that was satisfying beyond belief. However, after my invention, email became a commercial tool, and with that, we as citizens made some significant compromises to our own privacy, as we started using "free" email services.

The USPS is in a unique postion to provision and offer email as a service to all citizens to ensure privacy and security, which the private email providers such as Hotmail, Google, and Yahoo cannot. When we sign up to those services, we give up our privacy and tell them that they have the right to tamper with the contents of our email, our electronic letters. We would never think of giving such rights away to anyone to open and read our postal letters. The USPS ensures that this does not happen. There is a whole body of law, hard fought, which ensures that citizens' mail is not tampered with

The USPS is poised, if it takes ownership of email, to ensure that such privacy and security are maintained for email. Gmail, Yahoo, Hotmail, and others profit by reading our email! They have full rights to read the content, and today reuse that content to deliver advertising. We have given up our privacy to these private organizations in return for their "free" email services. I believe when we become aware of the implications of this implicit transfer of rights, we will recognize the importance of privacy and real security, and realize the need for email to be provided as a civic function not dissimilar to the highways and public water systems.

USPS Can Offer Email Management

The USPS can also offer another important and valuable service: Email Management. Email management services can be offered to small and mid-market businesses, which would likely pay as little as $1 to process an email. The thought of postal workers, who previously processed postal print mail, now processing email may initially sound odd. When one considers how many companies are routinely outsourcing their email processing to companies in India and the Philippines, who have built teams of "electronic" postal workers to process email, the opportunity will not sound that odd. If you send an email to a major credit card company, for example, where does it go? It goes to email processing centers in places like India or the Philippines, where in conjunction with intelligent technology, which can do sorting and analysis of the email, your email is then opened and read by humans, who review and respond to the incoming email. If you go to the website of American Express and fill out a complaint or a question on their "Contact Us" form, or directly send an email to the email address support@aexp.com, that email is routed to email "postal" workers, based in India, for example, who are opening, sorting, routing, and processing your confidential email, with your personal information and financial details. Sounds a lot like what USPS workers were trained to do with postal mail. While USPS workers today do not actually open up your postal mail, there is an entire infrastructure within the USPS designed to do such processing more securely and in a trusted manner. Think about it. Would you rather have someone half-way around the world processing your email, or the USPS, which has a long and trusted history of processing mail, long before the founding of the United States? What doesn't make sense is why the USPS is not offering those email services using USPS workers, who are perfectly trained with the right core values of trust and integrity to do the same job.

Think about this: corruption in developing nations such as India is rampant. It would not be that hard for a competitor to your company's business, for example, to pay a few extra rupees to some nineteen-year-old email worker in Gurgaon, India, to download all your customers' email. The trusted brand of the USPS, across its 500,000 workers, however, provides a policing force through the USPS Office of the Inspector General (OIG) to monitor, deter, and prosecute such incidents. We, as consumers, would never think of such a situation when it came to the USPS worker. These USPS workers have been trained, imbued by more than 200 years of experience with the mail service ethos of respecting confidentiality, and know how to handle the mechanics of sorting, handling, and delivery. For $1 apiece, smaller enterprises in local communities could hire USPS people to manage their email. USPS workers could be situated in their existing local post office locations, manage, analyze responses, and send responses based upon predetermined answers. The value to those enterprises using such a professional service would be immense. Nearly 70 percent of companies today do not respond to email effectively. Research shows that if one does not respond back to email, there is nearly an 85 percent chance of losing a customer for good. We all know our postal workers can be trusted and counted upon to be timely. They never miss a heartbeat delivering the mail. In this solution, rather than fire 100,000 workers, close down half the nation's 461 mail processing centers, end Saturday delivery, and raise postage rates, with about two weeks of instruction the USPS could retrain an employee to be a knowledgeable worker, as India and the Philippines are doing, to handle email, scan and process documents, and do things they already know how to do.

USPS OIG Gets the Value of Email

Benjamin Franklin, and other forefathers of the printed word, had already done the hard job of designing and implementing the USPS production system of mail pickup and delivery; and more importantly, they had established a deep and trusted cultural ethos, a core part of its brand today. That postal infrastructure framework is ready to be used for email. The USPS already possesses everything necessary to include email in its services. In spite of the logic of the two solutions mentioned above, my personal attempts in 2011 to reach out to USPS were not getting anywhere. However, in November 2011, a feature article in *Fast Company* magazine appeared, in which I related the accurate history of my creating email, and how email was different from TXT, SMS, and other forms of digital text-based communication. More importantly, in that article, I once again attacked the USPS bosses for their ineptitude in embracing email. That attack in *Fast Company* magazine finally resulted in my receiving a call from the USPS OIG. The OIG is the ombudsman for the American public, overseeing and auditing the functions of the USPS.

The OIG, like me, wanted to save the USPS and was seeking and willing to explore innovative and even out-of-the-box solutions. In my discussion with them, the focus was on getting back to basics: What is Email? and why should the USPS be in the mail business, be it print or electronic? The OIG sincerely seemed to understand. That strategy demanded that the USPS live up to its brand promise of being a provider of mail services—print or electronic. Even if the OIG supported my recommendations, the USPS bosses could turn a deaf ear and did not have to implement those recommendations. In late 2012, my research center, the International Center for Integrative Systems (ICIS), was commissioned by the OIG to write a detailed report on how Email Management could generate new revenues for the USPS. The nearly sixty-page report was accepted by the OIG. The report projected, conservatively, that the USPS could generate $250 million in additional revenue annually by providing email management services. Did USPS officials do anything with this report? Ultimately, only when the public becomes fully aware of the importance of the USPS as a foundation of American democracy and innovation and raises a massive outcry, will the USPS management fall in line and fulfill the brand promise of this amazing institution.

Saving the USPS Is About Innovation and Freedom

For me, helping the USPS was a personal endeavor. My own struggle against the corrupt Indian government in 2009 to unleash freedom for Indian scientists to innovate had taught me the close link between innovation and freedom. In 2008, I had gone to India on a Fulbright Scholarship Program to study traditional systems of Indian medicine from the perspective of modern systems biology. After completing my Fulbright Scholarship Program in India, I was recruited by the Office of the Prime Minister of India to head up a new initiative within the Council of Scientific and Industrial Research (CSIR), India's largest scientific institution, to drive innovation among its 4,500 scientists across nearly forty national laboratories. CSIR was set up by Jawaharlal Nehru, India's first prime minister, to be a translational institute to create tangible technologies and solutions to serve the broader masses of Indians. However, after nearly seventy years, it had devolved into an organization publishing papers, many of questionable integrity, and filing patents, less than 10 percent of which were of any value, creating an archaic system of promotion, which failed to promote the original mission of Jawaharlal Nehru: to innovate new technologies to serve the masses of Indians. During those nearly seven decades, CSIR had degenerated, producing only $2 million in revenue from its patents, less than $25,000 a year, while consuming billions of dollars of the public's money. Significant portions of it were routed through illicit means for self-serving purposes. What I witnessed, as I traveled across these labs and met nearly 1,500 scientists, was a consistent theme: the lab structure was set up as a continuation of the feudal system left by British colonialism. There were many incredibly smart scientists and innovators who were trapped by this feudal and oppressive leadership structure.

If one studies Indian history carefully (as I had the opportunity to do while an undergraduate at MIT with Noam Chomsky), it becomes clear that India never really got Independence. Instead, India transferred power from "white men who wore crowns" to "brown men who wore white hats," as denoted by the *Transfer of Power* documents signed between the new Indian ruling elite and their British brethren. Unlike America, there was no Declaration of Independence, clearly defining a new nation independent of the British crown. The Indian bureaucrats continued to run India's internal machinery in the same resolute manner as the British feudal system of patronage, at best making India a flawed democracy, with little transparency and openness, the necessary ingredients for innovation.

The labs within CSIR reflected this. And this is why relatively little innovation was taking place in those labs. Consider this, that since the so-called Indian Independence of 1947, for nearly seven decades, not one Indian scientist had won a Nobel Prize *while living in India*. Ironically, the two Indian scientists who won Nobel Prizes, while living in India, won them during the pre-Independence era, prior to 1947, during the British occupation of India! It is only after leaving India and migrating to America that Indian scientists seemed to flourish from the fundamental and relatively greater freedoms and merit-based system afforded by the American way of democracy. Har Gobind Khorana, an MIT professor, for example, was not even able to get a job as an instructor in an Indian educational institution. After coming to America, Khorana not only became a full professor at MIT, but also went on to win the Nobel Prize in Medicine. There are many such stories.

In October of 2009, after my deep frustration with CSIR and in solidarity with the 4,500 scientists of India, I published a report called "The Path Forward," describing what I had observed within the CSIR: the rampant corruption, the feudal order which suppressed the creativity and innovative capabilities of brilliant scientists, a system which recognized obsequiousness over competence, and barriers that inhibited the ability for innovation to be translated to the public. Within moments of publishing this report I was fired from my post, ousted from my government house, and I was literally forced to flee India, through Nepal, Katmandu, to Qatar, and back to the States, under threat of physical violence as well as incarceration. So much for freedom in India! So much for innovation! Subsequently, I wrote an invited Commentary article for India's *Nature* magazine, entitled "Innovation Demands Freedom: Why America Innovates and India May Never," in which I laid out my thesis that without Freedom there cannot be innovation in India, along with the details of the corrupt behavior I had observed. The Indian government banned this article and demanded that *Nature* remove it, under threat of a libel suit. *Nature*, fearful of libel laws in the United Kingdom, complied. However, by then, the article was across the Internet for everyone to read.

So for me the USPS was an amazing institution—representing the fusion of innovation and freedom. From my experience in India, the failure of the USPS would be significant—it would send a global and reactionary signal, and deal a blow to those core elements of innovation and freedom inherent to the foundations of America's inspiring developments in science, technology, and the arts. The USPS had to re-innovate itself, for it was not just a mail communications company but also a symbol of that freedom and democracy. The USPS was borne out of the American revolutionary war against British colonialism, as a need to communicate orders and information to Patriots across the thirteen colonies, and it afforded each citizen the incredible services of the postal mail system, where every citizen could communicate across space and time, connect with loved ones, business associates, and friends, for pennies, no matter where they lived or what their background. Such an institution was about providing the fundamental tool of democracy: the right to communicate freely. The trusted brand of the USPS made each of us feel comfortable, knowing any mail we sent or received was handled with care and security. Our local postal worker was a symbol of that trust that implicitly connected each citizen directly to the fabric of the hard-fought gains of the American Revolution.

The USPS Still Can Innovate

However, unlike Benjamin Franklin and other American revolutionaries, Postmaster General Donahoe, in 2012—a thirty-five-year veteran of the US Postal Service who managed the organization primarily using fiscal solutions instead of through vision or innovation—did not really understand the depth of the USPS as that shining pillar of innovation and freedom. Throughout the decades, when email began to cannibalize snail mail, in a new world where email and information technology were rising, and snail mail would predictably decline, he never chose to lead the USPS away from the physical and into the digital. He emphasized services like Priority Mail and First Class Mail as revenue generators instead. USPS officials were happy to be generating revenue from their consistent portfolio of products. But email was right there for them to own, had they wanted it and had they wanted to fulfill the USPS brand promise. Email was postal mail in electronic form, the "electronic letter," being received, sorted, transmitted, and done with reliability, speed, and efficiency—the core rubric of the USPS's core functions of processing mail. Instead, the USPS saw themselves not as a communications organization, but as a narrow paper mail delivery company.

Lora asked me during that *Fast Company* magazine interview was, "Is it too late for the USPS to capitalize on email now?" I still felt that there was time, given the sheer size of the USPS and the existing infrastructure of personnel and real estate. The USPS, because of its trusted brand position, could still offer email services, such as the email management service described above, to millions of businesses overnight, generating enough revenue to cover costs and make a profit without layoffs. In addition, the USPS could also lead the charge in other email services such as email validation to solve a host of problems being faced by email marketers. Such service would drastically reduce the spam in our inboxes.

Email Has Nine Lives

Within the context of Zuckerberg's strategic moves, and the USPS's slowness to act, there was a deeper issue: a *zeitgeist of misunderstanding* of what email really was. We all used email like we drink water. However, a fundamental misunderstanding of what email really was existed in nearly everyone's psyche. This ignorance of email was the source of the confusion and why Zuckerberg or others were able to get away with comments of "Email is Dead." This ignorance was also the reason why brands like the USPS and other companies failed to use email appropriately. Email was becoming indistinguishable from other digital text-based communications (real-time chat, text messaging, SMS, Twitter, online forums, discussion threads, blogs, and wall posts) because of that ignorance and misuse of the term email, in all its variations, to refer to "electronic messaging," and the lack of clear distinguishing between email as the platform, and email as the medium which flowed between email platforms.

The trend of predicting email's death was not new. I recall how industry analysts, experts who are paid to watch and predict trends, as early as 1997, had started to proclaim that email was dead, with the emergence of each new form of digital text-based communications. For example, in the late 1990s, they were sure that real-time chat services would replace email and boldly declared email's imminent death. Since then, there has been a consistent stream of news heralding the death knell of email at the inception of each one of those new mediums. When SMS grew, in early 2000, again email's death was predicted. Zuckerberg's proclamations were in that same lineage. However (a big however), he was far more clever than other industry experts. He had an ulterior motive in riding and promoting the death knell of the email story. While he was declaring that email was dead, he was fully integrating email into Facebook, to foster what he called *conversation*, recognizing that email was necessary (had the stickiness factor) to keep his viewership from moving to Google+, which was Google's response to Facebook; and with Google+, Google was in turn integrating social media features into their pervasive email application Gmail. Zuckerberg's comment that email was dead was really not about email's dying, but about attacking Gmail, which dominated email services. What he was really trying to say was that he hoped Google would die, once he incorporated email into Facebook. Zuckerberg, unlike the industry analysts who were truly misinformed about email, knew the power of email and the fact that social media needed email, which was why he incorporated email into Facebook.

Email Is Here to Stay for a Long, Long Time

Mark Zuckerberg's comments and events surrounding the USPS situation are what compelled me to complete this book, though many chapters were in process for nearly a decade. That urgency was not out of some parochial or possessive interest to save email, as its inventor. My intention was to inform you, to help you understand what email really is on a much deeper level, and for you to recognize its unique power for branding and building connections, so you can rediscover the medium in a completely new way, and realize why organizations such as the USPS should be providing email as an important civic function to protect our democracy. My hope is that you will realize that email is here to stay for a long, long time and recognize its immense power for building true connections, and that email offers ways to strengthen and to extend your brand, through the intimate and formal conversations that email uniquely affords.

In part 1, "What Is Email?" we begin our journey. Part 1 opens with chapter 1, entitled "Smoke Signals to Email," to explore the history of messaging, to place email within its modern context, and to understand how it differs from other media, for which it has been historically confused. In chapter 2, "Electrified Paper," I share my adventure, starting as a fourteen-year-old in 1978, at the University of Medicine and Dentistry of New Jersey (UMDNJ) in Newark, New Jersey, challenged to create the world's first email system, by translating the interoffice postal mail system to its electronic equivalent. That adventure leads us to chapter 3, "The Pulse of Email," and to the world of modern email, starting in 1993 as the World Wide Web (WWW) comes into being, making the Internet accessible to billions of people. Even in 1993, long before email volume overtook snail mail volume, there were those who really understood email for what it was—one of these people was former President Bill Clinton, who should have passed his understanding on to the USPS. President Clinton had an intuitive grasp of the value of email as a vehicle to connect with constituents and build a brand. His understanding is contrasted with that of a major corporate brand such as Toyota, who learned about email too late, costing them billions. Part 1 ends with chapter 4, "The Ten Commandments of Email," which offers a convenient summary of ten key principles of email.

In part 2, "The Power of Email," we present eleven chapters. Chapter 5 through chapter 12 provide a detailed account of how some of the leading companies such as Nike, Calvin Klein, American Express, Allstate, Citigroup, Hilton Hotels, QVC, and public figures such as Senators Ted Kennedy and Bill Frist, and even former President George W. Bush, used email to build brand in ways that few of us still exploit. Chapter 13 shows how the Guggenheim Museum, a leading arts and nonprofit organization, uses email to build relationships and memberships. Those stories will inspire you and hopefully get your own creative juices flowing. You will learn how these brands consciously and appropriately used the medium to build close relationships by integrating email with existing modes of broadcast advertising, paper mail, face-to-face conversations, and much more. In chapter 14, we focus on how the lessons from these large and eminent organizations are relevant to small and mid-market businesses. The large organizations, during the early period of email's growth, pioneered many amazing uses of email, which many simply have forgotten. Those uses are unearthed and provide valuable lessons for millions of small and mid-market organizations that now ubiquitously use the Internet and email. In chapter 15, I share my experience in working with two personal brands, Oprah Winfrey and Deepak Chopra, to integrate television's reach with email's intimacy, in order to deliver a timely email-based curriculum for millions to learn meditation in twenty-one days.

In part 3, entitled "Email Takeaways," I've provided two additional chapters to summarize key elements of the book and to give you some of the best utilizations of email. Chapter 16 reviews "10 Reasons Why Email Is Here to Stay." Chapter 17 offers those best utilizations as "50 Tips on Using Email."

In the Afterword, I emphasize why the US Postal Service must embrace email for its future and why the demise of the USPS is the demise of democracy.

As you journey through this book, you will have learned:

1) Innovation can take place anywhere, anytime, and by anybody. The invention of email, by a fourteen-year-old immigrant kid working in Newark, New Jersey, serves as an important reminder of what can happen if the right infrastructure is put in place even in the most impoverished cities of our world.

2) Email is really the interoffice, interorganizational paper-based mail *system* in electronic form. The true nature of the email medium will be discussed, as well as its origin and its unique characteristics in relation to other media.

3) Why should the US Postal Service be embracing email? Not only to save itself but also, and more importantly, the USPS can save democracy by providing a civic function, such as the highways and water systems, ensuring that all of us can communicate, anytime, securely and privately.

4) Unearthing the lost history of email's use, by pioneering companies and businesses, during 1995 to 2003, provides us today with important and relevant lessons on using email for what it was really intended: to create a strong brand by making deep connections that are trusted, deep, and sustained.

5) Email is here to stay for a long, long time.

I hope that this journey through *The Email Revolution* will help you value the medium for what it is, so you can appropriately use it to develop your brand and the kind of relationships you deserve.

PART ONE

WHAT IS EMAIL?

Smoke Signals to Email

"Email is the full-scale electronic emulation of the interoffice, interorganizational paper-based mail system, a system of interlocked parts by which all offices in the world are run."

So what is email?

Email is the full-scale electronic emulation of the interoffice, interorganizational paper-based mail system, *a system of interlocked parts* by which all offices in the world were run. The US Postal Service (USPS) was also a *system*, the paper-based version of email. Had the USPS clearly understood this in 1997, when I first advised them, then likely many of us would be using an email service, much like Gmail or HotMail, but brought to us by the USPS, which would likely be far more secure and private than its privatized counterparts, protected by the same governing laws that ensure our mail is not tampered with.

In 2011, when the USPS reported that it may go bankrupt, I wrote a series of articles sharing my frustration on why they had not followed my advice nearly fifteen years earlier. Those articles got the attention of the USPS Office of the Inspector General (OIG). The OIG is the ombudsman for the US public, and oversees the USPS. In many ways, the OIG polices the USPS on behalf of the public. The OIG was keen on also understanding how the USPS had gotten into this mess and was far more open than the USPS was in finding new ways to generate revenue.

My initial discussions with the OIG in the fall of 2011 resulted in the OIG formally engaging my research center, the International Center for Integrative

Systems (ICIS), to write a report on how email could generate revenue for the USPS. Over a period of nearly six months, our center developed a detailed sixty-page report entitled "Email and Its Potential Revenues for the United States Postal Service." The OIG accepted our report and published summary results where we projected nearly $250 million in new revenues from the offering of email services by the USPS.

As of the writing of this book, it is unclear if the USPS management will actually take action on the report's findings. However, in that report, we developed a clear analysis for the USPS to help them understand why they should be in the email business, and core to this analysis was the detailing of the origin of email, so they could clearly see *why* they should have always been in the mail business, be it print or electronic.

Systems and Media

Different types of *media* flow through different *systems* of communication. For example, a *letter* is a medium that flows through the *postal mail system*. Similarly, a *text message* is the medium that flows through the *short messaging system* (SMS). A *tweet* flows through Twitter, a system for transacting a particular type of short message. An *email message* is the medium that flows through *email*, an electronic system mimicking the interoffice paper-based mail system. The terminology used for the *medium* (e.g., email message) should not be confused with the terminology used for the system (e.g., email, the system).

Just as a "letter" is not the postal mail system, an "email message" is not an email system. Systems are comprised of interconnecting parts. The kinds of interconnections and parts determine the unique nature of a system. One could start with the same set of parts, but connect them differently to get different types of systems. For example, one may have a set of rubber tires, gears, an engine, some steel, and seats—connect them one way to get a car or another way to get a motorcycle. Different interconnections yield different systems.

A system, in its most general form, is defined as a set of interlocking parts consisting of a combination of three fundamental elements: *transport, conversion, and storage.* The media that flows through these system elements can be in one of several forms, such as: *information, matter, or energy.*

In the cells of Table 1, three different system examples are provided for each of the three different types of system elements, in order, for you to appreciate how this generalized approach to systems and media provides a foundation for understanding the nature of *all* systems. Within any form of media, information, matter, or energy, there are various instances. For example, information may

Table 1—System Elements and Medium in Most General Form

System Elements and Media	Transport	Conversion	Storage
Information (e.g., email message, digital document, text message, tweet)	Ethernet	Computer	Hard Disk
Matter (e.g., oil, rock, cup, glass, water)	Oil Tankers	Refinery	Storage Tanks
Energy (e.g., electrical, magnetic, mechanical)	Copper Cable	Power Plant	Battery

appear as a book, a digital document, a text message, a tweet, or an email message. Matter may be a rock, a cup, oil, or a glass of water. Energy may be electrical, magnetic, or mechanical.

The core elements of transport, conversion, and storage act upon these forms of media to create the particular system. For example, when it comes to information, the Ethernet system provides a mechanism for transporting information; a computer converts information to let us add, subtract, divide, and multiply numbers; and a hard disk stores information. Similarly with matter, tankers provide a method of transporting oil; the refinery converts oil to gasoline; and storage tanks provide a method for storing oil. Transport of electrical energy is done using copper cables; a power plant converts mechanical energy from turbines to electrical energy; and, batteries are used to store electrical energy.

A Relational Taxonomy of Information Messaging

Over time, human civilization has manipulated systems of communication to provide more accelerated means of transferring information. The core functional elements of transport, conversion, and storage have remained unchanged, but through technological advances, their methods of implementation have produced significantly different types of systems of communication. The US Postal Service is itself a complex system of communication, which emerged from the interconnection of multiple subsystems of transport, conversion, and storage of paper-based mail. And, as we will see below, email is another system of communication, which emerged from the "electronification" and interconnection of multiple subsystems of transport, conversion, and storage of the interoffice, interorganizational paper-based mail.

To understand and define the nature of email, as a system, a relational approach is required. If one subscribes to the philosophy that nothing in life is defined by itself, but only in relation to other objects, then the nature of any media and its associated system will be defined by its relationship, both contextually and historically, to other media and their systems. Early forms and systems of communication, for example, were rooted in myth, primarily in oral tradition, and relied on the persistence of memory. Without the use of the written word, stories were shared through direct face-to-face contact, preserved through repetition and adaptation, sometimes, using poetry, music, and dance.

In India, the great epics of the Mahabharata and the Ramayana are such examples. In Western culture, the residues of these traditions can be found in the works of the Greek epics such as the Iliad and the Odyssey, which were traditionally sung by minstrels, and adapted to the needs of new generations. The persistence of communication was sometimes visible in large structures, demonstrating the importance of time and tradition. The Parthenon and Rosetta Stone trade their great weight and immobility for such persistence in time. Similarly, the paintings in France's Chauvin Cave—the oldest known paintings in the world—are the work of several artists, collaborating in a shared, visual narrative, though separated in time by several thousand years.

The development of writing systems, the proliferation of papyrus, and the invention of the printing press made it possible to commit that oral tradition to permanent record, and to distribute it widely. The shift in power from time-oriented oral tradition and myth to the systematic, linear media of books, mass newspapers, and radio had a significant role in human development, and indicated a strong shift to a new form of long-range communication, where information could traverse and be dispersed across both time and space. This was particularly valuable for administration and commerce. It is no exaggeration to claim that the entire modern world, everything we see around us, is built from, and dependent on, a fundamental control over movement of matter and information across space and time: books, newspapers, radio, telephone, TV, email messaging, text messaging, community forums, trade routes, railroads, automobiles, airplanes, and space travel. However, the channels and extents of these spatial media and their systems are not identical, and an exploration of their properties can reveal the underlying assumptions and cultural effects in the modern world of both print and digital text-based communication systems.

Such a relational understanding of information media requires a "space." We define that relational space by proposing three independent dimensions or modes of text-based communications and their associated systems: short messaging, community messaging, and intimate (or formal) messaging.

These three modes of messaging appear to be invariant across both print and digital media, and in fact have analogs to premodern forms of human communication as summarized in Table 2, below.

Table 2—Different modes of messaging and their exemplar mediums and systems

Modes of Messaging	PreModern	Print World	Digital World
Short Messaging	Smoke: Smoke Signal System	Sticky Note: Note passing System	Text message: Short Messaging System
Community Messaging	Cave Walls: Cave Drawings	Comment: Bulletin Board System	Post: Blogging system
Intimate (or formal) Messaging	Papyrus: Scribe system	Memo: Interoffice Mail System	Email message: Email system

Table 2 provides a perspective of how, over time, human development of different systems of communication across each mode of messaging has served to evolve the particular information-media within the invariant messaging modes. Each mode of messaging in our modern print and digital worlds has its origin in premodern times. Table 2 also provides a metaphorical approach to understand the nature of these different modes of messaging.

Short Messaging, the Sticky Note

The sticky notes are the common 2" by 2" yellow pieces of paper. They are good for writing short messages of ten to twenty words. They are convenient for exchanging short messages between an assistant and a boss or between partners: "pick up the milk" or "don't forget your 10:00 AM dentist appointment." The limited space requires one to be parsimonious, to think before writing, and to use abbreviations and mnemonics or drawings, like the smiley face. Some use sticky notes, placed along the edge of their computer screens, to serve as urgent reminders to get certain tasks completed, sooner rather than later. Since they are for short messages, they are typically used to convey a singular thought or instruction and likely are informal in nature.

Community Messaging, the Bulletin Board

Anyone who has passed by a community bulletin board where posters, sugges-tions, or offers are posted using thumbtacks knows the value of that medium for community messages. Community messaging is different than short messaging. Community messages are shared through a bulletin board. They are public and typically accessible for many others. They encourage others to participate within a confined topic or discussion, started by one individual. They allow one to post suggestions or ideas and to receive open feedback from others in a local com-munity. Physically, such a bulletin board is much larger than the sticky note, and typically stands five feet high and seven feet wide and provides the conversational space in which community messaging is accomplished. Most schools have them in the hallways and retail establishments have them near the checkout counters to get customer feedback. The bulletin board at my local retail food store, for example, has posts such as "Hey, can you have more organic fruits?" and "Why is there no chocolate milk?"

Other community members who see these posts can respond by posting responses next to them, in a proximal "thread" of communications. For the post on organic fruits, other organic fruit lovers demanded, "Yeah, get the Washington State apples," and "Please make sure that they are really 100% organic." These posts are open, transparent, and available for all to see. They foster a collective and participatory behavior, and let others gain a better understanding of con-cerns being raised about the establishment. The owners or managers of the estab-lishment can moderate the boards and respond, so the community knows that they are responsive to the needs of the community. They reflect a sense of open-ness and transparency.

Intimate (or Formal Messaging)—Letters (or Memos)

A letter or memo, either received at our home mailbox or at work, is an example of an intimate (or formal) message. Unlike short messages and community mes-sages, intimate (or formal) messages serve a very different purpose. These mes-sages are typically more structured. They consist of fields such as: "To:," "From:," "Subject:," "Date:," "Body:," and sometimes with "Cc:," "Bcc:," and attachments such as photos, documents, and other media. Letters and memos require greater thought in their production. A love letter, a legal termination notice, and noti-fication of changes to policies and procedures are examples of such thought-ful and formal communication. These letters and memos could be personal or official communications. They are typically more than twenty to thirty words, and are generally not for public consumption, but for individuals or targeted groups of individuals. Security of transacting, acknowledgement of receipt, and prioritization are other features of letters and memos. They may have salutations such as "Dear Bob" or "To Whom It May Concern" or "Hi." It is generally accepted that when you write a letter or memo, it is directed to someone or sometimes to a group and such a salutation aids in personalizing the message.

The above examples from the print world provide a concrete understanding of the three messaging modes. This understanding is the first step toward providing clarity in the digital world where email is misunderstood. Popular sites such as *Wikipedia* wrongly and broadly contribute to this misunderstanding by defining email as "a method of exchanging digital messages from an author to one or more recipients." Such a broad definition lumps short messages, community messages, and intimate (formal) messages together. According to *Wikipedia's* definition, this would mean that a tweet, a Facebook post, and a text message are all considered emails, which we all know not to be true.

Imagine if we defined a letter as "a method of exchanging handwritten messages from one author to one or more recipients." With such a definition, we would consider the sticky note, a bulletin board, and a letter the same thing, since they all exchange handwritten messages from one author to one or more recipients. Such a definition could lead to erroneous conclusions of the future of the letter, and an issuance of proclamations such as the "Letter is Dead," if one were to observe an increasing number of people using community bulletin boards or sticky notes.

This sounds absurd. A bulletin board and a sticky note each serve a very different purpose than a letter. But this is exactly what has been occurring in the digital world, as TXT, SMS, blogs, and wall posts appeared, expert after expert declared, "Email is Dead," assuming that an email message is the same thing as a TXT or a blog post.

Email, we will see in the next section, as a system, was intended to facilitate an already well-established social process (memos and letters), to address the existing needs of scientists, engineers, and doctors, as well as secretaries, politicians, and civilians. Email is a great poster-child adage that the original content of any new medium is the product of an older one[2]: the content of an email message is the same as that of the interoffice mail. Email, therefore, is literally the interoffice, interorganizational paper-based mail, or Postal Service Mail system, in its electronic form.

Email—A System of Interlocking Parts

What we know today as "email" is really a system of interlocking parts, each part of which is essential for ordinary people to communicate effectively with one or many others, in an environment where different kinds of information must be shared (memos, documents, files, etc.), an environment such as the modern office.

Many people over the age of forty will remember the interoffice paper mail system, which was the basis of how offices around the world operated, from the level of secretary to CEO. The interoffice mail system had the following interlocked parts, which are the now-familiar components of email: "Inbox," "Outbox," "Drafts," "Memo" ("To:," "From:," "Date:," "Subject:," "Body:," "Cc:," "Bcc:"), "Attachments," "Folders," "Compose," "Forward," "Reply," "Address Book," "Groups," "Return Receipt," "Sorting," and many other parts that I observed while working as a fourteen-year-old kid at the University of Medicine and Dentistry of New Jersey (UMDNJ). These components are shown in Table 3, in the next chapter. This system was not only used within offices but also for communicating between different organizations, across the three campuses of UMDNJ.

The interoffice, interorganizational paper-based mail system was therefore an interlocked system of parts. If you took away any one component, such as the ability to attach other materials or the use of folders, send attachments, or make carbon copies, then functionality between coworkers would be greatly impaired, and the system itself would break down.

The definition of email as the full-scale electronic emulation of the interoffice, interorganizational paper-based mail system is an important one, as it clearly sets forth that email is a system of interconnected parts which has its origin in the paper-based mail system, a system similar to the Postal Service. In 1978, when I created email, I implemented all the features of the interoffice paper mail system I observed at UMDNJ (as shown in Table 3 of the next chapter) in the computer program I created. Table 4, also in the next chapter, provides a detailed list of the major features inherent in the system, which I called "email," that defined the system as we all know it today.

Why the Postal Service May Now Embrace Email

The origin and definition of email, as discussed, should clarify why there may be an opportunity for the Postal Service still to embrace email. The postal mail system consists of a set of interlocked parts with direct correlations between the paper method and the electronic method: mailboxes (inbox), registered mail (return receipt), security, notifications, retries, sorting, address books, transport and delivery, universal accessibility regardless of skill (e.g. no one needs to be a postmaster or a computer scientist to send a paper mail or an email). So the reasoning that email is a natural extension of the Postal Service is easy to understand. As the use of email systems has grown worldwide, so has the volume of email messages, as indicated in the graph below.[3]

The usage of email systems has grown exponentially, with a significant marked increase in 1997. Nearly 550 billion email messages were sent in 1997.

During this same period, 191 billion postal mail pieces were sent. This important development reflected a significant change in the behavior of interhuman communication. This is why, in 1997, I had urged the Postal Service to embrace email.

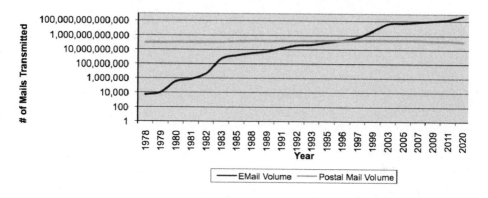

Growth of Email Messages Vs. Post Mail Messages

I still do not believe it is too late. Today, in a world of privatized email messaging service providers, where privacy and security are in question, the unparalleled history of law and jurisprudence for managing paper mail provides the Postal Service with a unique opportunity to potentially offer email through the goodwill of its trusted brand.

2

Electrified Paper

"Hearing those two words 'electronic' and 'mail' juxtaposed in 1978 evoked Star Trek's *transporter dematerializing paper and beaming it across the ether."*

The first time I heard about "electronic mail," I thought it was about sending electricity through paper. Hearing those two words "electronic" and "mail" juxtaposed in 1978 evoked *Star Trek's* transporter dematerializing paper and beaming it across the ether. When Dr. Leslie P. Michelson, formerly a physicist at Brookhaven National Laboratory, then director of the three-person Laboratory for Computer Science at the University of Medicine and Dentistry of New Jersey (UMDNJ), told me those words, I was intrigued and thought we were going to build some nuclear powered system to blast paper into vapor and then somehow transmit it over electrical wires.

Dr. Michelson, however, held up one of UMDNJ's off-gray Interoffice Mail envelopes and asked me if I'd like to "create the electronic version of the interoffice mail system?"

Michelson was a pioneer in bringing computers to medicine. My mother, Meenakshi Ayyadurai, an incredible mathematician, educator, and systems analyst, who worked in the computer department at UMDNJ had introduced me to Dr. Michelson hoping he would guide me on the right path. Earlier that summer, I had been admitted to a special program at New York University, designed by Professor Henry Mullish to introduce young people to the world of computers. My mom's friend Martin Feuerman had told us about the unique NYU program.

Mullish was a visionary who had recognized the importance of computers early on and had the brilliant idea to train select youths of America to lead a workforce of future computer programmers. He had received funding from the National Science Foundation (NSF) to develop an intensive program for such computer programming education. In that NYU program, we were exposed to several different programming languages, including BASIC, COBOL, FORTRAN, SNOBOL, PL/I and ARTSPEAK. Most are rarely used today with the exception of FORTRAN. In those days, software was written on punch cards and used to operate enormous mainframe computers.

Learning Programming in New York

The New York University course was an adventurous and intensive eight-and-a-half-week program. NYU was situated in the heart of Greenwich Village, known for artists, great ethnic food, creativity, and all sorts of spectacles. I had never traveled to New York alone. The only way to get there was to take a bus from my home in Livingston, New Jersey, to the Newark Port Authority. From Newark, I took the PATH train to New York Penn Station, and then the A train to Bleeker Street. If I missed the bus, which did happen at times, my poor mom would have to drive me at 5 AM to the Newark train station. Walking from Bleeker Street to NYU in the 1970s was a daily adventure. Cutting across Washington Square Park, local dealers advertised their wares: "Try before you Buy." During the early part of my adventure, a man called Jenkins, who I would later find was a bronze molder, was concerned for me, a young fourteen-year-old boy walking among those hustlers in Washington Square Park. He befriended me, becoming initially a bodyguard, and later a family friend. I remember one day going to his forgery, watching liquid light, molten bronze being poured in molds that hardened into amazing sculptures. On one occasion, walking uptown on Christopher Street with Jenkins, I saw two men jumping out and smashing through a jewelry store glass window. They had just robbed the store. One passerby started chasing one of the thieves, and another passerby started chasing the other thief. What a spectacle—I loved it! It reminded me a lot of the bazaar-like atmosphere of Bombay—wild and free. The NYU campus was in the heart of all of this chaos and creativity.

There were forty of us who had been admitted to the NYU program. The teachers of our classes were NYU professors and graduate students. The teaching was wonderful, and they put in a lot of effort to make the material understandable. In retrospect, having the opportunity to learn coding, programming, and digital circuitry in 1978 was incredibly good fortune. I remember painstakingly writing my first program in FORTRAN on those punch cards. There was a great sense of wonder in seeing a set of instructions being carried out by a computer. The first programming assignment was to simulate the classic game of life: predator and prey relationships in an ecosystem. Programming was also shown to have artistic applications. We were introduced by Mullish to ARTSPEAK, an innovative language to create artistic drawings. A computer art competition was run to see who could create the best artwork. During this exercise, I had made a programming error, which resulted in very wild and abstract shapes that resulted in my winning the award. ARTSPEAK was one of the earliest computer-aided drawing packages, without any type of easy-to-use graphical interface, long before Microsoft, Paint, or Photoshop. NYU's program provided invaluable training in programming, as good as or better than any undergraduate courses at MIT.

My Mentor, Leslie P. Michelson at UMDNJ

Dr. Michelson, director of the lab at UMDNJ, was responsible for three mainframe computers, located on three separate campuses. UMDNJ was both a facility of medical practice and of medical research, so thousands of medical students and doctors were spread across the three campus locations in New Jersey: Piscataway, New Brunswick, and Newark. Time-sharing was how each user was given access to the mainframe computer. At each of the three locations, each user accessed the local mainframe computers using keyboards and terminals, which were attached to the centralized mainframe computer. At that time, the computers ran software to support various applications pertinent to running a medical school and supporting medical research. For example, there was software on the mainframe to do basic statistical data analysis for use by medical researchers. There was software for managing patient records and accounting information. In this model of time-sharing, each mainframe had various software applications. A user was able to access the mainframe through a terminal. They logged in to the mainframe, ran particular software, and logged out. Their user session on the mainframe was charged to their account at $.05 per minute.

Some scientists in Dr. Michelson's lab in Newark were writing new software for biomedical engineering applications. One research fellow by the name of David Ritacco was writing software for doing presentation graphics, the predecessor to products such as PowerPoint. In this time-sharing networked environment of users spread across three campuses, Dr. Michelson's challenge for me was to create a system that was the electronic version of the interoffice mail system for the full range of managing the creation, receipt, transmission, and processing of paper memos within a user-friendly, network-wide, high-reliability framework. Up to that point, researchers had succeeded in building various components of systems necessary for creating such a potential system. For example, IBM had created, in the 1950s, the first programming language, FORTRAN. Others had created early database systems to store and retrieve information in the early 1960s. In the early 1970s, networking protocols were developed. However, no system yet existed that enabled the full range of processing, mimicking the range of features extant in the interoffice postal mail process. Moreover we wanted it to be user-friendly, network-wide, and easy to use for any ordinary citizen, and feature-rich to capture all the elements of the interoffice postal mail system. In 1978, even sending short text messages electronically was limited for use by highly technically savvy computer scientists and engineers. Sending text messages involved very hard-to-use commands. Those text messaging systems were nowhere near being easy to use like SMS or Twitter is today.

However, no one had attempted to build a full-scale version of the interoffice, interorganizational mail system, as far as we knew. It would be many years later in 2012, when we would unearth documents to prove that others were not attempting to do this at that time, since they had found such a development "almost impossible." As Dr. Michelson revealed in the Foreword of this book, we found an important document written by David Crocker, an early electronic messaging pioneer, which made this amply clear. Mr. Crocker had written a RAND Report in December of 1977, a few months before I joined the lab, where he stated:

> At this time [December, 1977], no attempt is being made to emulate the full-scale, inter-organization mail system. To construct a fully-detailed and monolithic message processing environment requires a much larger effort than has been possible. . . . In addition, the fact that the system is intended for use in various organizational contexts and by users of differing expertise makes it almost impossible to build a system which responds to all users' needs. Consequently, important segments of a full message environment have received little or no attention . . .

The challenge that Dr. Michelson had given me was to specifically do the "impossible" and create such a system, which would meet all the "users' needs" across the three campuses of UMDNJ.

Email

I named the system I created "email." I used upper case because in the Fortran IV programming language, variables and subroutine names had a six-character limit, and the five letters E, M, A, I, and L juxtaposed together fit that limit. In addition, the operating system only allowed five characters for program names. In retrospect, adding "E" to "MAIL" may seem obvious, but it was not in 1978.

On August 30, 1982, I received the first US Copyright for email, the computer program of the electronic mail system. In fact, today, the *Merriam-Webster Dictionary* and the *Oxford English Dictionary* place the origin date of email as 1982 and the 1980s, respectively.

Our goal with email was to create a system such that any nontechnical person, for example, medical doctors and students, could use it to send electronic letters, email, with equal ease as they would with print-form memos, across the three campus sites. At that time in UMDNJ, all mail that had to be sent from one site to another was done only through typewritten or handwritten paper mail. The concept of creating a complete system to send, receive, and manage electronic versions of letters was nonexistent. When I first made a formal presentation of email to doctors and other technologists at UMDNJ, they had no desire to even use electronic mail, because they thought their method of sending print mail was absolutely fine, efficient, and it worked. They felt email was not necessary.

In this office situation environment, it was clear that any email system that was designed would have to be easy to use and offer sufficient features on functionality, equal to or better than their interoffice postal mail system, to entice these early users to take advantage of it. To meet these goals, it became important to use the same language, or lingua franca, from the print world of interoffice mail, so they would become as comfortable in sending email as they were with writing and receiving Memorandums (Memos).

At that time, I was still a sophomore at Livingston High School. In order to work on this project, I needed to get special approval from my high school to leave in the middle of the day and travel nearly thirty miles to Newark. The high school's principal first had to approve this request. Later, the superintendent of all schools in Essex county also had to get involved in order to authorize this special independent study program. Fortunately, one teacher, Stella Oleksiak, a visionary educator, persuaded the principal and the superintendent to support this independent study. Without her persuasion, I would never have been able to get such authorization. Since I had completed most of my high school course work, Stella was able to make a strong case.

A World of Paper

The doctors at UMDNJ mainly communicated through written memos. The medical community was, for the most part, technologically illiterate. There were secretaries to write and handle their letters and memos. The idea that doctors could now write their own memos, through email, was a new endeavor and a tough sell. They were happy having their secretary do their work. This is different from today, where doctors cannot live without email. The way doctors and researchers relayed information across these three campuses was through print mail, written and delivered through couriers. Our job was to figure out how to digitalize the interoffice mail process. Typically, a doctor would dictate to a secretary, who would write down the letter or memo. The memos were structured in a very precise manner: the letterhead of the university at the top; the word MEMORANDUM in the center; then came the doctor's FROM NAME:, SUBJECT:, TO:, FROM:, Cc, and Bcc: fields; beneath that line was the main text, and at the bottom there was a field call ENCL:, where the doctor could enclose attachments. The FROM NAME: was the official name of the doctor, "Dr. James B. Smith, MD." The SUBJECT: was the title of the memorandum: "Meeting of All Cardiologists." The TO: field allowed a memo to be sent to one person or broadcast to multiple people. The interoffice mail system had the concept of an individual recipient or a group. The Cc: in those days literally meant "carbon copy." When a secretary typed a letter, she would place a piece of carbon paper in between two pieces of paper. As she typed, a carbon copy would be generated. Bcc:, or "blind carbon copy," meant that others did not know about the person receiving the message on the Bcc list. Just as Cc was a literal term, so was the "box" in Inbox and Outbox. Secretaries would put these memos in envelopes and put them in one of two physical boxes. The Inbox was meant for incoming memos that they received from others. The Outbox was for outgoing letters. External mail, in the Outbox, would go out daily by post. For internal mail, someone would diligently do pickups in the morning as well as in the evenings. The mail would then be sorted. Memos traveling within the building would be separated from those bound for one of the other campuses, and finally all would be delivered to a recipient's Inbox. At the Newark campus in the building where I worked, they were able to also deliver interoffice mail through these clever rubber canisters using hydraulic air, through ducts and tunnels, which were interconnected throughout the building. It was quite amazing.

The logistics of the operation were complex. For example, consider a memo with a TO: field with five recipients. The secretary would make five copies of this Memorandum. Once they were copied, each would be placed in the secretary's Outbox. A courier would pick them up and bring them to the sorting room. There, they would be sorted by destination. The ones bound for people in the same building would be delivered first. The others had to wait for another courier to pick them up and deliver them to the indicated remote locations. At the remote locations, they would again be sorted on site before being delivered locally. This was a replica of the USPS mail processing system. Each of the three locations of UMDNJ had such a processing center.

Goal: "Electronify" Letters and Memos

The goal was to convert the structured interoffice memo, including the process and memos, to an electronic form. Clearly, if there was a way to make this process easier, by creating a system through which mail could be dispensed electronically, a lot of expensive and time-consuming processes could be avoided. In an electronic world, there would be:

- No need to physically transport mail
- No more reason to do physical sorting
- No more reason to physically create carbon copies
- Savings in both time and gas
- More efficient delivery of enclosures and attachments
- Huge savings in paper and ink
- Savings in cost and labor
- Ease of filing and archival

The value of creating an email system became apparent. It would be revolutionary. What would make these medical doctors and others, who were so used to paper, want to switch to an electronic medium?

The adoption of email would only occur if there were a clear understanding of its unique characteristics. They and others had to become convinced of its value. Today, however, we take email for granted, and many of us, ironically, still use email as a print or phone medium. We do not appreciate the real nature of email. In 1978, I had to educate the future users of email on the nature of this medium.

The Nature of Email

Education on the particular characteristics of email was a critical part of the process toward email being used effectively. There are multiple adjectives that describe email. Here are important ones that we all tend to forget or do not fully appreciate:

- Asynchronous
- Flexible
- Targeted
- Cost-effective
- Immediate
- Costly to manage
- Ubiquitous

Let's review what we mean by these terms so we can better appreciate the nature of these fundamental characteristics, which will be key to understanding email as a platform and rediscovering email as a medium.

Asynchronous means a user of email can decide if and when he or she wants to respond to an email. In contrast with phone or instant text messaging, email does not require both parties to be present at the same time for communication to take place. Think about it. For example, with instant text messaging, two parties are expected to be online at the same time to have a conversation. If one party does not write back quickly, that can be taken as lack of interest. With email you respond to it when you want to respond. If you don't want to respond, you don't have to; and, for that matter, one can simply delete the email.

Email is a *flexible* medium. This means email can be written and distributed far more easily than other media. For example, unlike print mail, one can send or forward a message to one person or a million without any significant difference in cost. Think about the effort it takes to distribute a piece of print mail such as a brochure. It has to be copied on a photocopier or at a printer's, then put in envelopes, mailing labels added, and delivered to the post office. With email, one can simply distribute the electronic version of a brochure instantaneously to thousands of people. And, those recipients can cut and paste portions of it and send it to others in a matter of seconds.

Email is a *targeted* medium. For those wanting to use email for marketing, this is a very powerful feature. A single email can be tailored to targeted groups of people. Consider two groups of recipients: males and females. One can create email with three paragraphs, and the first paragraph of that email can be dynamically changed, with the right technology, to tailor the content based on the gender of the recipient, with the remaining two paragraphs being unchanged. In contrast, consider Television or Radio, where one message is broadcast to many people. The targeted nature of email allows us to send different customized and targeted messages to many people. In this sense, email is a wonderful medium for *narrowcasting*, unlike TV and print mail, which were originally designed for *broadcasting*, the same message to many people.

Email is *cost-effective* and can be accessed relatively free of charge. It is almost free to receive and send email, unlike print mail, where we have to pay a cost for mailing an envelope or postcard. Today, email services are available through freely accessible websites such as ones that offer email as free service. Compared to sending a package through the United States Postal Service, email is a fraction of the cost. However, we will need to consider the implicit privacy we give up for such free service.

While email may be cost-effective to send, for those receiving email, it can be *costly to manage*. For example, processing an inbound customer service email costs a business between $5 and $18, depending on its complexity. Why is it this costly? Handling email properly requires reading the email, analyzing its contents, crafting a proper and accurate response, and ensuring that it is sent out in a timely manner. Many companies, as we will discuss later, do not handle email well. To handle email well requires the right process and technologies. Trained customer service personnel are needed who can read and write clearly and effectively, not a readily available commodity. The costs of such personnel are more expensive than those handling a phone call. Trust is perhaps one of the most underestimated elements in email processing.

The email medium is relatively *immediate*. Messages sent arrive almost instantaneously. In contrast, the USPS may take many days, depending on destination. Of course, if there are problems with the computers and network, there can be delays, but that is the exception. Most email messages take less than a few seconds to send and receive.

Finally, email is *ubiquitous*. Email can be accessed using email systems anywhere in the world. As of the writing of this book, there are nearly 2 billion email users and 500 billion emails sent each day. For those of you who read this book ten years from now, nearly every human being will have access to email across laptops, PDAs, cell phones, and other yet-to-be-invented devices.

Shadows of Email

Many of the positive features of email also have their shadows. For example, while email is immediate, it does not mean one should write an immediate response. The immediacy of email encourages speedy replies. Therefore, users tend to write hastily and to press Send without editing. Email will also get integrated with other applications.

Yes, email is asynchronous, but that does not mean we should wait forever to respond, when you want to, forgetting that someone else is waiting for a response. Responding to friends and customers in a relevant and timely manner earns loyalty. In business cases, for example, recent studies have shown that if organizations do not respond in less than twenty-four hours, they have an 85 percent chance of losing the customer. In 2012, less than 35 percent of organizations responded to email within twenty-four to forty-eight hours. Most organizations do not respond within seventy-two hours. What an opportunity to succeed! Organizations that simply respond in a timely manner with quality and accuracy can have a significant competitive advantage.

As a flexible medium, email can be widely distributed with ease. This feature can be dangerous if used impulsively. We have all probably heard of, or experienced, many instances of employees going home after an argument to write a long diatribe and email it to everyone in the office. The next day, the parties involved walk sheepishly around the office, embarrassed about the email exchange. While the immediate nature of email offers many benefits, this does not mean one should write back a hasty reply, unless one is willing to handle the resulting fallout, which could be significant: loss of friendships and customers.

Email is costly to manage, and doubly so if used ineffectively. Reading and responding to an inbound email is costly enough; however, given that many companies treat their customer service department as a cost center, they tend to respond poorly and thus hurt themselves. For example, in most customer service centers, from the legacy of responding to phone calls, customer service representatives (also known as CSRs) are motivated to resolve complaints one at a time, and as fast as possible. Their goal is to talk to a customer, "solve" their problem and get them off the phone, fast!

Why? Well, a single call is costly. Too many calls can affect a company's bottom line. For example, in the hotel industry, a decent hotel room is priced at $150 to the end customer. The profit a hotel makes from that room is typically $25 to $30. However, every customer service phone call costs a company $15 to $20 to handle. If that phone call goes beyond thirty minutes, the costs go to $25 to $30. This means a long customer service call for the $150 room destroys the profit of that room, reducing it to *zero*! The hotel management, therefore, motivates representatives to handle the call quickly. We will see later how companies such as Hilton manage email effectively to achieve first-time resolution. This makes customers happy and builds a great brand.

This similar approach when used with email without care to responding can be devastating also. Why? Bad, hasty, or generally poor email responses will likely, according to recent studies, be forwarded to twenty-seven other people. A bad phone call, according to similar research, is only told to five other people. Thus, a bad email response is five times more harmful. Furthermore, as we said earlier, a poor email response has a nearly 85 percent chance of losing a customer for good. Thus, even though email is costly to manage, it can be far more costly if proper infrastructure and processes are not put in place to handle inbound email effectively.

Since email is ubiquitous, perhaps more so than even water, we often take it for granted. As a result, we treat all email equally. All emails are not equal. Informal personal exchanges are different than business exchanges with customers. Failure to recognize this difference leads many to transfer their personal exchange style to business emails. In a business context, using a colloquial personal approach may not work: emails with spelling mistakes, grammar errors, and abbreviations may affect the sender and the company's brand. With text messaging, one can get away with it—as that is part of the culture—but not with email. Such emails may result in a very poor experience for the recipient. Consider this exchange I experienced many years ago with a rent-a-car agency. I was flying to Atlanta for a few days and needed to rent a car. I wrote this email to a major rent-a-car company and asked, "Hello, I'm coming to Atlanta, I'd like to rent a car from you. Do you carry any car equivalent to a BMW?"

The response I received was "No, we don't." Period.

There was nothing like a salutation or a "thank you." Nothing. It left me with the impression that this company didn't care. I had wanted to rent from them. Their email response not only lost them my business, but also potentially other customers; since then I've told that story to many others. Here is a company, which spends millions training its representatives to greet and process your transaction face-to-face, but fails to understand the importance of investing in email interaction. Despite the cost of managing email and its ubiquity, it does not mean that replies should be rushed in an unprofessional manner, as in this case.

The current high cost and low performance of customer service centers in this respect highlights how email is not used effectively. There are still a few companies that handle email by responding via paper mail! The leaders of these organizations view email as a print correspondence. However, many pioneering leaders recognize the importance and prominence email is gaining and are making efforts to implement advanced technologies and innovation to manage and streamline email processing.

Herein lies the opportunity: If a customer sends you an email and you respond well, they are going to tell more people about that experience. They are likely to forward the email to many others. What better advertising!

Inbox, Outbox, and Much More

In inventing email, I realized that there were many components necessary for sending, receiving, storing, and securing email in a networked environment while retaining accessibility in a user-friendly manner. Transmitting electronic messages was one thing dating back all the way to the Morse code telegraph and some work in the 1960s and 1970s in exchanging electronic messages across computers using very cryptic codes, but creating an email system to capture the entire interoffice mail system was another.

What is an email system? In 1978, when I began the development of email, here were the main design features of email:

1. **User-Friendly Interface.** A very easy-to-use interface was needed to send an electronic letter by creating an environment that would be reminiscent of the familiar protocol with which memos were written. This environment had to fit in a small space. At that time, the screen only

supported fifty characters across the screen and twenty characters vertically. The menu had the concept of Inbox and Outbox, and allowed the user to create a message, receive email, procure online help, broadcast messages (early email marketing), and the ability to contact the system administrator.

2. **A Rich Set of Features.** The system was a full-scale emulation of the entire interoffice, paper-based mail system, and as such offered the ability to sort and view the Inbox and Outbox, to create Folders, even the ability to send Registered Mail, what we call return receipt today. Here, the system was also mimicking the USPS (versus Tom Van Vleck, who was afraid of and concerned about the USPS, and was told by his CTSS management *not* to do that). The system provided an editor, the ability to save a Draft, Send and Receive Messages. It also offered settings for retries if there were network issues. Email could also be archived, stored, and deleted.

3. **Network-wide.** The system enabled users to reside across three geographical locations, each of which had three different servers (nodes) and multiple users at each location, with their own computers, connected to the servers. Various checks and balances were put into email for ensuring transaction of email across locations (e.g. if one server went down, what to do, when to resend). Administrative tools and reports for managing network email transactions were part of email. All of this had to be built and tested. My programming staff was *me*: responsible for writing the code, writing all documentation, testing for bugs, and training users.

4. **Security and Login.** This system assigned each person a username and password. This was a necessary step in enabling one to send and receive email, as well as access their folders, regardless of the location of the terminal they were logging in from. Each of the different geographical locations had access to the master user and password tables, enabling a login flexibility we take for granted today.

5. **Enterprise Email Management.** Once such a system was built, many other administrative features were added, such as what to do if a person forgot their username and password, archival and email retention policies, limits on how long an email message would be stored, when to clean up the system, and so on. These were not always evident to the user, but on the back end of most systems, such issues were addressed.

6. **Database and Archival.** Email needed a way to store all the information. Email incorporated emerging database technology in a relational data store to index email and users and to sort and rapidly transact email. Without a relational database, email would not have been possible.

However, text messaging systems can be implemented using just simple files, which Van Vleck and Tomlinson used. Since they did not create an email system, they did not need database technology. But an email system needed the ability to link and sort each user with their Inbox, Outbox, archives, and more—all needing a database. The incorporation of such a sophisticated database structure provided the ability for email to offer many of the rich features already described.

Elements of the Interoffice, Interorganizational Paper-Based Mail System

When I first started at UMDNJ, Dr. Michelson allowed me to explore the entire UMDNJ interoffice mail system. I made a detailed list of the various parts of the paper-based mail system, which are summarized in Table 3.

Table 3—The System of Interlocking Parts of the Interoffice, Interorganizational Paper Mail System[4]

Part Name	Part Description
Inbox	This was the physical inbox where a secretary received incoming documents. It was usually made of wood, metal, or plastic. The courier or "office boy" or "mailroom clerk" would deliver documents—postal mail or internal memos came to the Inbox regularly, such as twice per day.
Outbox	This was a physical box of metal, wood, or plastic, for memos that were composed and edited, ready for delivery to the recipients. The courier or "office boy" or "mailroom clerk" would come and pick up the mail from the Outbox regularly, sometimes twice per day.
Drafts	A memo, sometimes, was saved for review prior to sending. A secretary or another person would write the memo and put it in a Drafts folder, which a superior would review and provide "red-line" feedback in the Drafts folder.
Memo	This was typically a piece of 8½" by 11" piece of bond paper. At the top of the Memo was written, "++++++ MEMORANDUM ++++++" and below that were the following fields of information: "To:," "From:," "Date:," "Subject:," "Body:," "Cc:," "Bcc:," (only for view in the sender's original) and an indication with "Encl.:" if attachment(s) were included.

Attachments	A Memo could sometimes indicate "Encl.:" if attachments or enclosures such as another file folder, another document, a drawing or photograph, or even a parcel, were included.
Folders	Mail sometimes was organized and filed in separate folders based on some subject matter.
Compose	A new memo was typically composed on a typewriter. Sometimes whiteout (a white liquid or white paper) was used to erase mistakes.
Forward (or Redistribution)	A person receiving and reviewing an incoming memo could forward or redistribute it to others. Forwarding literally involved adding a list of other people to review the memo. Sometimes the forward list was just paper-clipped on the received memo.
Reply	Sometimes instead of writing a new memo, an employee replied to a memo received in the Inbox. The memo that was being responded to would be attached.
Address Book	Every office had an address book, which listed each person's first and last names, campus location, group (e.g. surgery, pharmacology), room number, and phone number.
Groups	At UMDNJ, different groups were at different locations, such as Surgery, Pharmacology, ICU, IT. Each location had different people in different groups.
Return Receipt	This was a formal receipt that a delivery person would make sure got signed by the recipient who had been sent a registered memo. This return receipt would then have to get sent back to the original sender.
Sorting	Different locations had mail sorting facilities, where the mail would come in, be sorted by groups, departments, locations, zip code, office numbers, so the delivery was easier.
Send	A memo to an individual meant that the "To:" field had only the name of one recipient.
Receive	Memos were received in the Inbox by a secretary.
Scanning Mail	Visually reviewing the mail was the process of quickly reading the envelope or top portion of a memo, such as the "From:" and "Subject:" lines to get an idea of which memo to read first, which to put for later review, or sometimes to discard altogether.

Forwarding with RETURN RECEIPT Requested (or registered memo)	This was an important feature of the office. Sometimes, a manager, for example, would receive an important letter, from a director, and that manager wanted certain employees in his group to read it and make sure that they did in fact read it. So forwarding with return receipt enabled the manager to know exactly who got and who did not get the memo.
Editing	A memo sometimes would be edited after it was composed. Editing could be iterative based on the feedback received.
Broadcast Memo	Sometimes a memo would need to be sent to multiple recipients, not just one individual. This meant having multiple names of recipients in the "To:" field. This was a complicated process, since copies had to be made (carbon copies on a typewriter). A check mark was put next to each copy's intended recipient, so the envelope would be addressed correctly.
Sending Memo to Group	In a large organization, like UMDNJ, there were different faculty departments—Pharmacology, Surgery, etc.—and one may want to send a memo to a Group. Again, copies were made, and an Address Book used for a secretary to correctly address each envelope.
Deleting	Sometimes a memo would be thrown into a trash folder for disposal.
Purging	The contents of trash folders, by request, would be collected and permanently destroyed.
Updating Address Book	Address books were updated as employees came and left UMDNJ. New people were added, and those who had left were removed. Sometimes a circular was sent out which was the update to the existing Address Book, and one would have to manually insert the changes.
Prioritization	When mail was left in the Inbox, it sometimes was sorted based on some basis of priority, and so marked.
Archiving	Memos to be kept were often put into an archive file cabinet and organized for long-term record keeping.
Carbon Copies	A secretary would typically place dark blue carbon paper between two Bond pieces of white paper and roll them into the typewriter, to create copies. The Bond paper on top was the original, the ones below were "Carbon Copies"

or CCs. Sometimes, several Carbons were used, and sometimes if the CC list was long, the original would be mimeographed on a mimeograph machine. Then the original To: recipient would get the original, and each person on the CC list would get copies. This got more complicated if there were multiple recipients or a Group in the To: field.

Blind Carbon Copies A Bcc list, in the header of the memo, was kept by the Sender only, and others who got Carbon copies did not see the one with the Bcc list. So only the sender knew who was on the Bcc list.

Registered Memo In the hospital environment, this was a very important feature, because certain memos had to be acknowledged as received. A Memo could be flagged as a "Registered Memo," this would mean that it was treated differently. For instance, the delivery person could put it in a different color envelope and ensure that the recipient signed for it.

Undeliverable Notification Sometimes a memo could not be delivered even after many Retries. In this case the delivery person would take the memo back to the sender with a note on it saying "undeliverable."

Retries All mail had to be delivered, or a real effort made to keep trying before being deemed undeliverable. This meant instituting a policy of "retries," as many as three or five times, before the attempts stopped. The number of retries was a policy decision.

Securing Delivery All mail had to be securely delivered. This meant that only the designated recipient could get it. Typically this was ensured because the delivery person knew everybody and all the secretaries. Moreover, most memos were put in individual sealed envelopes with string closures or tape binding it shut.

Transporting All mail needed to be transported. At UMDNJ, there were many ways of transport. The delivery person could physically pick up and deliver from local office to office. Another form of transport was a pneumatic tube, forming a system on train-track-like rails. Mail addressed to different buildings and campuses was transported by cars or trucks.

The design and development of email relied on several earlier developments in technology:

- The development of FORTRAN in 1954 by John Backus at IBM
- The development of ASCII naming standard in 1962 by Bob Bremer
- The invention of database technology in 1969 by Charles Bachman
- The creation of TCP in 1973 by Vinton Cerf, Robert Kahn
- The development of Ethernet in 1973 by Bob Mercalfe
- The development of TCIP/IP by Danny Cohen, David Reed, and John Shoch

A text messaging system could have been created without the above developments; however, in 1978, the earlier work of other pioneers, from Backus to Danny Cohen, was necessary to have the foundational components to develop email. Text messaging systems didn't need these kinds of foundational technologies. In 1978, the first version of the email system I built offered doctors the ability to send and receive email in a user-friendly, network-wide manner, emulating their interoffice postal mail system. I continued to evolve the system over the next few years. Table 4 below itemizes all of the features of email, which I implemented to mimic the physical features I observed (as itemized in Table 3 above).

Table 4—Email: The Full-Scale Electronic Interoffice, Interorganizational Mail System[5]

Interoffice Mail System Parts and Related Email Parts
Inbox
Outbox
Drafts
Memo
To:, From:, Subject: (70 characters in length), Date:, Body:, Cc:, Bcc:
Registered Memo
Folders
Compose
Forward (or Redistribution)
Reply
Address Book
Groups
Return Receipt
Sorting

Send

Receive

Scanning Mail

Forwarding with RETURN RECEIPT (or registered memo)

Editing

Broadcast Memo

Sending Memo to Group

Deleting

Purging

Updating Address Book

Searching Address Group

> By Group, By User Name (short name), By Last Name, By Zipnode (node or location)

Prioritization

Archiving

Undeliverable Notification

Retries

Secure Delivery (Using username and password)

Attachments

> Attaching to a memo, Creating attachments from scratch, Saving attachments, Attachment editor

Transmission of memo

Multi-Level User Access—User, Manager, Postmaster, System Administrator

Memo Formatting—Functions were included to make sure that a memo on the screen when printed looked somewhat like a typewritten memo.

Printing

> Print all mail; Print selected memos; Print only the "envelopes," To, From, Subject, Date; Formatted printing—memo looked like typewritten one

Exporting of Mail

> Export a single memo to a file; Export a set of memos to a file

Group Management—Postmaster/Administrator Level

> Creating Groups; Deleting Groups; Placing User in a Group; Deleting User from a Group; Displaying Groups; Restricting Group Access— which users could not send to certain groups. E.g. Only the Postmaster could send to "ALL"

Postmaster & Systems Administrator Functions

> Reports on mail usage by user; Deleting aged mail; Shutdown of the entire system; Startup of the entire system; Deleting Users; Adding Users; Adding a "Zipnode," new network; Deleting a Zipnode; Disabling a User from logging in to the user interface; Direct starting of mail transmission

Integrated System Components

> Easy-To-Use User Interface; Word-processor; Integrated Attachment Editor; Relational Database Engine; Modular Inter-Process Communication Protocol; Print Manager for Formatted Printing; Systems Administrator Console; Post Master Console

---

Beyond reproducing the functional parts of the paper mail system (Table 3), I also incorporated a set of *Integrated System Components* (the latter part of Table 4) to make email a truly usable system at UMDNJ. All of these components, such as the Easy-To-Use User Interface, Word-processor, Editor, and so forth, were not "off-the-shelf" parts, but ones I had to build from scratch, except for the Database Engine. The Integrated System of Components made email network-wide, highly reliable, and easy-to-use so anyone from secretaries and doctors to technical folk and business executives could transition from the typewriter to the keyboard. The creation of email—with all these familiar features we take for granted today in programs such as Gmail, Hotmail, and others—by definition was and is the the full-scale electronic emulation of the interoffice, interorganizational paper mail system.

In 1979, I also completed the development of Email Maintenance and Management System which allowed administrators, or "Postmasters," to manage the system (e.g., change forgotten usernames and passwords, clean up junk mail). Once email was deployed other infrastructure was required, which needed to be managed, so more tools had to be written into code. Infrastructure was required to ensure that email reached its destination without failure. At that time, such an assurance or tracking mechanism did not exist. Email included the right software to send and receive communications. Each location could receive email from any other location, and the software ensured delivery to the Inbox of the correct person. Every user had a username, password, and location. The email system needed to know who logged in, and once they pressed Send, the email had to be accurately transmitted to the appropriate person. These are things we take for granted today. If the sender and receiver were at the same location, say in Newark, then it meant moving the data from the sender's Outbox to the storage of the recipient's Inbox. If the sender and recipient were at different locations, say one in Newark and the other in New Brunswick, then email had to be transmitted from one local server to a remote server. In our case, we did something quite novel, instead of "transmitting" the email, we simply pointed to the email data in the remote database server. Many things could go wrong in the transmission, such as the servers or the lines going down. This required the need to keep track of which servers were up and which were down. If an email did not get transmitted, we needed to know that an error took place and to retry. As the first email Postmaster, I was responsible for ensuring that every email got transmitted. Any errors would make users question the system's value and reliability and take away their motivation to leave their paper world behind.

Once the system was up, we needed to train the users. In 1980, I wrote a formal user's manual and an online Help section to make it even easier and more instructional. In 1981, the Westinghouse Science Awards, considered the "Baby Nobels" (known today as Intel awards), recognized the invention of email with an Honors award. Since the development of email, from 1978 to 1981, the core features of email remain unchanged in modern products such as Gmail, Hotmail, Yahoo, and others. One will notice that the core features in these tools, which we all use today, are from the interoffice postal mail system.

The History of Email: From Newark, NJ, to the World

The evolution of email is summarized below. The appendix contains a visual diagram, which also summarizes this history.

1978—A fourteen-year-old high school student becomes a research fellow at UMDNJ in Newark, NJ, and begins to create email, the electronic version of the interoffice postal mail system.

1980—Local news of email's creation appears in the *West Essex Tribune*, a Livingston, NJ, newspaper.

1981—Westinghouse Science Talent Search Honors Award is given for Email.

1982—First US Copyright for email is issued.

1985—Development of "offline readers." Offline readers allowed email users to store their emails on their own personal computers, and then read them and prepare replies without actually being connected to the network— sort of like Microsoft Outlook can do today.

1988—Eudora is developed by Steve Dorner.

1988—Vinton Cerf arranges for the connection of MCI Mail to the NSFNET for "experimental use," providing the first sanctioned commercial use of the Internet. Made possible through the Corporation for the National Research Initiative (CNRI).

1990—Compuserve offers its email, connected to the NSFNET, through the Ohio State University network.

1991—Lotus Notes is released.

1992—Microsoft Outlook is released.

1993—America OnLine and Delphi offer global Internet Mail. Their solution makes it easy for an ordinary citizen to get an email account and use an email system.

1995—EchoMail for email management to AT&T launched.

1996—HotMail is released.

1997—Yahoo Mail is released.

1999—The Blackberry comes out.

2003—CAN-SPAM Act goes into effect.

2005—Email address verification, SPF deployed.

2007—Gmail is released.

2009—iPhone 3G and other smartphones are released.

2011—"E-mail" now becomes officially "email" (to match original copyright of V. A. Shiva Ayyadurai) per the Associated Press (AP) Style Book.

Chapter Summary

The features created for email in UMDNJ in Newark, New Jersey, still exist in present day email systems. Those features were derived from the interoffice, interorganizational paper-based mail system. Email is the electronic version of this paper-based mail system. The email that flows through email systems, moreover, has unique characteristics, different from other medias such as phone technology. This chapter has clearly delineated those characteristics to enable you to consciously see email for what it is. That understanding will enable you, as well as your organizations, to effectively use the medium to build brand, create new connections, and develop relationships. And, in a world where a customer is the lifeblood of one's future, the optimal use of email can drive superior customer service.

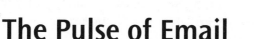

The Pulse of Email

"Clinton got email as early as 1993 and used it to build his brand. Toyota learned the hard way in 2010 after losing $30 billion in market value and 16 percent in sales."

On February 22, 2010, Aiko Toyoda, the chairman of Toyota Motor Corporation, admitted that his organization had failed to "connect the dots." Consumers had experienced a disastrous flaw in Toyota's brake pedal design, which resulted in catastrophic accidents and deaths. As early as December 2008, Toyota knew about the brake pedal matter—their customer service department had been receiving communications from consumers, in email as well as other media. By failing to "connect the dots," he meant that his internal organization had failed to connect the complaints being received by Toyota's consumer call centers with the other "dots" or parts of Toyota's internal organization, such as product development and manufacturing. The results were disastrous: consumers died and were injured seriously—deaths and injuries that could have been avoided far earlier.

Why did Toyota's call centers not notify product development and manufacturing of the brake pedal matter? It would have been easy for them to forward and route those recurring email complaints—far easier than phone calls or print mail. The reality is they did not take email seriously. They had treated email as though it were a phone call and did not understand email's unique characteristics. Even today, nearly 70 percent of organizations do not manage and use email effectively. So the Toyota incident is not that surprising. When a new medium initially appears, we tend to treat it in the same way that we treat other mediums with which we are more familiar. This is the case with email. For example, in the 1920s, during the glory days of Broadway, when film, a new medium at the time, first came into being, most early filmmakers simply pointed the camera at the stage and "made a film." They thought that by simply putting a camera in front of a theatrical set and shooting the actors onstage, they were making a film. It was not until many years later, once filmmakers recognized that a camera could be panned, zoomed, taken on location, and so on, that real films with "shots" and "editing" were done. Realization of the medium's potential finally enabled the creation of films that went beyond just pointing a camera at the stage. More importantly, a new art form developed, far different than theatrical stage performances. Today, we still use email like early filmmakers made movies. Many do not understand the nature of email's characteristics. They simply answer email like a phone call, or respond to it in a delayed manner like print mail, and express other old habits.

The White House

Had Toyota understood the properties of email, they would have organized the email into categories, tracking them to see if there was a trend or recurring pattern of complaints, and would have escalated them appropriately. In 2010, there were enough examples of large brands starting to handle email. What is startling is that such a major brand as Toyota failed to integrate its customer communications effectively. President Clinton, however, started using email as early as 1993 and used it to build his brand. Toyota learned the hard way in 2010 after losing $30 billion in market value and 16 percent in total sales. As early as 1993, President Clinton had sought and found solutions to manage and sort email as a way to listen to his "customers," his constituents. At that time, the White House was receiving 5,000 emails per day. Interns would read these emails manually, sort them into 147 different "buckets" or categories, print them out, and send a printed mail response to those with postal addresses. The White House was looking for a more efficient way to sort and manage incoming email. A Clinton staffer by the name of Jack Fox had the idea for a competition. The rules were simple: they would send a set of several thousand White House emails to qualified contestants. Each contestant, using their software, had to automatically categorize those emails. Fox and his team would score the results, and select a winner based on whoever had the greatest number of emails categorized correctly. Examples of the categories included Death Threats, Education, Drugs, Environment, and Iran.

The concept was that an incoming email would always fall into one of these categories. If an email could be automatically categorized, then it would save an incredible amount of time in sorting and filtering. The categorization could be used to select the correct templated response. At the time, the process of reading, sorting, and responding was done by White House interns. With the accelerated growth rate of email, the entire White House would have become an email call center, filled with hundreds of interns. There were six companies that entered the competition. While at MIT in the midst of my doctoral research, I was asked to participate in this competition. I had developed a highly unorthodox approach to classify all types of objects, and that approach could be used for classifying email.

The competitors were companies, with programmers, infrastructure, and staff. I was the only one participating as an individual and not as a company, and I ended up winning the White House competition. My approach had resulted in the highest accuracy of automatic categorization. For Jack Fox, this meant he could give real-time reports to the Executive Office of the White House, identifying which topics or categories were top priority to the American public—these reports would serve as a pulse to allow President Clinton to feel the heartbeat of the American public. Had Aiko Toyoda done the same thing in 2010, he likely would have seen a big spike even as early as December 2008 in the "Brake Pedal" category, from the inbound email analysis.

In 1993, the World Wide Web was getting more accessible, making it easy for many to use the Internet. If the White House was receiving growing volumes of inbound emails and needed such a solution, was it not likely that many larger companies would face the same situation? Clearly, such a solution must have a wider market. I sought MIT's permission to get rights to my work. The MIT Technology Licensing Office (TLO) was surprisingly amenable and gave me a waiver. The TLO only wanted MIT to own things developed at the Institute if they saw it had a huge market poential. At that time, they felt that technologies for managing email were not of any market value. Such was the perception of email in 1993, even by the world's leading educational institution for technology.

AT&T—First User of Email Management

At that same time, I had been fascinated with the Web. While in graduate school, I had already begun experimenting with creating web content. Websites may have been rudimentary at that time, but building them was an art. There were not many businesses looking to the web in 1994. Arts-Online.com was one such experiment, a web portal for artists, which I began developing with several others. Many of my friends were struggling artists, and it seemed that the web could offer a direct marketplace for them to sell their art, without gatekeepers. I managed to convince the mayor of Cambridge, Massachusetts, to loan us a small 200 square

foot space in the Cambridge Multicultural Arts Center (CMAC). In return for
the space, we gave CMAC an Internet connection. That Internet connection was
obtained for free by my bartering with NETCOM, an Internet service provider, in
exchange for placing their advertisement in a book I was writing called *Arts and
the Internet*. When Arts-Online.com went up, it was the first interdisciplinary
artist site on the Internet. We put up nearly 5,000 artists, musicians, filmmakers,
and photographers on the site. At that same time, we were hosting Arts-Online
on our own web servers, and with the growth of hits to the site, we were thinking about moving the servers to The Internet Access Company (TIAC). While at
TIAC for a business meeting, I met Tom Zawacki, one of the founders of a company called Modem Media.

At the time, traditional advertising agencies did not concern themselves
with the Internet. Modem Media was the first such company. When I met Tom,
I shared with him the events of the White House competition and Arts-Online.
Tom asked if we would put an "ad banner" on Arts-Online. The concept of an ad
banner itself was new. Tom himself had barely gotten started and had just won
the Zima account. Zima was a new brand of liquor designed for Generation X,
and Tom had built their website. They were looking for ways to draw hits to the
site. The Arts-Online site seemed to attract the kind of crowd Zima needed. He
asked me to formulate a pricing scheme for the ad banner. I looked at the price of
physical banner ads on the Massachusetts Turnpike, a full-page ad in *PC Week*,
and a 30-second ad on TV as benchmarks, and asked for $.06 per impression
(a view) of the banner ad. I estimated 700,000 impressions over the year and
asked for about $40,000. Tom loved the analysis and agreed to the price. This
kind of transaction was as new to him as it was to us. He published the pricing
analysis in *Internet World*, and, for many years, that pay-per-impression pricing
was the standard in the industry. The $40,000 was more than enough to fund
Arts-Online. We even had some extra cash, which we used toward developing
EchoMail, the name we gave to the software based on the White House experience of email sorting.

At this time, few large companies saw the importance of investing in web
presence. The few that had a website spent no more than a few hundred dollars
on it. However, there was a revolution under way. In 1994, AT&T, seeing the
Internet's exponential growth, understood it was quickly becoming a powerful
force. They were the first to decide to make a serious investment in online marketing. They wanted to hire a company to build websites for the entire AT&T enterprise including all of their forty subsidiaries. The budget was an unprecedented
$10 million, and Modem Media was selected to build AT&T's web presence. Each
of the forty websites they were building would be receiving email. Tom and I had
remained friends. Familiar with the White House story, Tom thought this would

be a great opportunity to have EchoMail process the influx of email that AT&T's websites were likely to receive. He introduced me to Lisa Gillingham, the head of the Business Marketing Division at AT&T. Despite Tom's recommendation, AT&T did not immediately see the value of managing email. I took a bumpy $20 bus ride from Boston to New Jersey and met with Lisa nearly thirty times, finally convincing her to employ EchoMail (the technology for managing email) for all of AT&T's forty websites. AT&T in 1995 became the first commercial customer of email management—the first customer of EchoMail.

The AT&T contract with us was for $40,000. Our services would be used to receive all inbound email from each of the customer service contact forms on the forty websites. We were expected to analyze the email, sort it, and make it available for the proper customer service representative to respond. Unfortunately, the IT department of AT&T did not want to deploy the EchoMail software within their infrastructure. Lisa was caught between a rock and a hard place. She wanted EchoMail's software, but the internal IT department would not cooperate. I suggested that she forward each of the AT&T emails to EchoMail servers in Cambridge, where they would be automatically categorized, and that we provide a web-based interface (like we all use today in popular web-based email browsers) to make the processed email available for the representatives at AT&T to review and send back to customers. She agreed—it resolved her internal IT politics. The IT department was happy since they didn't have to manage hardware or software. EchoMail was deployed on a server out of that 200 square foot room at CMAC. Imagine this, a small company in Cambridge, located in an Arts Center, was receiving all of the customer emails of the largest telecommunications company in the world!

EchoMail was not only the first email management company, but also the first Application Software Provider (ASP). Today, people call this concept Software as a Service (SaaS). AT&T did not have to buy hardware or software, we provided it all. All they needed to do was log in and use the software over the web. We had one small server, hosted in our small room at CMAC, which we could barely maintain 70 percent of the time, and this was considered good. Today EchoMail wouldn't be in business if the servers were not kept up and running 99.99 percent of the time.

The Guts of an Email

The AT&T account was a great first customer. For me, the irony was not only that I had created the first email system in 1978, but also that I was deploying the first email management system, EchoMail, to address the success (or problem) of email: its growing usage and volume. EchoMail involved a fusion of two fields: email and pattern analysis. My love of both had begun at UMDNJ. In my pattern analysis work at MIT—studying patterns in ultrasonic waves sent through materials to map their internal structures—my thoughts were on the digital world as much as the physical one. I had this idea that the same techniques for analyzing physical matter could be used to analyze information. With physical matter, ultrasonic (high-frequency) waves are shot through a piece of material. Techniques are then used to observe the reflected waves coming out of the material. By comparing properties of the reflected wave patterns with what was originally inputted (e.g., frequency shift, amplitude changes), one can attempt to understand the internal characteristics of the physical material. Could not information be conceptually treated as a piece of physical material for which one could derive similar properties? The White House contest was the bridge that provided me the opportunity to test this theory.

I was reading thousands and thousands of emails, and realized they are not all that different. In fact, looking below the surface, email tended to be almost robotically repetitive with some high level patterns. Maybe email had fundamental properties that could be recognized like physical matter? Consider the following message someone may send AT&T:

Dear AT&T,
I love your website. However, I am upset with my wireless service, with poor connection in certain areas. Furthermore, my son is graduating college, can he have an internship at AT&T? I'm a school teacher and would also love a copy of your annual report.

Sincerely,
Mark

EchoMail was built to scan this free-form message for key words and phrases, within a bounded context, which I called the "five fundamental properties of email," for which I received three US Patents. The first property is the *attitude* of the email. EchoMail can classify the writer as negative, neutral, or positive, or a combination, by honing in on key words such as "terrible" or "superb." I recall that one client's messages included the words "da bomb." EchoMail initially classified it as negative, then we learned "da bomb" meant "you're cool"; the classification needed to change.

In the above email, the attitude is both positive (for the website) and negative (for the wireless service). A second property is the *issue* of the email. There are two issues in the above email: website and wireless service. The email could also have been about other issues such as a billing problem or merchandise return or a legal problem. A third property is the *request* the writer is making—for example, the location of the nearest outlet. In the example, the request is for an annual report. The fourth property discovers which *products (or services)* the writer is interested in. In the example, it is wireless service. Finally, the fifth property is the *customer type*. This determines what sort of person is sending an email. Writers often give away information like whether they own a boat, their home address, or zip code. EchoMail can scoop up and add this information to the client's customer databases. In the example above, it's clear the customer type is a school teacher, likely a male due to the name "Mark."

Using a number of sophisticated and not-so- sophisticated techniques, EchoMail applied a dictionary of key words and word relationships known as a "semantic network," to extract these five properties of any email. If EchoMail finds the words "website" and "problem" in close proximity, it might conclude that the email's issue is an online ordering problem. Depending on how an email gets classified, EchoMail can choose either to reply from a selection of prewritten responses or forward the email to one or more departments for humans to address.

JCPenney and Email Crisis Management

In an article in *Technology Review*, "Dr. Email Will See You Now," the writer Deborah Shapley began her story by saying, "I'm gay!" with a big picture of me on the front of the article. So, rightfully, many of my friends thought I was coming out of the closet. But the story was not about me; it was about how JCPenney was using email to support their crisis management efforts after TV actress Ellen DeGeneres announced her homosexuality during her prime time *Ellen*. That ABC broadcast fueled a nationwide controversy, which spilled over to JCPenney, a major sponsor of *Ellen*. JCPenney found its fledgling presence on the World Wide Web inundated with email of a kind and quantity it had never seen before. Anti-gay critics flamed DeGeneres and belted JCPenney for supporting her show. Supporters were just as vehement. At the time, Middle America's favorite apparel retailer had just implemented EchoMail. Not only did EchoMail go on routing and replying to regular queries about orders and returns, but also recognized that the *Ellen* messages didn't fall into a preset category. Of course, people working in JCPenney stores and catalog call centers were also getting calls about *Ellen*. But the volume of complaints to any one site couldn't compare with the power and immediacy of the signal received by JCPenney's email department. The EchoMail program was reporting a sudden spike in the number of angry incoming messages, and headquarters knew it had a major customer relations problem. Right away the PR department drafted a statement for the company to use in reply to the ornery *Ellen* email.

The *Ellen* brouhaha caused the show to lose JCPenney as a sponsor, as the retailer declined to renew for the next season. EchoMail, however, fared better. The system's early alert over *Ellen* during the testing period helped convince JCPenney to sign up for the service. The JCPenney site's goal was to "surprise and delight" visitors, as Ron Hanners, executive vice president of JCPenney Commerce Solutions, had explained. As the visitor moves through links, Ron's vision was that "the experience should become an emotional surge" that leads to a purchase. But the sale was only "the first part of the loop," according to Hanners. His vision was that JCPenney must make a "return loop" by speaking back to that customer, "offering them additional products at a fair price and added convenience." And for this, Hanners saw email and EchoMail as a way to save money by "multiplying our personnel's effectiveness." At the time of the *Ellen* furor, JCPenney received about 1,200 emails per month. By late 1999, the number had grown to 30,000. Yet their Internet customer service staff only needed four people, because of the power of the EchoMail technology to sort and process email. Back in Cambridge, we had conducted time-motion studies that showed the average cost for a human to read and compose an answer to a single email was $4.23. EchoMail received about $1 for each message successfully decoded and replied to automatically. The client saved about $3 per message.

The Growth of Email Management

The success of customers like AT&T and JCPenney helped garner EchoMail many other blue chip customers such as Nike, Citigroup, Procter & Gamble, Unilever, American Express, Calvin Klein, and others for email management. EchoMail had a solution and the market needed it. The White House's recognition of the importance of email is what had led to EchoMail's existence. During the period from 1993 to 2003, EchoMail defined email and email management. Major press in the *Wall Street Journal*, *Technology Review*, *US News and World Report*, the *Boston Globe*, and others continually provided news stories on how companies were using email with EchoMail in new and incredible ways.

William M. Bulkeley of the *Wall Street Journal* wrote very favorable comments about EchoMail:

> Send an email to your Senator, and there is a growing likelihood that it will first be read by a computer system called EchoMail. The program, developed by EchoMail Inc., of Cambridge, Mass., sorts, analyzes and even answers some of the email sent to companies such as Kmart Corp., American Express Co. and Calvin Klein Inc. Now, after two years of pilot programs, more than 30 US senators have installed it under a deal signed by the Senate sergeant-at-arms.

Bulkeley went on to share how David Archambault, president of B3 Corp., which runs Internet promotions for companies such as AOL Time Warner, used EchoMail to reduce customer service costs. "I read about Shiva and tracked him down. I became enamored with the technology," Mr. Archambault told Bulkeley, ". . . how EchoMail analyzed and forwarded email automatically to the right department."

Archambault shared, "Questions about a promotion become very similar: How long is it running? What are the terms and conditions? We've trained [EchoMail] to respond to hundreds of questions. It's smart enough to tell us when it's got something it can't answer." Archambault explained that as new questions arose, his team could train EchoMail just as it would an employee. "We had more inconsistency with our live service reps," he concluded, as an important aspect of email management. In his tests, he shared that EchoMail answered as much as 95 percent of all emails correctly.

Bulkeley went on to tell how EchoMail sorts out and immediately deletes random "spam" or unsolicited pitches with such phrases as "I hated your product" or "please send me a replacement." Bulkeley found how some customers were using EchoMail to sort mail and route it to the right person, and many other customers found it smart enough to respond to most of the regular emails and to forward to humans the things it didn't understand. When reporting on EchoMail's success with the US Senate, Bulkeley said that most email from constituents still gets a glance from staffers, but that Sen. William Frist, a Tennessee Republican and technology enthusiast, had told him, "that's not going to last for long" and that EchoMail is good enough to categorize most email and send appropriate responses.

Companies sometimes started using EchoMail because they were inundated with mail on a topic. Kmart signed on with EchoMail when Kmart was starting to deal with letters protesting its decision to stop carrying handgun ammunition. Since EchoMail could batch and categorize email together by similar categories, EchoMail was able to get a consumer's email quickly routed to the appropriate department. Similarly, when NASCAR driver Dale Earnhardt was killed, EchoMail sorted email from customers who wanted to buy memorabilia from Kmart.

Many companies were educated on the characteristics of email and its benefits. These companies learned to use email effectively to interact with their customers and partners. Calvin Klein utilized integrated email with TV advertising to generate one of the most "innovative advertising programs," as stated by *Wired* magazine. In Calvin Klein's use of email, an integrated marketing program allowed viewers exposed to the cKOne TV ad to send email directly to the characters in the commercials. The viewers were allowed to continue that conversation online. Companies such as QVC, the second largest TV network and the number one online electronic retailer globally, conducted an electronic dialogue with the customers through email to convert one-time customers into lifetime customers. QVC did not see customer service emails simply as complaints, but rather as opportunities to further satisfy customers through accurate and well-thought-out responses. While resolving customer complaints, they cleverly found a way to embed a marketing offer within the response email. QVC gave life to the ethos "a complaint as a gift."

The United States Senate took one step forward and two steps backward in their use of email. Initially, they deployed sophisticated email management technology to sort incoming email to various senate offices. EchoMail made senators more accountable to their constituency by being able to automatically filter and categorize their constituents' emails, enabling them to know the real-time concerns of their constituents. However, email's accountability became a threat to various senate offices. Prior to the use of email, a senator could easily state that they were not fully aware of what their constituents thought. The filtering, categorizing, and organizing of email provided unadulterated reports of constituent concerns requiring action on the part of senators. Senators, by and large, except forward thinking ones like Bill Frist and Ted Kennedy, were not ready for such accountability.

Other organizations such as Nike and JCPenney used email to avert crises, and Calvin Klein to drive new integrated marketing campaigns. In the interest of their own benefit and that of their stockholders, Nike was one of the first to elicit feedback from customers as well as organize, categorize, and route email for superior customer service. Their use of email helped them to understand their consumers' concerns on Nike's labor practices, address those issues, and build goodwill among their consumers. By reviewing and paying attention to feedback from constituents or customers, email offered opportunities to improve a product and create innovations based on such feedback.

The Power of Email

A company's Inbox was literally a treasure trove of raw data that could be analyzed to find new product ideas which could generate billions of dollars. Analysis of email revealed potential and egregious product and service issues such as the Toyota brake problem. Detecting trends in email could serve as an early warning system to "connect the dots" and avert such fiascoes. In this sense, email could foster transparency and accountability within an organization, leading to trust, internally and externally. Email could be used to strengthen existing relationships through creative communications. Customer email contained personal likes and dislikes which could be quickly and cheaply extracted, such as gender, age, or buying habits. Using this data, a company could engage in customized communication and tailor a promotional message to a customer's individual tastes. Email provided an ideal platform to conduct such one-on-one dialogue.

Customers themselves were sources of innovation. Incoming email could be cheaply filtered and analyzed with the aid of software. Once categorized, the email could be forwarded to the right customer service representatives in an expeditious manner, so at the very least the sender received a timely and accurate response. More importantly, suggestions to fix or improve existing products could be dually routed to both customer service representatives and product developers, the latter being able to gain direct feedback from the customer, to affect product improvement. Early adopters of email such as Nike used it to identify creative input for new product design directly based on customer feedback. This kind of customer feedback is invaluable, and if used right, far cheaper than any focus group or marketing research. When used successfully and incorporated appropriately, such feedback can lead to the creation of new commercially successful products.

During the period from 1995 to 2003, EchoMail defined both email and email management with such major brands. These brands were beginning to see email for what it was, and learning how to use it in powerful ways. However, that would all change. The period after 2003 became starkly different, when other large software companies such as Siebel (now part of Oracle), witnessing the growth of email, began to work hard to confuse the world and the entire marketplace on the essence of email, to ensure their own long-term survival.

Siebel Confuses the World of Email

In chapter 1, it was discussed how one source of confusion, surrounding the origin and unique characteristics of email, was the lack of fundamental understanding as to the nature of the three major forms of text-based messaging. Hopefully, that chapter cleared up that confusion, and put email in the right context. However, starting in 2003, a second source of confusion arose. This was not from ignorance but from a conscious and willful effort to confuse the market by purposefully lumping the email medium and the phone medium into one category. If there was one company I would blame for this confusion of email (and perhaps indirectly for Toyota's fiasco), it would be Siebel, a company started by Tom Siebel. Siebel dominated the Customer Relationship Management (CRM) software market by selling a core product for managing inbound phone calls into call centers of large Global 2000 brands. Siebel's price tag for an enterprise installation could easily be upwards of a whopping $6 million. Siebel's growth relied on the need for call centers to manage phone calls. More phone calls meant more reasons to buy Siebel software.

However, the rise of email sent fear through Siebel. A small company in Cambridge, Massachusetts, EchoMail, a fraction of Siebel's size, was getting big customers—winning brand after brand for managing email. And, email volume was increasing quarter after quarter—a threat to Siebel's revenues. In 2003, Siebel decided to get into the email business in a big way, without a product anywhere near the functionality of then email management products. To do this, they would somehow have to convince the leadership of Global 2000 brands that Seibel's software, built for managing phone calls, could also handle email.

The Corrupt World of Industry Analysts

Industry analysts came to Siebel's rescue. In the world of technology, as mentioned earlier, industry analysts, such as Forrester Research, IDC, and Gartner to name a few, make money by writing industry reports on their "independent" third-party analysis of products, vendors, and technology trends. They then sell their reports to other companies, who need such "independent" third-party advice. Consider the VP of technology at General Motors who wants to know which software platform to buy for a new accounting system. The VP contacts industry analysts for help. There may be many vendors of accounting systems, and he doesn't have time to speak to all of them and wants to invite the top five for a competitive selection process. Industry analysts may have written a report surveying the top accounting systems. After paying the analyst for the report, the VP is able to identify the top five vendors. If you are a vendor and are not included in that top-five list, GM may never select you. In this manner, the analysts work hard to become gatekeepers of technology selection by the Global 2000. Vendors are forced to be "nice" to analysts, so they get included in these reports. Analysts do not look kindly on vendors who get selected without their "blessings," for it diminishes their business model.

In early 2000, EchoMail was growing at an explosive rate, being selected by senior executives at major Global 2000 companies based on its merits, without the need for blessings from industry analysts. Forrester Research, for example, contacted EchoMail, stating that they were doing a survey on the best email technology companies. In Forrester's 2000 report, EchoMail received a near perfect score, as *the best* product in the industry. A few years later, Forrester contacted EchoMail to be reviewed for inclusion in the next report. However, a few days before their review, a call "requesting" EchoMail to become a customer was also received—this meant paying up to $250,000 a year to get subscriptions for Forrester's industry reports. EchoMail refused and expressed its concern on why a sales call was related to the "independent" review process. The result: EchoMail never appeared in that year's report. The number one company in the world for email was wiped off the Forrester reports. This form of corruption in the technology world goes on each day. Since EchoMail was not willing to pay to play, this meant EchoMail would never get called in for any competitive reviews, so woe to EchoMail if decision makers relied on Forrester reports alone.

That is the game of industry analysts, and Siebel knew how to play that game. In fact, some vendors, to get their names in reports, fund analysts to perform customized "research" projects—another way to get money to industry analysts. With the growth of email and with a lack of real products for email management, Siebel contracted many analyst firms to do research and write white papers to preach a new mantra: email and phone were just channels of communication and a single platform (their Siebel CRM platform) could handle both. The reality of the nuances and fundamental differences of email and the phone medium were purposefully ignored. The analysts created a new theory called "blended media"—they parroted Siebel's mantra that a single technology could handle both email and phone—claiming that there was no reason for independent email management systems. All of this in theory sounded good, but anyone running a call center knew that it was absolute rubbish—managing and responding to email was different than handling a phone call. For one thing, email was asynchronous; phone was synchronous.

However, the deep pockets of Siebel, combined with the questionable business model of analysts, proliferated the equivalence of the email and phone myth overnight. Siebel was implementing the approach of "if you can't convince, then confuse." Following this, many customers would ask, "Why don't I just buy Siebel? Their phone product can also handle email." Siebel's ability to confuse the email and phone issue under the umbrella of CRM and "blended media" won them email customers, and more disastrously, it made executives in senior-most positions think email and phone were the same.

On a cultural level, managing a phone was different than managing an email, for the many reasons previously discussed. The misinformation that Siebel and analysts spread resulted in major brands not using email as it was to meant to be used and forcing email to be managed like the phone. The culture of treating email like the phone affected many companies and was a setback to the educational efforts that EchoMail had done on email and email management during the decade prior to 2003. Toyota, in my belief, in 2010, was a direct victim of this kind of misinformation. The care President Clinton showed in 1993 to organize, categorize, and be responsive to email was because the White House rightfully compared email with their existing postal mail letter correspondence process, *not* their phone call management process. Customers who bought Siebel products, investing millions of dollars using their approach, took many years to figure out the lie of the email and phone equivalence. The email channel could not just be "blended" with phone. Citigroup initially got caught in this myth, as related later in chapter ten, and eventually broke out of it after losing much time and money.

Chapter Summary

My hope is that this chapter, combined with the earlier two chapters, has made you aware of the opportunities of email, its origin, and the sources of confusion surrounding it. With this awareness, you are in a position to consciously appreciate and resuscitate the power of email as exemplified by those early companies, which we will detail in chapter 5 through chapter 15. Their pioneering use of email is still valid today. The next part provides those stories so you can reclaim email for what it is and move beyond the confusion that still persists.

Ten Commandments of Email

These ten "commandments" will ensure that you use email the right way. They will save you time, money, and a lot of heartaches.

Before moving on to the detailed stories of major brands and their uses of email, *The Ten Commandments of Email* are provided here to serve as a summary of the core set of principles governing email. These ten commandments will ensure that you use email the right way. It will save you time, money, and a lot of heartaches. These principles are supplemented by *50 Tips on Using Email*, in chapter 17.

First Commandment

Email Is Not "Private"

You may think that any email you send is only received by the recipient; however, email can be easily forwarded, or the recipient of your email can reply to you while copying or blind copying a host of other people. On a different level, following the attacks on Septermber 11, 2001, and the Homeland Security initiatives derived from them, all of our email is accessible by governments at any time and any place regardless of the level of security and encryption. From a corporate perspective, a company owns any and all email transactions made on the company's server. Also, those sending email must be aware of hackers and thieves. Be particularly careful to avoid sending passwords, credit card numbers, and other personally identifiable information via email. If you use free email services, read their privacy policy, for you will find that your email is not so "private."

Second Commandment

Email Reflects You and Your Organization

When you write an email, you are mirroring your thoughts and feelings in the electronic medium. It is important to understand the difference between writing an informal and a formal email. Remember email is not text messaging. Sometimes it is okay to be funny and joking; however, in business communications, err on the side of formality by checking spelling and grammar and following proper etiquette of writing with appropriate headers and footers on all email communications. For organizations, every email sent to a prospect or customer reflects your organization's brand. Set standards, protocols, and templates to ensure that the millions of emails that are sent do not erode your brand, but rather enhance it through each communication. Within each communication, be concise with clear objectives and the results you hope to achieve.

Third Commandment

Email Has Permanence

Each email you send is more than likely saved or archived on your computer system or on the recipient's system; therefore, do not assume that an email message no longer exists, even if you delete what you received or sent. Your thoughts and interactions with others, via email, are archived and saved, potentially for posterity. In financial services organizations, all data must be saved for a minimum of seven years. Think about what you are writing and what legacy you are leaving through such communications. Email communications are subject to legal discovery and can be presented in a court of law.

Fourth Commandment

Email Can Be Confusing

While email is great for communicating quickly and easily, it can be confusing because the sender and receiver of such communications only see words, not gestures and emotions. Therefore, precision is central to email communications. Do not use capitalization unless it is necessary. Avoid sarcasm, as this can be very dangerous. For example, "What are you talking about?" can be construed in many ways: a joke, an attack, or a sarcastic remark. Use a clear subject line, signature line, header, body, and footer in all email communications. Think before you write. And, think really carefully before you hit Send.

Fifth Commandment

Email Is Not Free

One of the erroneous assumptions is that email is free. Email is not by any means free. There are many direct and indirect costs associated within this medium. It costs money for an organization to handle an inbound customer email. However, beyond this there are other costs. Spam or junk email costs money to read, process, store, and delete. Emails containing viruses have many side effects including loss in productivity and potential destruction of valuable information. Large attachments require additional space. Chain letters, forwarding of jokes, and participation in flaming debates via email add to these costs. Recognize that every email interaction has a cost, including your time, computer hardware and software costs, and IT personnel time to maintain the systems. Be frugal with email. If you're not paying for it someone else is or you may be paying indirectly when you use "free" services which may be reselling your personal information or using you to view advertisements.

Sixth Commandment

Email Is Personal

Email, whether formal or informal, is a very personal medium similar to personal conversation. If you send an email to someone and he or she does not respond, you will feel anxious and disappointed. Use auto-acknowledgment and out-of-office replies appropriately to let people know you received their email communication. If you are using auto-responders, avoid email loops by using varying "From" addresses. Use clear signature names at the footers so everyone knows exactly who is writing to them and how to contact the sender. In email marketing, the more you segment, target, and personalize your mailing lists and your content, the more you will be seen as personal and will be rewarded with higher open rates and increased sales. Your headers, language, and salutations will make your email more personal and intimate.

Seventh Commandment

Email Is Not Equal

Not everyone has access to the same technology for viewing email. This means that some people can view different formats of email, while others on old browsers and on many wireless devices can only see some parts of email. Thus, be concise when writing email. This will become more and more important for wireless interactions because many have to pay by character received or sent. If you are participating in email marketing campaigns, ensure that your outbound message can be read by the different browsers.

Eighth Commandment

Email Has Limits

Do not use email to avoid having a conversation. Do not send an angry, potentially inflammatory email when a heart-to-heart conversation either in person or over the phone is needed. Email is not good for debates, accusations, or personal attacks. Email is really designed for convenience, not for urgency. If you see an ongoing thread of email, back and forth, with no resolution in sight, step back, relax, and know you may have hit the limit with that email interaction.

Ninth Commandment

Email Contains Thoughts

Email contains the thoughts of those who write the email. Every email contains attitude, issues, requests, products of interest, and the type of customer sending the email, either explicitly or implicitly stated. By employing some manual or computer-aided filtering and intelligence, these thought forms, embedded in email, can be extracted and sorted, so you can better respond and connect with the other person and know what they are really thinking.

Tenth Commandment

Email Is Asynchronous

The great element of email is that you read it when you want to read it. Those who check email every five minutes are using email in an undisciplined fashion. Reading and responding to every email immediately sets false expectations for those to whom you send email. It may be valuable to set some guidelines, thus establishing some clear disciplines on using email effectively.

The above Ten Commandments are core principles that will support your creative, personal, and professional success in using email. There are other important elements of email usage. In chapter 17 of this book, "50 Tips on Using Email" supplements these Ten Commandments, which you may also find valuable in developing your own handbook of email's best practices.

PART TWO

THE POWER OF EMAIL

Anthropologists sometimes discover new findings in lost periods of human development that change preconceived notions of who we are and where we came from. Such lost history at times may provide new information and understanding relevant to modern times. The use of email from 1995 to 2003 is one such period. During this period, early adopters of email in large Global 2000 companies and major organizations explored dynamic and creative uses of email that few people are aware of, even today. Their experiments in using email were radical and revolutionary. This forgotten history of email provides valuable lessons for today and a unique opportunity to reclaim the power of email. Although those lessons emerged within large organizations, given the expansive growth of the Internet, those lessons are now equally important and relevant for small and mid-market businesses, which also seek to build brand, create new business, and make powerful connections through their growing online presence.

In chapters 5 through 12, the creative and strategic use of email by large organizations such as Nike, Calvin Klein, George Bush for President Campaign, Unilever, Cookie Jar Entertainment, P&G, American Express, Allstate, Citigroup, Hilton, and QVC are provided. In chapter 13, the Guggenheim's pioneering work in using email to build relationships with their members provides invaluable lessons to others in the arts and nonprofit community. Chapter 14 ends this part by providing practical approaches and methods for small and mid-market businesses, derived from the experiences of large organizations, so they too can build relationships and business through the effective use of email.

Brand Intimacy: Nike and Calvin Klein Style

"By integrating email with broadcast advertising, Nike and Calvin Klein created a new type of brand intimacy with millions overnight. That was revolutionary!"

Background

Brands like Calvin Klein (cK) and Nike are consistently great because they push the envelope. They seize the moment and push it beyond the ordinary bounds. And both understood the use of email as a medium for building intimacy. cK integrated email with broadcast advertising through the format of a transmedia campaign integrating email, TV, and print advertising that encompassed a soap-opera-like story, which *Wired* magazine called "revolutionary." Calvin Klein had followed Nike's lead. In an earlier campaign Nike integrated email, broadcast, web-based, and print advertising, featuring athletes, to build a similar intimacy to drive in-store traffic. In the late 1990s, this integrative approach was radical—and still is today. The story of how Nike and cK used email to build brand intimacy and connect with customers and consumers serves as a powerful lesson on how to build relationships by the integrative use of email.

Nike

The year 1997 became known as "The Year of the Sweatshop." The world's biggest clothing manufacturers reeled as one public relations disaster after another took place. Article after article came out exposing the horrendous working conditions, coupled with breathtakingly low wages, in the factories of some of America's best-loved brands. Even worse, the workers were often children, as young as thirteen, forced to work twelve-hour shifts, for up to seventy-five hours a week. Those making the Kathie Lee Gifford clothing line earned $0.31 an hour. The beloved cohost of *The Morning Show* became emblematic of the ruthless lipstick-clad capitalism practiced by American companies all over the world. Of these companies, none was more beloved or more emblematic of its country than Disney. In the first quarter of 1996 alone, Disney posted profits of $496 million and paid CEO Michael Eisner what amounted to $97,000 an hour. Meanwhile, all over the world, those who made the Mickey Mouse shirts were paid as little as $0.16 per hour.

In this milieu, Nike was yet another American icon that came under fire that same year. Started by Bill Bowerman and Phil Knight in 1964, the company was founded on outsourcing: the idea that they could compete with the German brands which dominated the market by producing quality running shoes in Japan. With nothing but $500 and a handshake deal, Bowerman and Knight ordered 300 pairs of sneakers, which Knight sold out of the trunk of his green Plymouth Valiant. The shoes sold. They ordered more from Japan. It also became cheaper to simply build their own factory. Soon they were building factories, and not just in Japan. As the 1960s gave way to the 1970s, it became too expensive to continue producing shoes in Japan. Nike built plants in Korea, then in Malaysia and Indonesia. Wherever Nike went, the economy boomed. Dubbed "The Nike Effect," this succession of investment, growth, and subsequent sale and resettlement was so solid that when financial analysts asked themselves which developing economy was next in line to boom, they looked at where the sportswear company was building its newest factories.

The year 1996 had been a great one for Nike. Stock price more than doubled from $32.50 per share in October 1995 to a stunning high of $76.38. Then came the articles about sweatshops and how companies like Nike profited from them. When they were accused of using sweatshops, the Nike initial response was all but confused: "It's an age-old practice," said spokeswoman Donna Gibbs, " . . . and the process of change is going to take time. Too often, well-intentioned human rights groups can cause dramatic negative effects if they scare companies into stopping production and the kids are thrown out on the street."

Profits were going up, sales were going up, they had just partnered with Michael Jordan on a new brand of sneakers, and expanded their scope yet again by recruiting a brilliant golfer, Tiger Woods, as their new spokesman. They were doing what they had always done. They had always been praised for it. They were not prepared for what was to come.

In her book, *No Logo*, Naomi Klein, an investigative journalist, wrote: "No story illustrates the growing distrust of the culture of corporate branding more than the international anti-Nike movement—the most publicized and tenacious of the brand-based campaigns. Nike's sweatshop scandals have been the subject of over 1,500 news articles and opinion columns. Its Asian factories have been probed by cameras from nearly every major media organization, from CBS to Disney's sports station and ESPN. As a result, several people in Nike's PR department work full time dealing with the sweatshop controversy—fielding complaints, meeting with local groups and developing Nike's response—and the company created a new executive position: Vice President for Corporate Responsibility."

Email for Crisis Management

In 1997, Nike learned a very expensive lesson in the power of new media and how bad PR spreads faster on the Internet. With earnings increasing to the tune of 40 percent, it was to be a record-breaking fiscal year. But the media storm did not let up. Anti-Nike websites sprung up all over the world. Using the Internet, activists' groups could communicate and coordinate internationally, then organize locally to create worldwide "Anti-Nike Day" protests. This was long before Twitter and Facebook. The boycotts were effective, and sales soon started to drop and stock prices plummeted. This spurred Nike to launch their own website: Nike.com. Soon they began to recognize that their consumer base wanted to communicate with them through email.

Prior to 1997, communications for Nike had been in postal mail letters, which would get handled by their consumer correspondence team who would open each one and respond. They would also get phone calls, which were also attended to by their consumer affairs staff. When they launched Nike.com, it marked the first time the company began receiving email. Nike realized that they would now have to offer real-time responses to this rapidly growing volume of inbound email. Emails were coming not only from their *customers* but also increasingly from *consumers* too. Consumers were the end users, who actually bought and put on the shoes. Customers were the retailers to whom Nike sold their shoes for selling to the consumers. Previously, Nike mainly dealt with customers: typically stores such as Foot Locker that would buy in bulk to sell to the consumers. Now, because of email, consumers that previously dealt primarily with the retail stores were in a position to take issues up directly with the manufacturer.

This was radical and new, especially considering the volume of consumer communication to Nike. This created a new issue for Nike, and Jane Flood was the executive who Nike charged with solving the problem. She would find her solution at a new media conference.

Tom Zawacki, one of the founders of Modem Media, the world's leading interactive agency at the time, was speaking at an Internet sports conference, when someone asked him: what were the technologies for handling email? Tom told the conference about EchoMail and the success of EchoMail's deployment at AT&T. Jane Flood was one of the attendees of this conference. Shortly thereafter, Brad Dupee, a vice president of business development at EchoMail, received a call from Jane. Brad gave Jane a quick demonstration of EchoMail over a web conference, and within that same week, Jane and her colleagues flew down to Cambridge. Within three days of seeing EchoMail, they began drafting a contract to have EchoMail process Nike's emails.

Nike showed the same attitude toward their website and email as they showed toward their brand, ensuring innovation and intimacy were integrated at every step. Their attitude toward email in particular ensured that they could effectively respond to their customers and their consumers. This was crucial because it was during this period that they began experiencing the media back-lash over use of sweatshops. They had to make sure that they kept good and open communication with their fan base in order to solve a major crisis.

There was a great amount of concern about Nike's use of potentially unfair business practices. As thousands of email came in every day on the subject of sweatshops, each and every one of them could be answered quickly, cheaply, and effectively. Not only that, but with EchoMail, Nike was able to generate reports about who was sending those emails. EchoMail's technology analyzed the email across five content dimensions: attitude, issue, request, products, and customer type. For example, if someone wrote the following email:

Dear Nike,
I love your website and my new Air Jordans, but am very upset with your labor practices. I am a CEO of a small company and would also like a copy of your annual report.

EchoMail would automatically analyze the content and characterize the attitude as *positive* and *negative*. In this case, the consumer is happy about the website and the Air Jordans, but is upset about Nike's labor practices. The issue in this case would be website and labor practices. The request would be for an annual report. The customer type would be CEO. Finally, the product would be Air Jordans. EchoMail would save this data for each email, and then use this analysis for automatic routing to the right department, and would also propose an intelligent response, by piecing together existing response paragraphs (based on the content categorization), which it would then send to a customer service representative (CSR) for review, editing, and final transmission back to the consumer. All of this was tracked so detailed reports could be created to know the "pulse" of the consumer in real time.

Phil Knight himself and his senior staff would regularly log in to EchoMail to get reports from the system. EchoMail also allowed Nike to organize those emails into groups, helping Nike address the individual consumers' concerns by sending messages from corporate communications. These messages could relay the reality from Nike's standpoint on worker treatment as well as new programs Nike was implementing to ensure more favorable treatment of workers. Email was used to tell Nike's version of the story directly to the consumers one-on-one—something they were not able to do before. This ability to directly respond to consumers was incredibly powerful. One noticed that first and foremost consumers gave Nike kudos for simply responding. Many other companies were simply ignoring email. Nike's commitment to get a response back to consumers was novel. Even in 2012, less than 30 percent of companies respond to their customers and consumers within forty-eight hours. Research reports show that there is an 85 percent chance of losing business if emails are not responded to within that forty-eight-hour window.

Nike was ahead of its time. This was revolutionary. Nike used email to do something unheard of: turn protesters into consumers. This not only proved the value of the EchoMail technology, but also the value of email as a direct one-to-one communications vehicle. Nike used the mined data from email communications to support Nike's brand by being proactive and being responsive to their consumer needs. Nike used EchoMail as an early warning system. Nike had always seen itself as creating products that represented a marriage between technology and design. Nike realized that within the content of email there was opportunity to not only address a crisis but also the opportunity to really listen to consumers and formulate new products and designs in a faster and cheaper way, from direct consumer feedback.

Email for Building Strong Consumer Relationships

Nike took incoming emails, categorized them, created standard responses, and routed them to customer service representatives who could look at them, edit them, and respond. This drastically reduced the cost of service. EchoMail's approach to analyze and sort email derived valuable data from the customer and consumer contact. The email, as aforementioned, contained attitudes (positive, negative, neutral), a myriad of issues (such as delivery, squeaky shoes, fitting), reference to different products (shoes, golf clubs, apparel), and different types of consumers (runners, skiers, baseball fans, hockey players). Occasionally, they would even find an email with requests, such as asking for an internship, or an autograph from Michael Jordan. As the emails came in, Nike developed a wealth of statistics gathered from the text analysis of the emails.

Even today, few in the senior leadership positions in organizations really understand what is happening on the front line of email communications. Consumers are writing to companies and those numbers continue to grow. Who receives that email? Typically a low-paid consumer care specialist who gets the email may read it, may delete it, and may write an appropriate or inappropriate response. Most CEOs and senior management officials have little to no idea of what is being written back, and this can be problematic because an email correspondence can be a legal document. Nike was a pioneer in recognizing the importance of knowing what people were thinking and saw email as an opportunity in the midst of the company's grave crisis. The CEO at Nike himself wanted reports; he was very interested in knowing the pulse of the consumers. The deployment of EchoMail created changes in the way email was dealt with from the lowest levels of customer service to middle management, and all the way up to the CEO. Everyone saw email as the connective tissue between the employees of Nike and the consumers and customers. This alerted Nike to imminent issues and potential future crises and allowed them to quickly and effectively address any matter requiring attention.

Email for Integrated Marketing

There are many uses for the data one can get out of email other than early warning systems and crisis communications. Email can be used as a sales tool. At the time, Nike spent half a billion dollars on traditional advertising. That included the money spent on TV ads, print ads, billboard ads, and so on. One of the brand goals of Nike was ubiquity. This means that advertising capital is spent on putting the Nike logo on all of the major athletes, in all different sports, as well as sponsoring major college and high school sports. It's hard if you're watching any sports game to miss a Nike logo. There is a very conscious effort by the company to ensure that the logo is everywhere and that it is broadcast widely. Primarily, Nike sends a common message: Just Do It. They send it through collaboration with a stable of sports stars and through their massive ad campaigns.

Email and the Internet offered Nike a very different way to communicate. This was one-on-one, no longer broadcast but *narrowcast*. In this effort, Nike saw the opportunity in email and a tool like EchoMail to accept inbound email and use its capability to understand the person's intentions from that email communication. They could organize and categorize the consumer by the attributes explained previously. Nike could thus track who someone was, what they wanted, and what their interests were, and proactively send out outbound communications targeted to those groups. For example, all the people who are into running and who liked their website may get a very different email than someone who was into baseball and wanted an internship. They could segment people in a way that was impossible to do through broadcast media. This is what is known as narrowcast, sending the right message to the right people at the right time.

To tap into the potential of both broadcast and narrowcast communications, Nike collaborated with other companies to create a marketing campaign integrating various forms of media. The collaboration between Nike, Wieden+Kennedy (Nike's advertising agency), and EchoMail was a pioneering effort in 1997. Nike knew how to bring the best of breeds together to create dynamic solutions. Wieden+Kennedy is known as the most creative agency in the business, taking on only a few clients, which at the time were Microsoft, Nike, and Coca-Cola. EchoMail provided the leading technology for email analysis, routing, and response. The goal of this effort was to integrate TV, email, print, and web. A series of twelve TV ads were set, one for each month, each associated with a different athlete, who got a unique email address and a unique website associated with a particular shoe or product. For example, Gary P. Jones would be associated with the Nike Air Ubiquitous shoe and his website was doyourazzup.com, complete with his own email address: garyp@doyourazzup.com. Wieden took out billboards where all one would see were pictures of the shoe and the athlete's email address. The intention was to evoke a passerby's curiosity to perhaps want to find out more and write in to the email address. In addition there were parallel TV ads running, such as Gary P. doing one thousand push-ups with the ad simply fading into the image of his email address. Again the goal was to inspire the consumer to talk with Nike on the email channel, intimate and direct communication.

Using broadcast advertising to entice people to write in email was unprecedented. Integration between print and web was radical. No one had ever combined media in this fashion before. Did it work? Yes. Consumers wrote in by the thousands. When they wrote in, email was analyzed, routed, and responded to using the same EchoMail technology originally set up for crisis management. The technology this time discerned the consumer's shoe of interest, and also extracted other valuable data. EchoMail formed responses that were tailored to the incoming request and also provided a link in the response to a local shoe retailer who would likely have that product in stock. The idea was therefore to use TV and print to engage consumers to interact through email, and then to use the email response to drive consumers to the local store. Nike served as the intermediary between their own consumers and customers. Consumers could communicate one-on-one through email and then engage with a local retailer. This campaign worked to close the loop between the end consumer, the product, and the retailer (customer) through an intimate interaction. In summary, broadcast media was integrated to drive one-to-one intimate email communications.

Early adopters like Nike were great to work with because they saw email as not just a vehicle for transmitting information, but also a vehicle for building connections across multiple constituents. Everyone noticed the Nike campaign, not only Nike consumers, but also businesses and the press. They used email, for purposes beyond just customer service, to show the power of email, to connect, and to grow business.

Calvin Klein

The Nike experience created a very close relationship between EchoMail and Wieden+Kennedy. Calvin Klein had approached Wieden+Kennedy in September 1998 to share advertising responsibilities for the cKOne unisex fragrance with their in-house agency. Historically, Calvin Klein rarely outsourced any aspect of their image or brand building to outside agencies. It had always been done internally through their in-house agency, CRK Advertising. However, Calvin Klein, seeing the power of email, to connect, from the Nike experience, was encouraged to potentially look at an agency to partner with that could similarly use email to build an intimate connection. In our discussions with the company, we learned that Calvin Klein, the designer himself, disliked the web; he thought the web was too dispersed and was not intimate. However, Calvin Klein loved email because it provided for one-to-one communication. He felt it was a thoughtful and an intimate medium, where people in the comfort of their homes could read an email and respond, at their own leisure.

Based on Calvin Klein's support of the email medium, cK offered us the opportunity to do a ninety-day pilot to prove the value of email to support the brand-building efforts of a new product called cKOne, a unisex fragrance line for the Generation-Xers of the time, between the ages of thirteen and twenty. The task was to prove to Calvin Klein that email was a medium by which to build relationships with that group through electronic means. It was a tall order. However, the Nike experience had built confidence among the Wieden and EchoMail teams, through the power of email and integrated advertising.

Email for Multichannel Marketing

Calvin Klein attracted many customers to their brand through their cutting edge broadcast TV and billboard advertising. But how could one leverage that to drive those same people to have an intimate conversation? Through a series of discussions, they decided to use the various media platforms in conjunction with one another and in an integrative manner. This resulted in creating a prototype concept of a soap opera. The soap opera would contain three characters: Tia, Anna, and Robert. Tia was Robert's girlfriend and Anna was Robert's daughter, and Robert was in his late thirties. And clearly there was a dynamic relationship between Tia and Anna.

The first TV ad, launched in a black-and-white, was a thirty-second mini-soap opera that exposed the dynamics of these three characters. The broadcast was limited to the United Kingdom. The ad ended in a cliffhanger. The only way one knew it was a Calvin Klein ad was at the end when the screen faded into the email addresses of each of the characters in black and white: tia@cKone.com, robert@cKone.com, and anna@cKone.com. The question was, what would make viewers even write into these email addresses? This was in 1998 and the number of email users was significantly lower than what we have today.

People did write! EchoMail was used to analyze and sort the incoming email. As the email came in, each email from the viewer was analyzed for its attitude, for what kinds of issues they talked about, and in this case, unlike customer service issues or the issues for the president, the issues were about Robert's hair color, what gel he used, or if they liked Tia's hair or the clothes she was wearing. The emails were categorized by these different issues and responded to with a follow-up email, designed as a continuation of the soap opera, which Colin Dodd, the former scriptwriter for Michael Jackson's *Thriller* video, had written. Email came in from people who had seen the soap opera ad. The emails were segmented and follow-up soap opera dialogues were sent, uniquely crafted for each character, via email. The conversation went from broadcast media to email.

In those first ninety days, hundreds of thousands of viewers sent emails and engaged with the three characters. These results were sufficient cause for Calvin Klein to fund another thirty-six-month period. The campaign went global. The advertisements were not only on television, but also on billboards. If you had been in Times Square in New York City, you would have seen a big billboard with the picture of the soap opera character and their email address. By the second and third year, a total of sixteen characters, in addition to Tia, Robert, and Anna, were involved. In 2002, *Wired* magazine said this was the most revolutionary campaign in advertising history.

The press buzz for this campaign was massive. As *Wired* magazine wrote, "In 1998, a dozen beautiful men and women began popping up on television, billboards, websites, and magazines in Europe and the United States. They were your typical, late-'90s beautiful people: Forlorn and apparently bored with their gorgeousness, they stared out at the world with a gaze that suggested thoughts that were either profound, or profoundly vacuous. It was not odd that these people looked somewhat mysterious—they were Calvin Klein fragrance models, models being a species that always appears to be a bit hard to figure out. What was odd, however, was that the ads— for Calvin Klein's signature fragrance, the 'unisex' cKOne—provided a then-novel way to peer into the enigma: an email address."

Email as a Soap Opera

Wired magazine presented the details of this email soap opera, which are shared in this section. The typical target of cKOne was a teenage guy or girl smitten by the model, who would send a quick note to tia@ckone.com, anna@ckone.com, robert@ckone.com, or any or several of the others, asking for information. In return, the teenager would get back a note that read like a letter to an old friend— it was personal, friendly, and it treated the reader as a confidante. For example, here's an excerpt from one of Anna's early letters entitled, "survived but barely," she starts (note the lowercase):

> I would have written sooner but i was scared my mom would walk in on my typing and catch me red-handed. shes gone off to the drugstore so i have about a half-hour window. you would not believe how screwed up an idea it was to have a party!!!!!!!

The letter went on to describe how much Anna loves a certain unnamed "he," and she adds that if "you want nothing more to do with me, simply title your reply 'get lost' and I won't bother you anymore. Don't worry, I'm used to rejection." That "get lost" was a hip way to "opt out" or "unsubscribe," which ensured compliance with anti-SPAM regulations.

Every few days, another letter would come from Anna and the others, confiding more details from the characters' lives—whom they loved, whom they hoped to love, how their dream somehow always fell short of coming true. Characters invited the reader into a world of their own, with the aim of emotionally connecting with the readers. "In my head, I took the universal themes of love, lust, etc., and combined it with the most modern thing actually 'connecting us,' the Internet, and email specifically," wrote Kevin Drew Davis, the creative director at Wieden who worked on the campaign. "Ten characters, each writing to you as if you're their personal friend about what they were going through. But on a macro scale, each one of the characters was somehow connected to the others. E.g., Robert was Anna's father, Robert was trying to have an affair with Tia, Anna lusted after Danny, etc."

Davis said, "It was supposed to be a discovery for the people who wrote in, and those first emails were great. They were asking a lot of questions about what this was." More than that, though, the campaign worked. "Hundreds of thousands of people went through the cKOne email," Davis wrote. Fragrance sales increased, and "because of the nature of the campaign and the time it was launched, it got a *lot* of PR. Some people loved it, some people hated it. But isn't that every Calvin Klein campaign?"

Eventually, Calvin Klein stopped the print and TV spots, but they wanted the email "to just keep going and going," according to Colin Dodd, a thirty-four-year-old fiction writer and bartender in Chapel Hill, North Carolina, who was contracted by the company to write the messages. Dodd had written a few short stories and had spent a long while turning one of his stories into a movie that wasn't panning out, "So I really needed the money," he said. "I was skeptical when I did it, and I thought it was going to take away all of my sensibilities. I was like, advertising—nothing but evil. But it was fun, and in the end it made me a better writer." And it's not hard to see how that happened. Here's the story that developed over the three-year campaign, as described by Dodd (after he warned, "this is going to be a run-on").

The initial story revolved around a commercial production company. Robert was the director at the production company, married to Patty, and they had a fifteen-year-old daughter named Anna, who had a crush on Danny, who was eighteen, who became a baseball player. Now, Tia worked for Robert as a producer, and he fell in love with her and left his wife. Ian was production assistant and he fell in love with Tia, too, and he eventually won Tia away—or Tia eventually fell for Ian, although Ian had help from Kristy, who was his best friend, until they realized that *they* were in love.

Also in the mix was Erica, a femme fatale who found herself in intimate situations with the males in the story.

Dodd said Calvin Klein laid down some ground rules for the characters—"no drinking, no drugs, no sex among the teenagers in the story"—but for three years, he had a fair amount of creative freedom. The one thing that the campaign never did was plug the fragrance. "If you're talking about big brands like that, it's more important that you get the idea across, get an image across more than mention the scent," Dodd said. "So there were no passages like, 'Gosh, Tia smells so good.'"

Calvin Klein urged Dodd to keep the situations relatively open-ended, "on the premise that if there was uncertainty, people would keep coming back." In an email, Dodd added that people kept reading the messages because the characters kept revealing their secrets. "Email can have a confessional tone, and I tried to have one secret revealed per email. Anna hating her father, Ian loving his boss, Tia losing interest in Ian, Kristy hating New York ... the things they couldn't tell anyone else," he wrote. Indeed, by her final message, Anna seems genuinely touched by her conversations with the reader. "It's so weird and funny how sometimes it feels like something doesn't really happen to me until I get home and write it to you in an email and tell you about it," she writes. Note how, three years later, her writing style has changed.

And readers, too, were touched, Davis wrote: "The thing that impressed me most is that teenagers completely got it right away. For example, there was a group of school girls in the U.K. (several signups from the same school) who took on Anna as a personal friend. They would write things like, 'We know you're just a machine, but you need to watch out for Danny....' They were letting the character in on what the other character had been saying to them. They were trying to direct the story! It was fantastic beyond my wildest expectations."

Chapter Summary

The Nike and Calvin Klein campaigns were powerful examples of where the email medium, integrated with an offline medium such as TV and print, explosively changing the nature of human interaction. Over 500 press articles were written about the cKOne campaign, generating a lot of brand buzz for Calvin Klein. What Calvin Klein received from this campaign was not just lists of email address contacts, but a whole buzz factor that they likely could not have received had they done broadcast advertising alone or email marketing alone. This integrative marketing approach was absolutely revolutionary and still is revolutionary today. The opportunity for marketers to recognize that integrative marketing, combining broadcast media with narrowcast email, opens virgin areas of creative branding.

The Nike and cKOne experiences further reinforce the fact that email is a wonderful medium for conducting extended and intimate communication with a target audience, one-on-one. This is where the power of email truly is reflected. Email allows a company to communicate intimately using different strategies for different target groups of people, taking into account that particular person or group's interests and outlook. This ensures a much more personal level of communication, which results in higher appreciation by the individual or group being targeted, making them feel more connected and intimate. The success of the Nike and cKOne projects resulted from establishing regular contact, through targeted email communication, with people who wanted that intimate communication that broadcast medium does not allow.

6

George Bush Ain't Dumb

"The Bush campaign was smarter than the Gore campaign. They knew what they didn't know. They wanted to use email to add muscle to their grassroots tactics."

Background

The success of the Bush for President Campaign of 2000 was in connecting people at a grassroots level. Led by direct mail expert Karl Rove, the Bush campaign committee knew the power of mobilizing people at the grassroots level. They learned that email communication is very personal and can be used as an excellent tool for one-to-one communication. The campaign team had a conscious strategy to collect email addresses of as many individuals as possible in each precinct and establish targeted one-on-one email correspondences with them. The campaign team identified with the "personal" nature of email, and used it to mobilize the power of grassroots supporters ultimately to win primaries and eventually the general election, which made George W. Bush the forty-third president of the United States of America.

The 2000 presidential campaign of Bush versus Gore was very close. Bush won the controversial election through the thinnest of margins. The election was noteworthy for the controversy that awarded Florida's twenty-five electoral votes to Bush, the subsequent recount process in that state, and the unusual event of the winning candidate having received fewer popular votes than the runner-up.

Although the campaign focused mainly on domestic issues such as the projected budget surplus, proposed reforms of Social Security and Medicare, health care, and competing plans for tax relief, foreign policy was often the most important issue. As the election night wore on, the returns in a handful of small to medium-size states, including Wisconsin and Iowa, were extremely close; however, it was the state of Florida that would determine the winner of the election. As the final national results were tallied the following morning, Bush had clearly won a total of 246 electoral votes, while Gore had won 255 votes.

Two hundred and seventy votes were needed to win. Two smaller states—New Mexico (five electoral votes) and Oregon (seven electoral votes)—were still too close to call. It was Florida (twenty-five electoral votes), however, that the news media focused their attention on. Mathematically, Florida's twenty-five electoral votes became the key to an election win for either candidate. Although both New Mexico and Oregon were declared in favor of Gore over the next few days, Florida's statewide vote took center stage because that state's winner would ultimately win the election. The outcome of the election was not known for more than a month after the balloting ended because of the extended process of counting and then recounting of Florida's presidential ballots. After an intense recount process, then Governor George W. Bush was officially declared the winner of Florida's electoral votes and, as a result, the entire presidential election. The process was extremely divisive, and led to calls for electoral reform in Florida.

Bush's platform had included compassionate conservatism, tax breaks for all, a humble foreign policy with no nation building, the "No Child Left Behind" education policy, energy policy including initiatives for use of con-serving technologies as well as decreasing foreign dependence on oil through increased domestic production, and redesign of the military with emphasis on supermodern hardware, flexible tactics, and less international deployment. Gore's platform included safe and legal abortion defending women's right to choose, continuation of Clinton's economic policies with limited tax breaks for working families, improvements to equal rights and opportunities—be it based on gender, race, sexual orientation, or disabilities—wider separation of church and state, transformation of the educational system including the hiring of more teachers, improved classrooms, increased public education and tuition savings programs, energy policy emphasizing use of new technol-ogy and strong control on global warming factors, strong agenda in foreign policy including leadership in response to violence and vigorous intervention abroad, and a strong push on technology, including policies supporting free-market Internet.

Email for Integrated Grassroots Communication

The 2000 presidential campaign proved that every vote counts. Hardworking supporters won each vote at the grassroots level through a door-to-door campaign. Any advantage could have a significant effect. Jeanniey Mullen, a business development executive at EchoMail, recognized there was an opportunity to use email for the presidential campaigns. Initially, she approached the Democrats thinking that if Al Gore "invented the Internet," his team would definitely want to use email for the campaign. However, something interesting took place. The campaign leaders at the Democratic Party were arrogant. They felt they knew everything about email and discounted it as real channel. They did not think email was significant. They were going to use other types of media, including the web, but not email. This was quite a letdown for Jeanniey.

Not giving up, Jeanniey approached the Bush campaign team. She noticed something significantly different. The Bush campaign, led by Karl Rove, who some consider as the "Devil," was actually very open to the idea. The Bush campaign was willing to explore new ideas. They wanted to learn how to really use email at the grassroots level, and saw it as a one-on-one medium that integrated well with their one-on-one philosophy of connecting with ordinary folks. The Bush campaign was smarter than the Gore campaign. They knew what they didn't know. They wanted to use email to add muscle to their grassroots tactics. They were interested and curious to learn, and EchoMail provided them opportunities to let them know how email could be used in the presidential campaign. EchoMail gave them examples of what they did with Calvin Klein, Nike, and the White House, and emphasized that email could be used as a vehicle to engage their "customers" at a one-to-one level, in an intimate manner.

In their case, the one-to-one communication would prove crucial to soliciting donations and to getting people in the neighborhood excited about rallying behind the cause. The campaign team achieved this through *viral email* marketing. Viral email encouraged one recipient to forward the email to another. This was a very new concept that few people were exploring at the time, and Karl Rove, who had built his entire career on the direct mail business and knew the power of grassroots marketing, saw viral marketing as a fast way to build new connections—a far cheaper option than print and postal mail. His team was therefore quickly able to understand the power of email and began to gather email lists and addresses. The Bush Campaign also targeted its bank of nearly 200,000 wealthy supporters and used the same viral process with them. They sent a series of targeted weekly email marketing campaign programs. In those email marketing campaigns, the recipients were encouraged to participate in receiving ongoing newsletters. The recipients were given up-to-date information on what Bush was doing, where he was campaigning, what he had said, and so on. The purpose of that consistent communication was to build an intimate relationship with each of the Bush supporters. Responses were also answered in a timely manner, and those responses always encouraged forwarding the email to others.

Email and Secure Integration of Data

The Bush campaign team had an elaborate strategy for volunteers to go door-to-door in their local neighborhoods. The volunteers visited each home with multiple objectives. Get the neighbor as an active volunteer or get the neighbor as a donor. Each visiting volunteer was encouraged to collect as many email addresses as possible from their daily visits. At the end of the day, they would return to the field offices with their laptops that had the information they had collected. The information in the laptops would be uploaded to campaign headquarters. This is an area where the campaign team faced multiple challenges. In the year 2000, Internet technology was not as developed as it is today and especially wireless technology for public access was in its nascent stages. This made uploading of the data from field offices extremely hard. Sometimes it would take hours for the data from some of the remote locations to upload. When it came to the day of a scheduled email campaign, it could get very complex with synchronization of data from different locations. With anti-SPAM rules developing, even in 2000, data had to be properly synchronized, so that a recipient's request to be removed from the mailing list was met promptly, especially in a scenario like an election where one does not want the person to get upset over a simple matter like opting out of an email campaign. With the data upload, synchronization of the data, and opt-out status updates all taking place, sending an email campaign at the predetermined time required near perfect orchestration, and the Bush team lived up to the task. Today, this is made far easier technologically; however, the commitment and need to integrate multiple databases and connect them together, like the Bush campaign had done with lesser technology, is still not fully realized by many organizations.

Another concern was information security. With information of people all over the nation, especially donors to the election, a lot of emphasis was placed on secure transfer of information from field offices to campaign headquarters to our facility. Even though they did not store any payment-specific information such as bank account or credit card numbers, personal information was still very important and the best security measures available of the time were employed to securely maintain the exchange and storage of data within our facilities. Being dispersed nationwide, collecting such campaign data in a decentralized manner, and using grassroots teams made this project very different from our corporate customers.

The recipients of Bush campaign email were also segmented. This was particularly important in certain districts where precinct-by-precinct, block-by-block, is how the election was going to be determined. Different areas, therefore, were sent targeted and customized content. For example, places like Ohio and Florida, as we all know now, ended up being highly contested. Those areas got very different information than the other parts of the country. Over the course of the campaign, the Bush for President team raised a significant part of their campaign funds through the use of email. They signed up huge numbers of new donors through the process of targeted viral email connecting the grassroots, door-to-door, as well as their wealthy donors.

Chapter Summary

This was a very close election with Bush as the final victor. Though one cannot definitively say that Bush's winning the presidential election was because of email, it is likely that their email effort gave them a huge advantage, particularly in those hard-fought districts such as Ohio and Florida. What would have happened if Gore had also embraced email? The Obama campaign of 2008 took many lessons from Bush's effective use of email. They hired specialists just for managing email communication and building a similar integrated grassroots model as Bush had done; it clearly worked for them.

At a time when many underestimated email, the George W. Bush campaign did not. Though considered by some as not the most intelligent candidate, Bush appointed smart people to run his campaign, people who had recognized the power of one-to-one marketing and embraced email. This attitude of being open to email, as a new medium, and exhibiting a willingness to learn its nuances and particular usage, is what gave the Bush campaign an important advantage over the Democrats, who did not value the email medium and thought the web by itself was sufficient for their traditional campaign activities. George Bush's campaign proved the power of viral email marketing, combined with door-to-door grassroots campaigning, to not only reach voters but also to build deeper connections, reinforced by email and face-to-face communications. George W. Bush's ascent to the presidency taught one of the most basic lessons of winning elections: all politics are local. The Bush campaign focused their attention at the grassroots level, collecting email addresses door-to-door, and communicating relevant messages, face-to-face and through email, with targeted content.

P&G Goes Neighbor to Neighbor

"P&G did a brilliant take on email. They used email to build participatory and neighborly relations, one at a time, pioneering brand understanding in a completely new way."

Background

Though Procter & Gamble (P&G) is considered the largest consumer goods company, they have recognized the value of maintaining a relationship with each individual consumer. P&G collects information about each consumer, analyzes it, and uses the analysis to offer more suitable products for their consumers. They are well-known for their unique brand-building activities. P&G, through the Tide Neighbor-to-Neighbor program, used a series of email communications to understand consumers' use of the Tide brand of laundry detergent and to explore how brand loyalty can be made stronger and even expanded to more consumers through the involvement of existing consumers. This program got neighborhoods involved at the household level, expanding to other households in the neighborhood through neighbor-to-neighbor email communications.

Procter & Gamble is a United States-based Fortune-500 multinational packaged consumer goods manufacturer, headquartered in Cincinnati, Ohio. With operations in eighty countries, over half of their revenue comes from outside the United States. Established in 1837 by the Englishman William Procter and Irishman James Gamble, P&G, as they are known around the world, is listed as one of the largest "fast-moving consumer goods" companies in the world.

P&G has over 300 brands available in 160 countries across the world—nearly two dozen of those brands are considered billion-dollar entities based on their annual revenue. Some of their top brands include Tide, Bounty, Fusion, Always, Braun, Charmin, Crest, Downy, Gillette, Mach3, Iams, Olay, Pampers, Pantene, Gain, and others.

My first job out of MIT was on a consulting project for P&G through a company named Information Resources, Inc. (IRI). Through that experience, I discovered that Proctor & Gamble is one of the most data-centric companies in the world. They analyze everything. On that project, they analyzed large volumes of data to determine whether a $0.50 coupon or a $1 coupon was optimal for selling more Tide laundry care products. P&G had hundreds of millions of data records on every Tide purchase, including when a coupon was used. During this project, which ran for almost nine months, massive amounts of multidimensional data were analyzed to understand which coupon drove consumer behavior. From the analysis of this data, it turned out that a $0.50 coupon was sufficient to swing the consumers; P&G did not have to give the $1 coupon away. This kind of analysis in the modern day is called the field of marketing analytics. Two MIT professors, John D. C. Little and Glen Urban, initially with Management Data Systems (MDS), were the pioneers of this new field.

Email and Surveying Consumer Behavior

P&G, therefore, really knew the value of data. In that context, in the late 1990s, P&G's advertising agency Saatchi and Saatchi had heard about EchoMail and its ability to conduct intelligent email conversation to gather consumer data. Saatchi convinced P&G that they could use email to understand consumer behavior and also develop branding via the email medium. At that time, P&G had a project focused on the Tide brand of laundry products and wanted to understand how different groups of Tide users, who were using the Internet, could be affected to change their usage patterns of Tide, solely through the use of email communication. More specifically, the idea was to learn how they could segment users of Tide to see how they could drive certain types of behavior.

Tide was P&G's number one brand worldwide. Tide was introduced first in the United States in 1946. Tide since then became one of the flagship products of P&G. Also known under the name of Alo and Ace in certain countries, it is widely used by a large population in Canada, Latin America, Europe, and Asia. The bright orange and yellow bulls-eye logo is distinctly recognizable. Tide is acknowledged as the first heavy-duty synthetic laundry detergent that includes chemicals necessary to make machine-washing with hard water effective. Over thirty laundry products are now available under the Tide brand along with nearly ten clothing care accessories.

The campaign for Tide was called Neighbor-to-Neighbor. The Neighbor-to-Neighbor program ran for three years as an exercise in intelligent email response and behavioral analysis. The campaign was developed in multiple phases. In the first phase, a website was created where consumers came in and answered a survey on their laundry practices. Based on the comments and responses in the survey, consumers were segmented into different kinds of Tide users. Tide has multiple products such as Tide for whites versus for colored clothing, Tide with and without bleach, Tide for different water types and temperatures, and more. From the survey responses, P&G began to know what type of Tide products were being used among those email respondents. The responses also showed them if they were heavy users or light users (i.e., who did a lot of laundry versus those who did lighter loads of laundry). Different segments of consumers were created with such behavioral information. Some respondents were not Tide users and this was also identified in the database of survey respondents. One key goal was to see what would motivate people who were not Tide users to become Tide users, and which Tide product they would want to use. In addition, the goal was to see if and how P&G could promote or cross-sell other products which the users had not known about.

The first phase of this program took almost six months to set up, figuring all the complex rules for doing the consumer segmentation, and actually implementing the acquisition program. After successfully executing the first phase, a campaign was launched to acquire "neighbors" to sign up. Respondents had the opportunity to win a year's supply of Tide as they participated in the program. People answered the questions about their laundry practices both at the survey website and by responding to the outbound email campaigns that were sent to them as part of this program. They were segmented based on their responses and further questions were asked based on previous responses. One goal was to not intimidate the user by asking all the questions up front, as most people dislike answering a long survey. Email interactions were configured so that any follow-up campaigns would be based on decision trees extracted from previous interactions.

Email for Conversational Dialogue

Based on a certain set of questions people were asked, and how they responded, the next campaign would include some incentives for the respondents to answer some more questions. Part of this exercise was to collect data through these series of email interactions, and to see how many people would keep giving information, and how many people would drop off. The goal, in the classic P&G style, was to really understand consumer behavior. Over the three-year period of this campaign, each person likely received a few hundred emails.

The P&G email respondents were tracked from the point of the start of the converation through the entire three-year period—who visited the website, who signed up for the campaign, what and how much information they were willing to provide, who did not want to provide information, how each person progressed through the campaign, which respondents switched from one brand to another or one product to another. Tide used this email interaction as a branding exercise to really connect with a pool of high-valued and low-valued customers and to understand how they could entice them through the email to participate in a dialogue. P&G collected valuable information that they could not have obtained by doing in-store surveys because in a store there is no way for the company to keep communicating with people in this pre-analyzed manner. Nor could they do this on the phone because it is far more difficult to get the people on the phone. People generally get weary when asked a long series of questions that may seem personal and private. With email, people could respond as they wanted and when they wanted. Furthermore, people felt more at ease in answering questions, such as details of their laundry practices, through email versus over the phone. Email was the perfect method for conducting this asynchronous conversational dialogue.

From a branding standpoint, Tide acquired a tremendous amount of information early on, which enabled them to understand how to dialogue with customers: when to dialogue, what to talk about, and how long to dialogue. They also learned how to implement brand loyalty (i.e., how and when to switch people from non-Tide products to Tide products, and within Tide, how to move people across different products). The Neighbor-to-Neighbor program also had a viral component. The program extended incentives for a person to sign on other Neighbors. In the Neighbor-to-Neighbor campaign, a person could sign up a friend. This also enabled P&G to see how many neighbors a person could sign on, and to what extent their degrees of freedom spanned—meaning how one consumer was connected to others, from one neighbor to another. P&G ended up collecting a significant amount of information on email dispersion across a set of neighbors. They learned how to use email not only as a survey medium but also as a medium for conversation and a medium for viral marketing.

Chapter Summary

P&G did a brilliant take on email. They used email to build participatory and neighborly relations, one at a time, pioneering brand understanding in a completely new way. Furthermore, they built their email list from the ground up, using the knowledge gained from years worth of data collected on their consumers.

They used the knowledge to identify those consumers who would get their neighbors signed up to the program and gave them the right incentives to sign up the neighbor. Their approach was similar to the grassroots-level, viral marketing approach of the Bush for President campaign. Through Tide's Neighbor-to-Neighbor campaign, P&G proved that the best way to acquire a following is not by buying email lists from third-party sources, but by encouraging current followers to sign up their neighbors and friends. Email proved to be highly successful at being visible in front of each follower, and the targeted intimate nature of the medium kept the follower interested in seeing what else P&G had to offer. As a follower's interest increased (because they received offers that were targeted at them), the person felt compelled, in a nice way, to continue to bring on neighbors and friends.

Unilever Makes It Personal

"Skin and email are both personal. Email allowed Unilever to distinguish their brand as being highly personalized—delivering the right product for the right skin."

Background

The Unilever brand of products either has mass appeal or is unique and personalized. They also have a unique approach to branding and marketing. Unilever learned about the power of email to deliver highly personalized messages to their consumers. They also discovered how email could help them conduct successful surveys, and how they could deliver personalized personal care information using the data they collected through surveys. Unilever's Dove personal care campaign was one of the most unique email campaigns of the times. It imparted knowledge of specialized care for different skin types in changing weather conditions to thousands and thousands of people, bringing specialized skin care to the common man or woman.

Unilever is a British-Dutch multinational Consumer Packaged Goods (CPG) company. Also called a Fast-Moving Consumer Goods (FMCG) company, Unilever manufactures and distributes affordable and quickly consumable packaged goods including food, beverages, household cleaning, and personal hygiene products. According to a Forbes Global 2000 report, Unilever is the fourth largest consumer goods company in the world, behind Procter & Gamble, Nestlé, and Anheuser-Busch, with over fifty brands and multiple products under each brand.

According to a Unilever investor fact sheet, two billion consumers in 180 countries across North America, South America, and Asia use Unilever brand products each day. Some of the well-known Unilever brands include Lipton, Dove, Caress, Ben & Jerry's, Knorr, Pond's, Slim-Fast, Suave, Vaseline, and Axe.

Email for Personalized Customer Care and Marketing

Unilever was particular on using email for doing both inbound customer care management and enterprise-wide outbound marketing for all their brands. On outbound email marketing, it is hard to appreciate the sheer size of the number of Unilever's brands, with each of Unilever's products being treated as its own marketing brand, with its own brand managers, and its own agency. Entering into the world of Internet and email, the brands were starting to define their marketing strategies. Several of the brands had traditional agencies, while certain other brands had begun experimenting with interactive agencies; however, most of them did not know how to enter into the world of outbound email marketing. On most occasions, these agencies were still learning how to design and develop email content as well as the operational processes for planning and executing their email campaigns. Working with multiple brands and their multiple agencies to ensure a standard email communications model while providing flexibility to the individual brands is a complex systems' problem, balancing centralization and decentralization of control.

Unilever recognized the importance of managing inbound customer service email, in addition to outbound email marketing. Unilever understood that email was a medium for dialogue, and that processing both the inbound customer inquiries and the outbound marketing was important, at a time when the concept of doing both was very nascent. Consider the Lipton brand. One may be exposed to the brand during an in-store encounter walking down the aisle. Alternatively, one may have been exposed to the Lipton brand when one received offers and coupons in postal mail, to encourage one to start consuming or increase the current consumption of Lipton Tea. By beginning to collect email addresses for the Lipton brand, Unilever could create a different channel to extend brand reach, to send outbound email to consumers. Through email, Unilever could directly communicate and converse with the Lipton users. The question was this: how and where do you collect email addresses? They, like Nike, were a consumer goods company with minimal access to the consumer, working historically with customers, the retailers and distributors.

This was a big issue at that time. On the Lipton website, one had to build enough content to keep it engaging for consumers who want to come back and to give their email address. Unilever could not just ask consumers to sign up for email, but instead had to build content that was engaging. Some brands like Dove and Gorton's began to learn to build such engaging content. In the case of Dove, people were asked to provide their email address and answer certain questions about their skin. The database software engine in the back end would use that input to determine the type of the consumer's skin. Then, based on the skin type, personalized emails would be delivered to them, with different content on how to take care of their skin, for different seasons of the year, and could be further specialized based on the region in which they lived. That personalized content softly promoted Dove as the soap that one could use for different skin types.

Skin and email are both personal. Email allowed Unilever to distinguish their brand as being highly personalized—delivering the right product for the right skin. Unilever similarly delivered email in a personalized manner for another one of their brands, Mentadent. Mentadent is a toothpaste brand, but Unilever wanted to brand Mentadent as a "solution for dental hygiene." This effort was part of Mentadent's effort to reposition the brand as a personal care product that continually helps a person with good dental hygiene, and not just another toothpaste. For this brand, an engaging website was built, which offered its viewers the chance to get dental hygiene advice. A person could actually ask a question about dental hygiene and care. Unilever had set up a network of dental hygienists to respond to these questions through the EchoMail platform. When a question came in via email, EchoMail would distribute it to those dental hygienists. The hygienists would log in and write back an email answering the person's questions. Dental hygiene is personal, and email afforded a private and personal medium to support interaction on such an intimate topic.

Using this same approach of personalized conversation, each brand's creative directors were encouraged to use email conversation as a part of their creative plans. Unilever had developed a mechanism to have a personalized conversation with consumers through email. A website was no longer just a sign-up form so you could get coupons or some other offer. A "story" was built around each brand's unique value proposition. For example, in addition to the Dove and Mentadent stories of skin care and dental hygiene, there was a "story" associated with Snuggle brand regarding fabric care. With Gorton's fish products, there was a story built about New England and the background and history of fishing in the United States, which is a large part of the historical identity of New England. The story promoted the value of the fish brand as one of the earliest companies that learned how to make and deliver frozen and breaded fish.

Email for Centralized and Decentralized Brand Messaging

From Unilever's standpoint, each of these brands wanted to enjoy both centralization and decentralization of control over their marketing program. This is an important part of brand management. Unilever, on the one hand, wanted to have unified branding guidelines delivered through certain reusable components distributed across all brands. For example, certain colors and themes of Unilever had to be used across all brands. The EchoMail technology gave them the ability to do that. On the other hand, each of the brands wanted local and decentralized control of particular aspects of their marketing program, which their brand managers could own. Thus, the central corporate marketing and communications group could control the overall branding, while the individual brands would present their particular composition of the campaign. This of course was delivered in conjunction with their agency helping them with the outbound content.

The inbound email management side was also very important to Unilever in this respect. Unilever had a centralized call center managed from New Jersey and this central call center had to process all email inquiries and respond to each email sent to each brand. To manage the inbound email flow arriving at each of these brands, individual email addresses for each brand's inbound email was set up. This again reflected the centralization-decentralization approach of Unilever. For the content of responses to email inquiries, each brand manager had the ability to build a decentralized library of possible responses, and the central call-center staff used this response library to reply to an email. Email inquiries would come in from people all over the world. EchoMail would receive them in each of the email addresses (starting initially with twenty email addresses, and at one point rising to seventy email addresses for the various brands) and would route them for each of the brands. EchoMail automatically analyzed the content of each incoming inquiry and assigned it specific categories based on the content analysis.

When a call center representative who was handling multiple brands opened the email, he or she would see the categories of email for that brand and, based on the particular responses set up by the brand manager in the library, would select a response and segment the email based on categories of that inquiry. This enabled Unilever to have a consistent response to the inbound customer inquiry. The responses that the call center representative would formulate, however, were not the same as what the marketing team sent in email to consumers submitting their information via web forms. The email content of outbound marketing campaigns had a certain flair, a feel, very different from the outbound email response that a customer service representative sent to an inbound email inquiry, which was more matter-of-fact.

For example, if you wrote to Dove saying you did not like their product, they would write back in a very matter-of-fact way saying, "Sorry to hear about that, we will get back to you." The customer service side had not integrated their responses with the marketing side. Even though they were using both aspects of email communication (i.e., response to inbound inquiries as well as proactive outbound email marketing campaigns), this variance in the writing style of message content was one of the challenges at Unilever. However, Unilever did recognize that the value of branding aspects of the outbound campaign was independent of the branding aspect of the inbound email response. But the lost opportunity was that they could have integrated both inbound and outbound programs such that it would appear seamless to the end consumer. The feel of those responses to inbound inquiries could have been done better, matching the flair of marketing campaigns prevailing at that time.

Chapter Summary

The Unilever projects were unique learning experiences on how one of the largest FMCG companies in the world focused on their consumers to deliver products personalized for their unique needs. Unilever learned that email was an optimal medium for delivering personalized communication to their consumers economically. They took advantage of this lesson with project after project—from Dove skin care, to Mentadent dental hygiene, to sauces and food products, Unilever wanted to deliver unique and personalized messages to their consumers. They also wanted to provide a conversational communication medium, which allowed Unilever and their consumers to ask questions and develop personalized messages. Email enabled Unilever to maintain enduring conversational communication, retaining knowledge developed from such enduring conversation, and delivering personalized messages based on such knowledge developed over time.

Kennedy and Frist: Smartest Senators in Congress

"Most of the Senate were afraid of email. It now forced a new accountability and transparency they were not ready for. Kennedy and Frist embraced it as part of their brand."

Background

"Responding to constituents' calls, letters, and emails occupies 30 percent to 60 percent of a US senator's time in many offices," said Richard Shapiro, executive director of the Congressional Management Foundation, a non-profit group that advises congressional staffers on running their offices. The group was urging congressmen to deploy EchoMail or other automated services to sort email. Shapiro said Congress was receiving five times as many emails as paper mail. That was in the year 2000.

Prior to email, United States senators were accustomed to paper mail. Each senate office was literally a USPS-like mail-processing center. Paper mail was received, sorted, tracked, and responded to. The success of paper mail handling determined how his or her constituency perceived a senator. As the World Wide Web became popular, inbound emails to US Senate offices began to grow exponentially. The lack of response to them was beginning to reflect poorly on senators. However, when it came to email, many senators were apprehensive about engaging this new medium.

Two senators, Ted Kennedy and Bill Frist, however, embraced the medium with enthusiasm, recognizing that using email reflected innovation, openness, and transparency. EchoMail, which was capable of processing many thousands of emails each day, was provided to the US Senate, while giving them the flexibility and security for each senate office to manage their own email.

The United States government has three arms for governance: the executive, the legislative, and the judicial branches. The US Senate is part of the legislative arm. There are one hundred senators in the Senate: two senators from each of the fifty states. In addition, the Senate has twenty committees, sixty-eight subcommittees, and four joint committees. The Senate is a large conglomerate of nearly 200 organizations. Each of those Senate offices, as well as each of the committees and subcommittees, has their own email address.

Email for Prompt and Responsible Constituent Communication

The problem of email surfaced during the time of John Ashcroft's hearings for Attorney General. President George W. Bush had recommended Ashcroft, which spurred a divisive controversy across America. The Senate was receiving over one million emails each day! The Senate majority leader at that time was Dr. William Frist. The floodgates of email communication were opened and the US Senate needed a platform to effectively manage it. At that time, the way the Senate managed email was the same way they had been managing postal mail—not that different from how the White House was managing email prior to 1993. Each senatorial office was its own minicorporation with a primary function to execute communication activities. A senator is constantly working on his or her reelection—starting from the day he or she enters office. How they communicate reflects how the public perceives them. A physical letter via postal mail was handled by each senate office's correspondence management system (CMS). When the letter came in, someone opened it, and sorted it into different categories, ranging from twenty to one hundred. Once classified, the right form letter response was selected and printed. A legislative assistant who had been given the authority to use the senator's signature signed the letter, and it was sent back. Each correspondence was recorded, and the statistics were used to get a pulse of the constituents. When email came along, the idea was that they would process it the same way as paper mail. They had someone, an intern, open an email, print out the email, and respond to only those emails that had a postal mailing address. However, this does not work with email, because people expected an email response to the email they sent in.

Why did senate offices initially want to respond to email with print mail? The US government afforded each senate office *franking privileges,* which provided them significant funds to communicate via print mail. If such communication moved to email, they would receive less funding, meaning less staff to process print mail.

However, this process of either not responding to email or sending printed responses to email was not going to be an acceptable solution in the long term. If a senator did not respond to email with email, they could be viewed as unresponsive, which hurts their brand and eventually jeopardizes a potential future vote. In the world of for-profit businesses, research had shown that if one did not respond to email within twenty-four hours, there was an 85 percent chance of losing the customer. Clearly, that research applied to the Senate would mean that a senator was jeopardizing many "customers" or votes by being unresponsive.

To address this problem, the United States Senate ran an RFP (Request for Proposals) to identify an email management solution. In Washington, companies typically hire lobbyists to win government contracts. EchoMail won the contract to deploy an email management solution at the US Senate without the need for such lobbyists, primarily because when it came to email management, no other tool had the rich set of capabilities for automatic analysis of the content, the ability to route, report, and respond—all of the items which the RFP had asked for, and more. After EchoMail was selected, the contract was not processed on time. EchoMail waited for five months. Finally a call was made to Ted Kennedy's office to seek his guidance. Kennedy's office was also concerned, as they had been waiting eagerly for EchoMail, and wanted to be responsive to the influx of growing emails from their Massachusetts constituents, who are known for being tech savvy. Senator Kennedy's staff was persistent and followed up on EchoMail's behalf, and the contract was processed.

EchoMail was contracted to find the solution for email management for all senate offices and committees. The EchoMail system would be installed within the premises of the US Senate Sergeant at Arms (SAA), and each Senate office would have secure access to their emails through a web-based interface. The office of the SAA had been in existence since 1789. The SAA is the protocol officer, the chief law enforcement officer, and the administrative manager for most of the support services at the United States Senate, including computers and technology support services, and is also responsible for Information Security. The computing data center where EchoMail would be deployed was located in the facilities of the SAA. While print mail was received and stored directly in each senate office, email would be received and stored in the computer infrastructure of the SAA. The implications of email being stored at the SAA would eventually lead to the adoption of email management in the Senate.

EchoMail's deployment to each Senate office was not direct, but under the auspices of the SAA as an intermediary. It was a challenging model. Here, unlike a corporation, the company was dealing with a government organization. People came in at 9 AM and left promptly at 5 PM. There was little sense of commitment to getting a job done on time or a culture of being entrepreneurial. The initial goal was for EchoMail to be deployed in two Senate offices. Those deployments were done on time with success, getting positive feedback and results. The next step was to deploy EchoMail across the other Senate offices. The setup for each Senate office required a tremendous amount of coordination. Over the next three years, EchoMail was implemented in nearly forty Senate offices. With EchoMail, Senate offices could identify common groups of incoming email with the same topic, aggregate them into "batches" and send one common response to those similar emails. What did constituents think about receiving a form-letter-like email? According to Shapiro, even though "people understood their communications weren't from the senator, [t]hey wanted responsiveness on a timely basis. They didn't care whether it was staff or whatever." Being responsive was the key, and with EchoMail, Senate offices were able to meet that need. Moreover, the Senate offices were building something even more valuable: email lists of their constituents, to whom they could "market" messages from the senator, on an ongoing basis.

In the middle of EchoMail's deployment, an administration change took place, and Democrats became the majority in the US Senate. As the Senate offices were getting equipped with email, we got word from a senior manager within the SAA that a number of the senators were getting concerned because the SAA was maintaining all their email. They did not like the fact that email was being stored at the SAA. For them, "their" email was with the SAA, a third-party entity. This had a very important legal implication. The SAA is wholly accountable to the American public, not to the Senate. Given the fact that courts were accepting email as evidence, if a senator was involved in a controversy, all the email stored at the SAA was subject to legal discovery, without the control of each senator's office, as is the case with print mail. This loss of control caused fear in the senate offices that had enjoyed their ability to control information access and flow. Culturally, it demanded that they become more open and transparent, since email had caused the transfer of power to the SAA (i.e., the American public).

Email for Responsible E-Government

In a sense, email forced the senators to have a far greater accountability to the constituents, but it also created the risk of "exposure" for them because their email could be exposed if there was an event where email discovery was requested. These events and fears coincided with the administration change, which also happened to be on the three-year anniversary of the EchoMail contract. It was clear that the new administration was anti-email, and preferred the old print mail days. Implementing email at each Senate office took a significant time commitment of the staff of each Senate office. Time that was taken away from doing what they knew how to do: responding to print mail and answering phone calls. Moreover, the fact that the email system was being implemented was a potential threat that did not bode well for the future of email management in the Senate. During this time, EchoMail received a call from a lobbyist. She said if the company wanted to continue as the vendor to the Senate, she knew the new SAA officer in charge (appointed by the Democrats), and could convince him of the value of EchoMail. There was a price: $200,000. EchoMail's answer was "no" and they knew their days in the Senate were numbered.

One of the senators who really understood the value of email was Senator Bill Frist, who was also a pioneering transplant surgeon. Another senator who embraced email and the technology for managing email was Ted Kennedy. When an opportunity arose to meet them, it was evident that, though one was a Democrat and the other a Republican, they both had the common ethos of transparency. They were not afraid that their email was at the SAA. This was not an issue for them, because they knew that technology and innovation, by their nature, could bring more transparency and accountability—it was their belief that this should be embraced. Unlike others who feared email, Kennedy and Frist saw email as part of their brand. The Pew Charitable Foundation conducted research that showed the value of email management for e-governance as well as for the American public through such transparency. From a branding standpoint, those senators who used email communication built tremendous value with their constituents—being seen as caring and responsive; those who did not lost a wonderful opportunity to connect. They failed to leverage email as a democratic medium to really listen and respond to their customers (constituents), out of a misplaced fear of losing control. The email project in the Senate was a great example of how email was a double-edged sword: a medium that afforded transparency and accountability, but on the flip side could cause one to lose some perceived control. Even many corporations were realizing this nature of email. A majority of senators, however, did not want this level of transparency. In that sense, EchoMail failed to deliver, not due to EchoMail, but due to the fundamental nature of the loss of control engendered by this medium, a loss of control that politicians feared in spite of the branding opportunity awaiting them.

Chapter Summary

Clearly there was resistance from a number of Senate offices to embrace email communication. What was really surprising was the reason behind it—it was not due to fear of technology, but it was the fear of openness and transparency. Email made senators accountable. They could no longer hide communication because email was received, processed, backed up, and stored in a facility outside of their immediate office and control. Even though their staff managed the reading and responding of email, the office of the SAA handled the physical storage. For senators like Ted Kennedy, Bill Frist, and a number of other senators who embraced it, they saw it as a way to understand the pulse of their constituents, similar to President Clinton's ideas. Email continues to exhibit the many qualities of postal mail: long, detailed, descriptive writing style, persistence of messaging through a history of prior communication, with the ability to store and archive in a systematic way for future review and response.

Building a Trusted Brand Through Secure Email

"Citibank, financial institution, and Cookie Jar, a children's entertainment company, both recognized the value of making it safe for customers. Their extra efforts created a feeling of trust and care."

Background

Due to the possibility of the impersonation of someone over email and with increasing instances of identity theft, security concerns have become even more important. Two of the industries that were most affected by this concern were those dealing with banking and children. Naturally, the government and the technology world sought to develop solutions to address this concern. Online safety became a matter of high priority for all of us. Government brought legislation into effect, technology companies started producing new security solutions, and all technology users started implementing security protocols to protect themselves and their constituents. Citibank, the financial institution, and Cookie Jar, a children's entertainment company, both recognized the value of making it safe for customers. Their extra efforts created a feeling of trust and care.

Citigroup

Citigroup is a United States-based multinational financial services company. Originally founded as Citicorp in 1812, Citigroup was formed in 1998 by the merger of Citicorp with Travelers Group. Citigroup has the world's largest financial services network, spanning 140 countries with approximately 16,000 offices worldwide. Citigroup, then Citicorp, in 1997 knew the value of email. Being ahead of other organizations in the use of technology for improving business processes, Citigroup wanted advanced technology to process their inbound customer inquiry email. They began a pilot project to prove that EchoMail was the right solution for Citigroup's inbound email management. The first Citigroup division to come on board was Salomon Smith Barney. The pilot project with Salomon Smith Barney was successful. Seeing how technology was able to handle inbound customer inquiry emails by automatically categorizing and routing them to the appropriate staff, Citigroup realized that it could save them tremendous amounts of money and staff time. Knowing that customers were going to rely more and more on Internet-based business, Citigroup was one of the early developers of online business portals for their customers. As the online customer base grew, so did new problems with maintaining security of customer information. Citigroup was determined to make their customers feel safe with online business transactions and inquiries.

Email for Trusted Communication

One of Citigroup's primary requirements was to provide a secure solution for email. Interestingly, after a number of discussions, it became clear that the best solution was to implement email management as Software as a Service (SaaS), which AT&T had proved to be successful. To prove the security of the infrastructure required audits of many different types. In fact, a type of security audit called an "ethical hack" was important. Such an audit involved hiring professionals who attempted to "hack" the system to force a security failure. Every year, Citigroup hired external resources to break into the email management platform used by Citigroup, in an attempt to expose any potential security holes. Citigroup did this regularly in order to provide Citigroup customers a highly secure environment in which to exchange email communication.

In addition to ethical hacks, various types of on-site and off-site audits were required. Citigroup set the highest standards in information security. On-site audits included site visits by various Citigroup security team members who inspected everything from the door locks to security cameras to physical access to computers to location of digital media that stored email and customer information. Off-site audits included reviews of processes and procedures such as emergency response procedure, disaster recovery, data center management, employee screening, and third-party contractor and visitor handling procedures. All of these off-site activities ensured that email communications were safe.

One of the most important aspects of email security is network security. Citigroup had to ensure that their network infrastructure at the hosting center was equally or better secured compared to their internal facilities, so that customer information would remain secure. The Citigroup customer service agents and managers located across the country accessed the email management platform remotely. However, Internet access is open to constant attacks from fraudulent operators, who are either looking to steal information or simply access the servers for frivolous or criminal activities. So the access from Citigroup customer service centers had to be highly secured. To ensure network security, a secure information "pipeline" was necessary to the email management system from the representatives who had access to customer email and the server infrastructure at the hosting center. A number of technologies including a virtual private network line (VPN), encrypted data exchange, and server credential confirmations were implemented to secure the information pipeline.

Email as Blended Media?

During this same time, Citigroup was also testing how to manage email using a "blended media" approach. This approach, as discussed earlier, was being promoted by industry analysts who had bought into Siebel's misinformation campaign, that email and phone were just channels and could be handled by the same software platform. Analysts had promoted this idea in their research reports, with an infeasible concept that customer service email should be merged with other channels to create what is called a blended media of customer service. On paper, with fancy workflow diagrams, it all looked good, but in practice it was devoid of any sense of reality. In the modern day call center, staff receives and handles customer service phone calls.

Significant technology and protocols, specific to managing phone interactions (beyond the scope of this book), have been meticulously developed over nearly 100 years to incorporate best practices to properly service customer phone calls. The process of handling a phone call, hiring employees, inducting them into the workforce, training them, etc., takes a significant effort. In spite of all the effort, call centers experience an employee turnover rate of 50 percent to 70 percent, due to the repetitive and high-intensity environment, where one is measured on how many calls are handled per hour. The entire incentive program in a call center is the drive to receive and close calls as fast as possible. Everyone from the customer service representative to the manager to the director up to the vice president of the call center is measured and compensated on how many calls, on average, they handle per hour. Various companies provided software for tracking and managing these phone interactions. Siebel was the largest such provider. Their business model was based on selling software licenses per customer service representative (CSR). More phone calls meant more CSRs, which meant more revenue for Siebel.

With the emergence of email and other media and new competitors like EchoMail offering technology for managing these new media, Siebel saw competition for their software licensing revenue. Email was becoming a popular channel for customer service. With multiple channels of customer service, the blended media theory was explored at Citigroup as the "cockpit of the future." Like the cockpit of a plane, here a call center representative was equipped to simultaneously handle phone calls, fax inquiries, chat requests, and email. When a customer service representative became free from a phone call, he or she could respond to an inquiry submitted via fax, or interact with a customer via chat text messaging, or open and respond to an email. Thus, the call center representative could handle multiple channels of service, *at the same time.* The idea was to use the intervening time when a call center representative completes his or her particular service task. In a call center, time is everything. From a merchandising standpoint, the goal was to maximize the utilization of that certain dollar amount the company paid to a call center representative for his or her time.

Citigroup had begun actively researching the possibility of this blended media to increase efficiency. EchoMail was asked to help blend the email channel with the phone channel through a phone switch. When a representative was handling a phone call, no email would be routed to him or her. If a particular representative was not handling a phone call, then the system would route them an email, and put their phone on a "virtual" hold, so no calls would be received. After the email was answered, the phone was then taken off the hold, ready to receive a new phone call or email. This way, the representative could work on email if there were no phone calls and vice versa. Technology-wise, this was feasible but a disaster from a human-capability standpoint.

The reality is that there is something called a switching cost. If one is working in one medium and has to switch to another medium, there is a cost for switching. Imagine you are writing an article using Microsoft Word and in the middle of your writing, you get a phone call. You stop your train of thought, stop typing on your keyboard, you pick up the phone and you start talking. You are now dealing with a very different channel, functioning in a very different mode. Let us say, you finish the call, and get back to the article in Microsoft Word. Now you have to spend some time rethinking and readjusting to start from where you left off prior to taking the phone call. This is the switching cost. The analysts who recommended "blended media" had not considered this switching cost. Speaking on the phone is very different than writing an email. It is literally using different parts of your brain and body. There is a significant switching cost associated with it, and the Citigroup experiment proved it.

Even though technology was developed to meet the challenge, the technology itself was inhumane in the way it further stressed the representatives, since the representatives would have to switch from doing a phone call, which had a certain type of dynamics, to an email, which had a different type of dynamics and later switch back. In an environment that already had a very high turnover due to job-related stress, this switching would make the staff even more stressed. In theory, the "cockpit of the future" seemed like a good idea; however, it did not include the poblems associated with the human component. What was better was to have agents, for a certain period of time continually answering phone calls, then to switch them to email for another period of time. The human mind and body were not able to handle the constant and immediate switching from phone to email.

Summary—Blended Media and Citigroup

If a company wants to deliver on its brand promise, then the human component also needs to be understood. Overstressed representatives do not talk well on the phone nor do they respond well to an email. The back room's ability to deliver has to be aligned with the objectives of the front room. Citigroup learned this early. Following the Citigroup experiment, it was clear that blended media was good in theory, but a disaster in practice.

Cookie Jar Entertainment

Cooke Jar Entertainment is a North American producer of children's entertainment, consumer products, and educational materials headquartered in Toronto, Canada. They have offices around the globe, including Burbank in California, Paris, London, and Tokyo, among other places. They are one of the world's largest independent producers of children's entertainment, branded merchandise, and educational products. They own and hold licensing rights to some of the most recognizable character brands. They are considered a leader in the creation, production, and marketing of animated and live-action programming with a library of nearly 6,000 half-hour episodes of television features, including award-winning shows and brands in over 160 countries. Some of the most recognizable children's television series include Caillou, Inspector Gadget, Arthur, The Doodlebops, and Johnny Test. A full-service international licensing agency within Cookie Jar Entertainment represents numerous entertainment, athletic, and design brands such as Strawberry Shortcake, Richard Scarry, St. Andrews Links, the Harlem Globetrotters, and Skelanimals. Cookie Jar presents numerous New Media endeavors including immersive worlds for kids. Some of Cookie Jar's immersive world sites include Jaroo.com, BusyTownMysteries.com, Caillou.com, Magi-Nation.com, JohnnyTestAndDukey.com, Strawberry-Shortcake.ca, Doodlebops.com, and others.

As one can imagine, a large number of visitors on Cookie Jar websites are children of all ages. Cookie Jar also conducts email communication with these children who visit Cookie Jar websites. However, all the website activities and email campaigns are strictly scrutinized under a United States federal law that was enacted to monitor such websites and email campaigns intended for children. The Children's Online Privacy Protection Act of 1998 (COPPA) is a federal law that was enacted in the United States in October 1998 and made effective in April of 2000. This act applies to websites that collect information online from children under the age of thirteen, to ensure proper privacy policies that protect the privacy of information of these minors. The act requires the online entity to include a clear definition of the collecting site's privacy policy, when and how to seek verifiable consent from the parent or guardian, and the responsibilities of the website operator in protecting the privacy of collected information. The Federal Trade Commission (FTC) has the authority to issue regulations and enforce the act. The act also includes "safe harbor" provisions to encourage industry self-regulation. Additional requirements regarding retention of such data and sharing with third parties were included in a September 2011 revision of the act. When Cookie Jar began to use email to communicate with children, it had to be compliant with COPPA regulations.

Email and Safe Communication with Children

Cookie Jar began with the development of web forms for collecting opt-in information from kids who wanted to join Cookie Jar's mailing lists. To be compliant with COPPA, the primary strategy was to make sure that children under the age of thirteen had a second opt-in from their parents or guardians. This "double opt-in" method ensured that Cookie Jar's email campaigns would not violate any standards. When a kid visited Cookie Jar's web pages, which led him or her to opting in to be on a mailing list, the site first asked for the kid's age and then redirected the rest of the opt-in process based on the age. Children under the age of thirteen were informed of the requirement to obtain consent from their parents or guardian and hence required a parent's or guardian's contact information. Those kids were included in the email list only after a parent or guardian explicitly consented to putting the child's name on the list. This may have prevented a sub-set of kids from joining the list, who wanted to join the list without their parent's or guardian's knowledge. The stringent measure ensured that Cookie Jar was not exposed to legal wrangling and penalties and fines at a later stage. It also built an online trust among the parents that Cookie Jar was willing to forgo easy sign up to ensure privacy and security.

A number of the outbound email campaigns included invitations to live performances by characters from the Cookie Jar television programs such as Doodlebops, Busy Town, Caillou, and Magi-Nation. This further involved the parents and guardians in the program, if the kid was under the age of thirteen. Other outbound email campaigns from Cookie Jar included information on merchandise, such as toys and accessories branded after the characters in the television programs. These outbound email campaigns were also an example of integrating offline television programs, live stage performances, online purchases, and email campaigns.

Summary—Cookie Jar Entertainment

Since Cookie Jar took care to ensure protection of the kids, their brand benefited from creating a sense of security. This was first reflected in the double opt-in pro-gram which parents and guardians really appreciated. For those parents, getting a communication from Cookie Jar about their kid's interest in joining Cookie Jar's mailing list, an invitation to attend a live performance hosted by Cookie Jar, or information about an online program Cookie Jar initiates was really helpful. On one hand they felt they were getting involved with their kids, on another level, they felt safe with Cookie Jar's attention to protecting the privacy of their and their child's information.

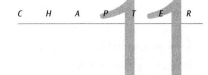

A Complaint Is a Gift

"Hilton and QVC knew one thing: handle email complaints right the first time around. They saved money, and ended up getting more business from complaining customers."

Background

One of the key elements of a successful service organization is resolving matters correctly the first time. There is nothing that builds brand loyalty better than *first-time resolution*. You have a problem, you explain your problem and your expectation of the resolution, and it gets handled correctly the *first* time. Such responsiveness builds incredible trust, which leads to more sales and substantial goodwill, and the benefits of that spread fast. Email helps to accelerate such goodwill (or malice). It is said that in the world of phone and paper mail communications, a bad customer service experience is relayed to five other people. A Hewlett-Packard study revealed that a bad email customer experience is relayed to twenty-seven people. Resolving customer complaints on email, the first time, becomes even more crucial. If you take good care of customers when they complain, you not only make the customer happy that one time, but also get more business from them longer term. This principle is what QVC and Hilton customer service teams understood in managing their customers. These organizations responded to customer complaints with precise resolutions promptly, converting the complaining customer to second-time and lifetime customers. Hilton and QVC knew one thing: the need to handle email complaints right the first time around. They saved money and ended up getting more business from complaining customers. Their demonstrated quality of service proved that a complaint is a gift.

With a brand to protect, QVC and Hilton used email to handle a complaint as soon as it was raised. But more importantly, they knew it was economically prudent to resolve it the first time. Organizations like Hilton, for example, lose profits from a room if their customer service team takes more than one attempt to resolve a complaint. Furthermore, a customer whose complaint is resolved right the first time is very likely to be satisfied with the service and be willing to remain a long-term repeating customer.

Hilton

Hilton Hotels & Resorts is an international chain of hotels and resorts under the company Hilton Worldwide. Started by Conrad Hilton with one hotel in Texas in 1919, the Hilton brands, which have ten brand names, now encompass 3,750 hotels worldwide spread across eighty-four countries on six continents. Focusing on business travelers, leisure travelers, luxury resort guests, and popular destination visitors, Hilton is one of the most recognized brands in the world. The company headquarters is currently located in Tysons Corner, Virginia. Hilton HHonors guest loyalty program is one of the largest of its kind with over twenty-nine million members and has developed a wide network partnering with airlines, car rental companies, credit card issuers, and other services. With its range of loyalty membership, Hilton HHonors is also a well-known brand across the world.

Hilton and Hilton HHonors pride themselves in delivering a high level of customer service. With call centers located worldwide in locations such as Scotland, Texas, and the Philippines, the organization strives hard to deliver the best service to their guests all over the world on a twenty-four-hour-a-day, seven-days-a-week basis. A reliable infrastructure based on advanced technology is essential for their customer service call centers to deliver this high level of service to their guests worldwide. They use different platforms for phone and email, having recognized that each medium is different. Hilton had experienced difficulties previously with certain poor choices in email management, having mistakenly thought that one platform could handle phone and email. Fortunately, Hilton learned from their mistakes. The technology team at Hilton worked hard to find the right email management solution to deliver on their brand promise of first-time resolution.

Email for World-Class Guest Relations

After conducting a very careful, in-depth, and thorough comparison of various solutions over a one-year period and carrying out multiple pilot projects, the Hilton technology team selected EchoMail. The key requirements for Hilton were the ability to support customer service agents located in multiple call centers in different parts of the world, the ability to route email written in different languages to different service teams, robust statistical analytics for real-time reporting for customer service team managers, and the ability to seamlessly integrate email data with other customer data stored elsewhere. Hilton's reason for these requirements was to ensure that they could deliver world-class email service. With EchoMail, Hilton was also able to increase productivity on the number of emails to which a customer service team responded per hour, while also providing accurate and prompt replies to their guests. This meant that instead of just receiving and closing emails fast, they also responded accurately, to achieve a high level of customer satisfaction.

One of the major needs of Hilton was the ability to integrate a customer database with email management. Customer service agents wanted to see additional information that was stored in the customer database at the instant and in the same screen they opened an email inquiry. Without this ability, when processing each email, the agents were spending extra time switching across different databases. To make matters more complicated, customer database was managed at another location by a team outside of Hilton technology. A novel approach was designed to make the additional information visible to customer service agents by connecting email in the EchoMail platform to data in the external database systems. This integration improved the customer service agents' ability to read necessary information about the sender of the email, such as the guest's membership in Hilton HHonors program, where the guest last stayed, and the length of the stay, for example. Not only did this additional information help the customer service agent to have all the necessary information in one screen, but it also enabled the team to move customers with higher levels of HHonors loyalty membership to a separate queue with higher priority. Since membership in the Diamond level of HHonors was branded with better services such as faster reservation time and quicker turnaround of service requests, this feature was reflected in the guest's ability to receive faster email response.

Email Interaction in Real-Time

Another key requirement came from the customer service managers. They needed real-time and periodic reports to manage their representatives in each division. Real-time reports needed to provide accurate statistics on each representative's productivity, including up-to-the-minute work status. These real-time reports helped managers situated in Texas know what each representative was doing in any call center worldwide, and reorganize the email queue to achieve their quality of service levels. These periodic reports provided daily, weekly, and monthly statistics. This assisted mid- and senior-level managers to determine the effectiveness of their customer service organization. It is an incredible experience to observe how managers in the call center in Texas deliver customer service by email in real-time, by dynamically reviewing and adjusting their teams.

Email Management in Real-Time

One of Hilton's other requirements included automatic routing of email to various service queues depending on the language in which the email was written, guest's loyalty card membership, and a variety of other parameters. The ability to route email to different service queues based on languages offered significant support to the customer service team. Another important factor that determined routing of email to specific service queues was the additional data obtained from customer database automatically. Information about the email sender's loyalty membership determined which queue that email was placed in—a high-priority queue or the standard queue. Information about the email sender's last stay such as which hotel and the length of the stay, for example, determined which group within the email service team processed that email. In addition, each email's content was automatically analyzed for sensing the sender's attitude, the issues he or she wrote about, and any specific request, so as to identify additional factors to determine which was the right queue to route the email to. This information also resulted in the customer service representative being presented with a suggested response, which made their response to the email faster and compliant with the standards set by Hilton. This implementation increased the number of emails each agent was able to process per hour, which is a key performance indicator of a successful customer service team.

The real-time reporting made a major difference in the instantaneous management of Hilton's worldwide customer service organization. Up-to-the-moment information on pending emails, knowing which agents were currently on duty, and which agents were actively processing email (versus agents on break), were available to the managers. The hospitality industry in general, and Hilton in particular, is very sensitive to providing quick and accurate resolutions for customer inquiries. This is not just prudent customer service practice; it also affects the hotel chain's bottom line. The up-to-the-moment information on service agents, routing of emails to appropriate agent queues, automatic analysis of emails, and selection of suggested responses based on the analysis, as well as additional information pulled from the customer database—all of them had a cumulative effect on the economics of Hilton's profitability. When a guest makes a customer service call to Hilton, the call could cost Hilton a significant amount of money. This amount is more-or-less equal to the profit they make from an average room rental. So, single call closure of service calls is a major factor for the Hilton customer service team. If multiple calls are made by a guest to resolve one inquiry, then Hilton loses a substantial amount of revenue. The customer service team has to respond to emails in such a way that it really addresses the issue the first time. Integrating the customer database with email helped the service team to see the history of each guest's stay at Hilton, which improved the accuracy of response, avoiding "multiple email resolution."

The additional information from the customer database regarding the guest's last stay also helped the customer service team to upsell the guest through follow-up targeted messages. In the email response, the guest is informed about their rewards program and how the guest could earn more rewards by taking certain action. This was a timely way to integrate marketing and service. Furthermore, this approach helped Hilton to establish its brand presence with guests, since the responses were not simply resolution of a question the guest had raised, but also provided additional information—a soft sell that was targeted and personalized to the guest.

QVC, Inc.

QVC, Inc. is a multinational company specializing in twenty-four-hour televised home shopping. Founded in 1986 in Pennsylvania, QVC televises its shopping network in five countries, including the United States, the United Kingdom, Germany, Japan, and Italy. The name is an acronym for the three words Quality, Value, and Convenience. It is estimated that QVC is telecast to approximately 195 million households worldwide, running a business of nearly $8 billion annually in sales.

QVC lives and breathes what is known as a "360-degree view of the customer." QVC integrates television and online media into one amazing customer and sales infrastructure. The studios are equipped with state-of-the-art communication equipment and information displays. Smallest details of sales are available to the telecast team and production staff on the studio floor. Everything is monitored and analyzed. The producer is monitoring up-to-the-second information on sales and he or she can prompt the presenter with what to say on live television. The scene on the studio floor is "real-time" action at its best.

Email for Integrated Inbound and Outbound Communication

QVC understood the value and need for integrating inbound and outbound communication. This was, sadly, an important aspect that Unilever failed to understand. QVC implemented the concept of *customer conversation* at all levels and EchoMail's ability to manage inbound and outbound email communication supported their brand goals. QVC used EchoMail for inbound service email management and outbound email marketing. With inbound email mangement, QVC not only addressed the customer's issues but also, like Hilton, saw it as an opportunity to market to the customer. Based on the nature of the customer's complaint about a particular product, QVC would not only address that issue, but also give leading tips on what other products would work best with the product that the customer had already purchased. They effectively used the opportunity to resolve a complaint and then upsell the right product at the right time. The idea was that those customers who complained were the ones who really wanted to be serviced. So the QVC team would address the complaint immediately and would also invite the customer to buy an ancillary product at a discount.

The EchoMail platform helped the customer service team to significantly improve response time. Television shopping customers are accustomed to the fast-paced environment of watching a product on television, ordering it on the phone, getting it delivered fast, and using it right away. Naturally, they also expect very quick turnaround when they submit a query or an email complaint. Using EchoMail's intelligent analysis of incoming email—automatic categorization, routing, and auto-selection of suggested responses—the customer service team eliminated a significant amount of manual work in responding to the service requests, dramatically improving the ability to respond to more customers in a shorter duration. Statistically, the customer service team doubled the number of emails processed per hour after they began using EchoMail. This was a significant achievement for the QVC customer service team.

From a data acquisition and utilization standpoint, QVC had amazing information on their customers and they used it to the best advantage possible. For example, if a customer bought a handbag from QVC, their data analytic engineers knew that it was likely for that customer to buy a piece of jewelry within three weeks, or if a customer bought a new jacket that he or she was likely to buy a matching scarf. QVC's intelligent use of data, based on customer behavior, drove more effective sales. Similarly, they used such analytics to send targeted outbound email marketing campaigns. Instead of sending out a blast of the same email to every person, they sent highly targeted email content to each recipient. QVC's outbound marketing email campaigns were never one single email message to the millions of recipients. Instead they were tens of thousands of different campaigns to highly segmented lists of recipients. The email content would vary based on a host of data that QVC maintained in their email list. The QVC marketing communications team created a large number of different sections of message content, and sections of the message content would be merged together based on business rules to form a complete email, appropriate for each recipient. The business rules were developed based on data analytics and historical purchasing patterns.

QVC received an incredible amount of experience by learning from other large brands. Lessons from Unilever provided knowledge on the integration of inbound and outbound email communication. Lessons from Citigroup provided ideas for the design of infrastructure to support the development of an automated email customer response system. Like Nike, QVC was another stellar example of a company which really used all the components of the EchoMail platform—inbound, outbound, analytics, data storage, and response management. They took the level of targeted email communication to a whole different level for their outbound campaigns.

Chapter Summary

The Hilton and QVC projects taught the valuable lesson of using the right tools to help customer service agents resolve customer issues correctly and quickly. With EchoMail's automatic analysis of each incoming email to identify the content of the email, to route the email to the right service team, as well as to construct the appropriate suggested response—and doing all of this quickly—the customer service team really improved the number of email units they were able to address per hour (a statistic classified as Units Per Hour or UPH). This improved UPH made a major contribution to the bottom line of these companies. Personalized and precise responses that resolved issues the first time and made their customers satisfied, contributed to that bottom line.

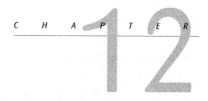

Watch What You Write

"With email, unlike phone calls, making false promises can be devastating. By using email monitoring, American Express and Allstate protected their brands and stopped problems way ahead of time."

Background

The financial service industry has been under scrutiny over the last two decades with regards to electronic communication with their customers. Financial service companies can be held legally responsible for making false claims or promises to prospects, customers, and investors. Prior to the banking collapse of 2008, there was a greater sense of implicit trust in banks and financial institutions. Financial services companies now need to go the extra mile to convince us that they are secure, safe, and honest. We, as consumers, take their brand promises seriously. Ensuring that the company does not make false promises and that it communicates properly in their offline and online conversations is critical to their brand. And email is where millions of those online conversations take place. Banks, credit card companies, insurance companies, and financial products merchants need to watch what their sales people, financial advisors, and other staff members say to consumers, particularly in email. If a staff member or representative makes a claim or promise regarding profits or returns, the company is liable for delivering on the claim or promise.

With email, unlike phone, making false promises can be devastating, and subject to serious legal claims in a court of law. Therefore it is critical to monitor, observe, and watch the conversation between customers and financial services personnel for ensuring best practices are followed and the brand promise of honesty, security, and safety are met. If there are breaches in communication, such monitoring will help alert compliance officers promptly so that corrective actions can be taken swiftly. Two of America's most well-known brands, American Express and Allstate Insurance, used email monitoring as a way of defining and protecting their brand, to monitor interactions between the customer and the people who represent the organization. Such email monitoring enabled them to strengthen their brand and prevent mistakes long before they might become an issue. Moreover, the technology for email monitoring also provided many other positive results.

Allstate

Allstate Insurance, a Fortune 500 company, is the largest publicly held personal-lines insurer in the United States. Founded in 1931 originally as a part of Sears, Roebuck and Company, it spun off in 1993 and established its headquarters in Northbrook, Illinois. In addition to providing thirteen major lines of insurance, including auto, life, home, and commercial, Allstate also offers financial services, including retirement products and investment products. Allstate also does business in Canada, and serves approximately sixteen million households in North America. Allstate has over 12,500 local agency owners and financial advisors. They sell products through their website and over the phone in certain states, as well as through independent agencies, financial institutions, and broker-dealers. Allstate agents function as independent contractors.

Email for Sales Lead Management

In 1997, Allstate built a simple but well-executed informational website. During the initial meetings with Allstate, the EchoMail team introduced the concept of augmenting their website for consumers to directly interact with Allstate agents online. The idea was to develop individual home pages for agents to generate potential sales leads, with email as the conversation medium between agent and consumer. Each agent home page would have the capability for the agent to receive email inquiries and respond to those inquiries, while storing the sender's email address in order to build the agent's email list for follow-up communications. While Allstate was open to the idea of agents having the ability to communicate with potential prospects and customers, they wanted to monitor the conversation to know *what* the agents were communicating with their prospects and customers. This was essential for Allstate, to ensure that no agent was creating legal liability problems for Allstate by miscommunicating and making false promises.

In addition to the agent email, there was also corporate email, being delivered directly from customers to the corporate head offices on more global questions and concerns, such as questions about stock price or how to get a job with Allstate. Allstate, therefore, had two parts to their communication strategy. Allstate wanted to enable their distributed network of independent agents to be responsive to the end customers, but they, at headquarters, wanted to be equally responsive to the emails they received in their corporate email box.

Email and Compliance Management

The communication between agents and prospects and customers was called "agent email." There was a need to implement a smart way for agents to communicate with their prospects and customers, while ensuring Allstate had the ability to review all email exchanges. To entice prospects and customers to interact with agents, an agent locator feature was deployed on the Allstate website. This functionality provided each website visitor the ability to find a local agent. If one typed in a zip code, for example, 07039, names of all Allstate agents in the Livingston, New Jersey, area would be displayed. By selecting a particular agent, the user was taken to the agent's particular home page, which included the agent's picture and contact information. This agent home page allowed the website visitor to send an email to that agent. The email sent to the agent was received by EchoMail, its content was analyzed to generate statistical information, and then it was routed to the agent while retaining a copy on the EchoMail server for Allstate to review. Similarly, the response sent back by the agent was received on EchoMail server, retaining a copy for Allstate's review, and was then routed to the website visitor who sent the original email. Allstate could analyze and monitor all communications between the agent and Allstate's prospects and customers.

This solution allowed Allstate to not only monitor the communications but also to identify leads for agents. The leads were a wonderful side effect and created new business for Allstate and its agents. Allstate agents were part of an extranet of resellers. The agents were *independent contractors*, and by law Allstate could not manage or dictate directives to them, but could monitor their behavior and ensure that the agents were compliant. The need for compliance was the driver for Allstate wanting to review communications because Allstate was responsible for what agents communicated regarding Allstate's products. Ultimately, a consumer experienced the Allstate brand and didn't care if the agent was an independent contractor or not. Therefore, Allstate wanted to know if any agent was writing incorrect information in their email correspondences with customers while carrying the Allstate brand. Providing false information, making harsh comments, and overpromising were areas of communication problems that Allstate wanted to avoid. This became even more important for Allstate when they added their new financial services division.

From a branding standpoint, Allstate wanted their agents to appear as an integral part of their brand, while providing them the ability to independently communicate with the public and, at the same time, Allstate would maintain centralized control, to observe and moderate all communications between agents and prospects and customers. When the agent responded, the response email went back through EchoMail. The EchoMail technology analyzed the agent's response, and stopped the response from going to the customer if the agent's response had any information that would negatively impact Allstate. Interestingly, a majority of the inbound inquiries were sales leads. The first rollout of this new email monitoring was in a small district in Texas. The pilot was successful on many fronts. New revenues from sales leads identified by EchoMail produced a multifold return on investment, relative to the cost of the project. Allstate proved to themselves that email could not only support their brand but also generate new revenue in the process. As Allstate added more agents, they could see the increased flow of sales leads. With the success of the Texas pilot project, the solution was deployed enterprise-wide for all of Allstate.

Allstate, through this email monitoring, was able to detect, in near real-time, which agents were more successful than others, who got more leads, and who was converting leads to customers. Allstate was able to monitor what the agents were communicating and control the agents who were poorly affecting Allstate's brand, sooner rather than later. This meant a lot to their legal departments in terms of risk mitigation and averting potential law suits—the indirect savings of which were incalculable.

Email for Corporate Information Dissemination

Independent of agent email, Allstate also had corporate email, through which people would ask general questions about Allstate's health as a company, request annual reports for shareholders, or inquire about their stand on social causes, and so on. Those emails went to Allstate service representatives and it enabled Allstate to be a brand-centric company responding promptly and accurately to the questions. The EchoMail platform served, similar to its role with Unilever, as both a centralized and decentralized communication system, becoming an engine for branding, lead generation, and customer service through email.

American Express

American Express Company is a United States-based multinational financial services company with its headquarters in New York. The company was founded in 1850 and is best known worldwide for their credit cards, traveler's checks, and charge cards. American Express accounts for nearly 25 percent of all credit card transactions in the United States, which is the highest percentage transacted by a single card issuer. American Express and the Roman centurion mascot are one among the top twenty-five most valuable brands of the world. When started in 1850 in New York, the company was involved in express mail business holding a monopoly of express shipment of goods, securities, currency, and more, which eventually included owning over seventy-one thousand miles of railroads. It was in 1882 that American Express expanded its business to financial services. Their first financial service product was money orders. In 1891, they introduced a new financial instrument called "traveler's checks" for making money available to people traveling from the United States to Europe. This offering set them up as a truly international company. From 1917–1918, during World War I, the United States government consolidated railway lines and American Express got out of the express mail business. In 1958, American Express entered the charge card business. It entered the credit card business in 1987 with Optima, which allowed a balance of unpaid credit to be carried over to subsequent months. Other businesses of American Express included brokerage, financial advisors, travel agencies, and publishing.

Email for Consistent and Constant Communication

American Express acknowledged a need for intelligent management of inbound email when they recognized that the volume of incoming email was increasing dramatically from their website. Initially EchoMail was deployed for one business unit based in the United States. Eventually, fifteen business units spread around the world were managing email using sophisticated analysis, routing, and tracking of each email. Email was monitored and tracked in many non-English languages, including Chinese and Japanese and some European languages. The implementation was truly global with the processing of email in multiple languages from multiple countries for multiple divisions. Each division worldwide could process and access their particular email. American Express's technology team, based out of Phoenix, Arizona, had centralized access, from a corporate compliance viewpoint. They could access any email, anywhere, in any country, at any time, to ensure that its brand was being treated right.

Email for Secure Up-to-Date Account Information

One of the key requirements of American Express was the implementation of *Secure Mail*—the word "Mail" refers to email. With the increase in phishing, identity theft, and online impersonation, Secure Mail is essential for a financial service organization to safely communicate account details through email. Phishing is a way of cyber-thieves attempting to acquire information such as usernames, passwords, and credit card details by masquerading as a trustworthy entity. For example, an email purporting to be from American Express is sent to lure the unsuspecting customer to provide details in the response email or at a fake website which carries a look and feel that is identical to American Express. When the customer provides requested information, the fake sender uses that information to make fraudulent transactions on credit cards or to use sensitive personal information for other criminal activities involving identity theft. Secure Mail makes sure that a customer's account specific information such as account balance, last payment, and transaction details are exchanged between American Express and the customer only via secure account access login.

Though the customer may send a request to American Express for information about his or her account via regular email, any email containing account information is only sent via the secure mailbox. A secure mailbox is an email communication system where a customer is provided unique account access to a secured server. All emails containing sensitive account information are kept only on this secured server. When American Express wants to respond to the customer with sensitive information, two emails are sent. One email is a notification sent to the customer's regular email address, instructing him or her to log into the secured server to read the sensitive account information. The second email is an email sent by American Express to the customer's Secure Mailbox, containing the sensitive account information. The first emails may carry a link to the Secure Mailbox, which is made accessible only when provided with the right username and password.

Financial service organizations such as American Express have been under the scrutiny of federal agencies for protecting investors and customers. Any promise or claim made by a credit card company, financial advisor, broker, et cetera, to the customer has to be fulfilled by the company for which the claim or promise was made. While it was easier for the company or the agent to deny such promises and claims when made through a phone call, email changed the game.

When the promise is written in an email, it becomes more or less permanent. In fact, federal regulations, including the Gramm-Leach-Bliley Act, Sarbanes-Oxley Act, and the USA Patriot Act, require an organization to retain email communication for up to seven years and produce them promptly for investigation when requested. Thus, financial service organizations such as American Express found it prudent, like Allstate, to monitor communications to identify inaccurate promises or claims. EchoMail's ability to automatically analyze the content of an email became a strong tool in supporting this effort. Email monitoring identified agents who were conveying inaccurate promises or claims. If the automatic analysis flagged an email with any message that read like an inaccurate promise or claim, the email was moved to a holding queue and a predetermined person or team was alerted. Such emails are held in the holding queue until a person with the right level of authority logs in and either approves or deletes the email. Such email monitoring made a major difference to protecting the American Express and Allstate brands and avoiding potentially costly mistakes.

Chapter Summary

The ability to automatically analyze the contents of an email became a significant component in watching what the salesman, financial advisor, or service representative wrote to a customer in email. Since even a small mistake carrying a false claim or promise can result in large legal fines for the company, this feature became very important for Allstate and American Express to monitor outgoing emails from their staff. To enable the staff to send approved email responses, EchoMail's response library of standard replies was used extensively; this resulted in another noteworthy advantage: consistency of messaging. The library provided the ability to push legally compliant and well-written messaging so the staff was compliant with corporate branding and legal guidelines. The banking collapse has in fact imposed even more formal and stricter regulations demanding more formal and accurate communication, for which email is perfectly suited.

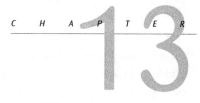
The Art of Email

"The Guggenheim mastered email to build membership and relationships that serve as a model for arts and nonprofits."

Background

The Solomon R. Guggenheim Museum is one of the most famous art museums in the world. The Solomon R. Guggenheim Foundation runs art museums in different parts of the world, including New York, Venice, Bilbao, Berlin, and Abu Dhabi. The museum in New York, often referred to as the Guggenheim, is located in the Upper East Side of Manhattan in New York City, overlooking Central Park. The museum building, designed by renowned architect Frank Lloyd Wright, is one of the most important architectural landmarks of New York City. The museum opened in October 1959 and underwent extensive renovations from the years 2005 to 2008. The New York location exhibits a renowned collection of Impressionist, Post-Impressionist, early Modern, and contemporary art and also features special exhibitions throughout the year.

Though Solomon Guggenheim had been collecting art since 1929, the foundation itself was formed only in 1937. The museum initially opened in a rented quarter on East 54th Street and eventually moved to the present location (88th street and 5th avenue) in 1959. The Venice museum, located in Palazzo Venier dei Leoni, an eighteenth-century palace designed by the Venetian architect Lorenzo

Boschetti, was opened in 1951 for public viewing. The Bilbao museum, located in Bilbao, Basque Country, Spain, designed by Canadian American architect Frank Gehry and built by Ferrovial, S.A. (an urban infrastructure development company) was opened to the public in 1997. Construction of the museum in Abu Dhabi is expected to be complete by 2013 in a building also designed by Frank Gehry. The Berlin museum called Deutsche Guggenheim, developed under a unique cooperation between the Guggenheim Foundation and Deutsche Bank, is located on the ground floor of the Deutsche Bank building, a sandstone building constructed in 1920 on the Unter den Linden boulevard in Berlin, Germany, and was opened for the public in 1997.

Email for Better Member Relations

From 2002 to 2003, the museum decided to find a solution for using email as a channel for enhancing member relations. The marketing and communications department took on the responsibility of finding a solution that would help them manage communication for all the different entities that wanted to communicate with the public and members. The entities included Marketing, Press Office, Corporate Development, Membership Services, Education Services, and Visitor Information. The director of marketing communication called for a Request for Proposal (RFP). She invited EchoMail based on an industry analyst report that showed EchoMail with a near-perfect score. Unfortunately, the RFP invitation came to EchoMail's marketing and communication manager who had suddenly taken ill and was out for a few days. By the time others found out about the RFP invitation, it was almost too late to meet the deadline. In a call with the director, and after explaining the situation, she agreed to extend the deadline by a couple of days to allow EchoMail to participate in the selection process. EchoMail ended up at the top of the selection process and became Guggenheim's chosen email communication platform.

The marketing and communication teams at the Guggenheim are highly sophisticated and technology-savvy. They are also proficient and skilled in creative design and writing. They keep up to date on all aspects of communication including new technology. As an organization that started out supporting artists during the Arts-Online.com days, the team at EchoMail had a special affection for everything related to the arts. EchoMail started by educating the Guggenheim team about the importance of maintaining member relations through email dialogue. Marketing and communications began their email communication program by setting up regular ongoing outbound email campaigns about various programs running at the museum.

Email Templates Need Care and Attention

The Guggenheim's email communication had to match the elegance of their brand. One way to ensure this was through the use of email templates. An email template is a design of the email with various text and graphic elements properly laid out. This design holds all the elements that are required to present a certain *look and feel*. The look and feel elements include the layout, use of certain fonts, size, position and selection of images. The template provides a seamless transition to pages in the website. When a template is produced, a number of technological considerations need to be incorporated into the programming of the template. For instance, some recipients may be limited in their ability to view a template, based on the browser being used. Furthermore, each browser has different releases and versions, and the different recipients may be using different releases and versions of browsers. Many of these browsers, and even versions of the same browser, render web pages differently even though the exact same programming code is used to present the email. Additionally, some of the recipients may be viewing the email in a text-only email reader that does not show the rich media in the email, but only the textual matter. Thus, the template needs to have programming code built into it that will consider these differences and render the viewing of the web page in the best possible manner, in the browser chosen by the recipient. In some cases, it may not be possible to meet differences in every single browser, a major challenge for any organization that sends emails containing rich media. The Guggenheim team extensively used EchoMail's creative team to produce email templates for every email campaign they sent. While the Guggenheim team provided detailed instructions of the visible elements of the template, such as images, fonts, and layout, the EchoMail team coded those requirements into templates that can be used to send email campaigns to the email list and have it appear as well as possible in the email reader of the recipient.

The Guggenheim Museum is well known for bringing some of the most interesting collections of unique artists and cultures from around the world for special exhibitions. They showcase work from Europe to Asia to Africa, in addition to the artists and culture of the Americas. These exhibitions are a unique opportunity for the rest of the world to see the exotic work of a people and culture that was little known or sometimes even completely unknown prior to these exhibitions. And these exhibitions needed to be publicized to the casual visitor as well as to devoted members of the museum. The marketing and communications team is very good at collecting email addresses and is successful in building a large email database of their enthusiasts. Working with EchoMail, they understood how seemingly disparate data collections could be integrated in EchoMail to generate mailing lists that could be used for these announcements.

Email for Growing Membership Through Targeted Communications

The marketing and communications team was collecting not only email addresses, but also other information about visitors and members, such as their level of interest in certain art forms. This additional information helped the museum in targeting their invitations to their visitors. EchoMail gave the museum the ability to use its personalization and targeted emailing capability to address and communicate with each visitor in a way that was personal to the visitor. Thus, the museum was now able to establish a new intimate manner of communicating with visitors who were dedicated to the museum. This made a big difference to increasing the commitment of those dedicated visitors to the museum. Show announcement emails became a regular ongoing communication channel for the museum. The marketing and communications team built what had started as a single email announcing an exhibition, into a series of announcement and reminder services for their members.

For example, when an exhibition of the unique early art forms of China was scheduled to show at the museum, the marketing and communications team started sending announcements to various subgroups of the member list announcing the arrival of the exhibition weeks or even months in advance. Then they proceeded to send reminders to the members leading up to the day of showing. All of these communications maintained a strict permission-based email policy, to be compliant with the anti-SPAM policies, which require a responsive opt-out option if someone says "take me off your list." Unlike solutions that required a waiting period of a few days to a couple of weeks to opt out of an email list, the EchoMail technology allowed the members to opt out of a mailing list immediately. This enabled the museum to be compliant with anti-SPAM regulations even before such regulation was made into a law under the Bush administration.

Another group in the museum that looked to have ongoing communication with visitors and members was the museum store. The museum is famous not only for its exhibits, it is also well known for the souvenirs and merchandise that go with the exhibits. The museum is so good with the merchandise that they even have a special merchandise sale when a unique exhibition is on show at the museum. For example, when a particular artist's work is showcased at the museum, the store will sell replicas of the artist's work as well as other merchandise such as scarves and mugs that depict the art. These objects are a big hit with the art enthusiasts, even with occasional visitors and tourists. As everyone likes to have a memento from a visit to a place as famous as the Guggenheim Museum, the museum store is always looking for ways to let the visitors and members know of the upcoming and ongoing special sales. They used email as a channel of communication for sending such notifications from the museum store. In turn, the store would collect email addresses of the store visitors, provided they were interested in receiving communication from the museum. The collected email addresses and related information were routed to the database management team in the Information Technology Department and the marketing and communications team would bring that information to EchoMail to enhance the email list.

Another function the museum used email on a regular basis for was disseminating press releases. Press releases are typically sent to lists of recipients in the news and publishing fields to publicize upcoming exhibitions and announcements from the corporate headquarters about new programs and other activities at the museum. Equally important are newsletters that are sent from the desk of the director of the museum. These newsletters are sent to visitors, donors, program participants, and many others, provided the recipients have already opted in to receive the newsletters.

Email for Raising Donations

The Guggenheim Foundation is a nonprofit organization. This means that the foundation meets its financial needs through donations made by individuals, family trusts, and corporate donors. The museum has a donor management group that handles donations and solicitation for donations. Even though the actual financial transaction in a donation is handled by a system that is built for secure financial transactions, the marketing and communications team is given access to information collected in the donation process to build their email list. Again, strict permission policy and communication preferences are applied when using information collected from a donation for future communication. In a manner similar to the way the marketing and communications team was able to support the museum store, they were able to support the donor management group as well in maintaining communication with the donors.

The corporate development group manages donations specifically from corporations and organizations that are interested in sponsoring the Guggenheim Museum's activities. The Guggenheim has a unique and interesting corporate development program, which affords many privileges to its partner organizations. Some of the privileges afforded to corporate donors include invitations to special opening days, free guest passes, access to halls and other areas in the museum for private functions, and access to other special programs that are not otherwise accessible to the general public. Email is used extensively to communicate with the corporate world, both for soliciting new donors as well as maintaining communication with existing donors.

Email for Event Management

The Guggenheim Museum provides extensive support to families and family activities. It promotes a healthy and safe family environment for activities involving parents and children. They conduct programs for children throughout the year, such as demonstrations and opportunities for children to express their artistic talents. Keeping the parents informed of the programs and schedules is a function for which email is used extensively. The communication program follows strict permission policy and respects recipients' communication preferences for these email campaigns.

In addition to working with families, the museum conducts educational programs for those who are interested in learning about arts and art forms. The museum also has a well-established internship program for youths. Such programs rely on a good communication backbone and email is a preferred channel of communication for the participants.

Many of the above programs are based on events that occur on a particular date and such events require that people register to attend. The museum made use of the event management capabilities of the email platform to manage this process. This feature gave the museum the ability to post information about upcoming events in the event management section of EchoMail and to let EchoMail manage the invitation and sign-up process with the participants. Not only did the event management feature allow them to send invitations, but also it provided the ability to send appropriate timed reminders to those who signed up and a second opportunity for those who did not.

Chapter Summary

As a nonprofit arts organization, the Guggenheim Museum required a reliable channel and robust solution to support their communication requirements. As a museum and as a nonprofit, communication plays a significant role in the day-to-day activities at the Guggenheim. Email proved to be the most reliable channel for their purposes. While the communications team was unable to determine if the direct paper mail drops were opened or read, they knew exactly how many people opened and read the email. Furthermore, they knew who opened the email and who got interested in a specific section of information in the email. This enabled the communications team to focus their messaging even more specifically on the recipient's interests. Some of the email campaigns also required a response from the recipient and the EchoMail event management feature handled it for the musuem. The Guggenheim, through a multidisciplinary approach, used email to manage communications and thereby acquire new donors and members while extending and deepening existing relationships.

Email for Small and Mid-Market Businesses

"The lessons from large organizations using email, nearly a decade ago, are now relevant and valuable for any business, small, medium, or large."

Background

Small and mid-market businesses can learn a great deal from the work of large organizations. Email has grown to be the preferred channel for most people when it comes to business communications, especially when the business is transacted online. The United States alone has over twenty-seven million small and medium business (SMB) organizations. These include one-person businesses as well as those organizations with less than 500 full-time employees. Even though small and medium businesses have fewer employees and may have smaller assets, most of the activities involved in the business process of SMBs are the same as large enterprises.

An SMB, like any company, has to obtain customers, vendors, and service providers; hire, train, and manage employees; produce and deliver products and services; and maintain customer relations. SMBs, like large companies, also need to establish communication with their customers to keep them and get new ones. And email is one of the best channels of communication for SMBs, for both marketing and customer service. Even though an SMB may receive and send fewer emails when compared with a large enterprise, there is still a need for strategies, best practices, and tools to effectively manage email within SMBs. The lessons from large enterprises can be extremely valuable in this regard.

Unlike large organizations, however, SMBs can benefit from email with far less investment. SMBs' requirements are less rigid and less specialized compared with large enterprises. SMBs' data transmission, security, and storage needs, for example, are more generic, compared to the big guys. This means that SMBs can gain significant value from email communications by simply replicating some of the best strategies, practices, and techniques used by big brands, as we have discussed in the earlier chapters of this part of the book.

Email for SMBs: A Two-Pronged Approach

As you would have understood from the previous chapters, there are two main areas in which email can provide great value to SMBs: (1) inbound email management and (2) outbound email marketing. Inbound email management focuses on the receipt of customer inquiries, taking proper action to address their issues and responding to customers in a timely manner. Outbound email marketing includes organizing customer email lists, creating attractive messages and offers, proactively connecting with customers, and tracking the customer interaction to understand what kinds of communication worked and those that did not.

From large organizations, we have learned about using email for managing crisis, maintaining good customer relations, managing account information, enhancing guest and member relations, ensuring prompt, trusted, and safe communications, creating a comfortable environment for donors and children, managing sales leads, being compliant, and managing events. Similarly, we have learned how large enterprises were able to use email to reach their constituents using integrated marketing, multichannel marketing, and personalized marketing for mobilizing at the grassroots level. Moreover, we've seen how email could be used for conducting consumer behavior surveys to gather detailed analytics on prospects, customers, and voters, for example. Our case studies have also shared the importance of maintaining one's brand by ensuring secure data storage, data integration, and centralized and decentralized message control.

Inbound Email Management

SMBs, like large enterprises, are continuing to receive a growing volume of inbound email each day from their customers. Creating a trusted communication channel for such questions and complaints to be handled promptly and communicated back to the sender is a significant part of good email customer care, whether the business is small or large. Volume of inbound email, however, is not the driving reason for implementing email management. In fact, even in large organizations, whether the volume was small or large, the motivating factor in implementing email management, which many find surprising, was to build accountability between the customer and the company.

Let us consider an SMB such as Taco John's. Taco John's is a small Mexican fast food chain in the Midwest. For Taco John's, it was clear that although the number of emails each day was not that many, according to their chief financial officer, their objective was to provide a prompt response to each email and take accountability for each issue. That was part of their business or brand promise. Commitment to such a promise required Taco John's to strategize and create a methodology using EchoMail to route incoming inquiries to both the local restaurant, which was referred to in the incoming email, as well as to the internal centralized customer service team. Taco John's, moreover, wanted to keep track of the statistics on the issues and locations so they could identify patterns and address issues before they became a bigger crisis. For example, if a particular branch of the restaurant consistently got lots of complaints, this would be an early warning signal to Taco John's headquarters to intervene and make the necessary adjustments.

The key elements of the Taco John's example are that even though email volume was low, they wanted to make sure each email was:

- Received and categorized
- Routed to the right person
- Answered with a proper response in a timely fashion
- Tracked to ensure service levels
- Used to understand trends or patterns of communication (to avoid a fiasco like Toyota's)

Any SMB can implement all of the above elements of inbound email management to ensure a solid email customer service program. Such an effort will serve to retain existing customers as well as build customer loyalty.

Outbound Email Marketing

Outbound email marketing includes the ability for an organization to disseminate information about their company and its products or services through the use of email. One way is to simply broadcast one email message to all. Alternatively, another way is to send personalized and targeted email messages via multiple channels, motivating recipients to take action within the email. The organization may or may not need to respond back, and they are then able to track all the actions, while ensuring that data from all sources are integrated and maintained securely. Such capabilities are now readily available in many email marketing services such as EchoMail and others.

Growing numbers of SMBs use outbound email marketing every day. This includes nonprofits, law offices, recruiters, artists, and small to medium financial service providers, to name a few. All of these organizations are able to take advantage of the same great features and functionality that large organizations have used, such as anti-SPAM compliance, secure data storage, data integration, personalized and targeted messaging, event management, surveys, and questionnaires. Above all, email marketing enables them, unlike print advertising, to track their investment down to the penny and make real-time changes to a marketing program. Such accountable use of marketing dollars is a significant advantage for SMBs with email marketing.

Chapter Summary

SMB organizations have requirements very similar to the requirements of large enterprises when it comes to email communication. The lessons learned from large enterprises are applicable to SMB organizations. Two important applications for SMBs are inbound email management for supporting customer retention and loyalty, and outbound email marketing for acquiring new customer sales.

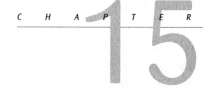
When Oprah and Chopra Meditate on Email

"The brands of Oprah and Chopra used email to connect with millions across the globe, as never before, and got them to meditate by delivering an email-based curriculum."

Background

The Chopra Center for Wellbeing, located in Carlsbad, California, offers a wide variety of programs, retreats, and teacher training programs that integrate the healing arts of the East with the best in modern Western medicine with the goal of helping people experience physical healing, emotional freedom, and higher states of consciousness. The Center was founded in 1996 by Deepak Chopra, MD, and David Simon, MD, and runs weekly programs, periodic events, ongoing subscription programs, and also sells merchandise. The Center offers an ancient Indian medical treatment program called Ayurveda, primordial sound mediation, and Yoga, a form of physical exercise and therapy program that alleviates certain physical health and mental stress-related problems. Their website, www.chopra.com, includes an online shopping site selling a wide range of products: clothing, jewelry, books, audio tapes, video, bath and body products, aromatic products, dietary supplements, herbs, etc.

Oprah Winfrey Network (OWN) is a multiplatform media company designed to entertain, inform, and inspire people to live in the best way possible.

Starting nearly twenty-five years ago with a one-hour television program, Oprah Winfrey has now evolved into a 24/7 cable network channel. The Oprah Show and OWN network are well-known for self-help and spiritual content. "The Oprah Winfrey Show" was nationally syndicated from 1986 to 2011 and, according to some estimates, was the highest rated program of its kind in history. According to Forbes.com, Oprah Winfrey is considered the most influential woman in media.

The 21-Day Challenge

In early 2012, I was introduced to Deepak Chopra by a friend. We remained in touch and in August 2012, Deepak invited me to his Center to speak at one of the events he was conducting. At the event, Deepak asked me to present Systems Health™, a new educational program I had developed that combined Systems Biology and Traditional Systems of Medicine. Deepak and I decided to have the Chopra Center offer my Systems Health program to MDs and other health care practitioners. While at the Center, I met Kathy Bankerd, the Center's head of Marketing. Kathy had been working with other email marketing providers and heard from Deepak that I had invented the first email system and had been the CEO of EchoMail. Kathy was mapping out a powerful strategy to work with OWN and to use television to reach millions to more broadly promote Deepak's 21-Day Meditation Challenge, through email.

Kathy's rich experience in marketing allowed her to recognize the power of EchoMail's enterprise platform, an integrated approach to conduct electronic conversations based on our earlier work with Calvin Klein. The conversation with Kathy and the subsequent review of EchoMail's capabilities led the Chopra Center to select EchoMail as their platform to deliver their 21-Day Meditation Challenge as an email-based educational program to teach millions how to meditate.

The 21-Day Meditation Challenge is a guided meditation program that Deepak Chopra was conducting remotely for participants all over the world. Thousands of people had earlier participated in the program and benefited from the positive results of guided meditation. The program ran for twenty-one days, during which registered participants received daily reminders for their meditation. Three to four weeks prior to beginning the twenty-one-day meditation program, people could start to register to participate in the program.

This time, however, Kathy wanted to do it in a much larger way by launching it on Oprah's network OWN, and encourage people to go from the TV announcement to a website, where they could register and then start receiving the email-based meditation curriculum. In addition to OWN, the program was publicized through a variety of other channels including the Chopra Center web-site, email marketing, and affiliate websites.

From Oprah to Chopra—Integrating TV With an Email Curriculum

In November 2012, the program was launched with Deepak Chopra leading a 21-Day Meditation Challenge program on Creating Abundance. Millions of people became aware of this program through "Super Soul Sunday," a television program Oprah Winfrey hosted with Deepak Chopra as her guest. The November Meditation Challenge generated hundreds of thousands of registrants.

The digital program included the following key features:
- Daily streaming of meditations guided by Deepak Chopra, approximately 15 minutes long
- Inspirational messages, centering thoughts, and images
- Mantras and their meanings
- Reflection questions
- A private journal to save responses and additional notes
- A Mindful Moment—a daily takeaway showing you how to incorporate Deepak's message into your life right now

The email-based curriculum had the following elements for a viewer:
- It was free to participate and there is no obligation to purchase.
- Registration was made possible via Facebook or email.
- Once registered, you would receive daily emails when the challenge started.
- Each email would have a link to log into the program.
- To ensure email delivery, registrants were encouraged to add meditationchallenge@chopra.com to their address book.
- One could access the program at any time from an Android or iPhone, iPad, tablet, or computer.
- The login URL for the Challenge was www.chopracentermeditation. com/login, and participants were encouraged to bookmark it on their browser for easy, frequent access.
- Meditations were made to be accessible for ten days—so if you missed a day, you wouldn't miss out.
- Meditations were emailed daily during the challenge and were to be in the inbox no later than 8 AM Pacific Standard Time or 4 PM UTC/GMT.

Registering and Participating in the Program

Registration for the online meditation program was free. It could be completed by signing up online with the website or through Facebook. The registrant was taken through a confirmation process in which they opted into the program as well as received a user name and password confirmation. Once registered, the participant signed into the program any time to view the information available in the program website. The program website was set up to assist the participant with the regular, ongoing signing in process, including retrieval of forgotten passwords, etc.

Starting from the first day of the program, registrants received an email in their inbox early each morning of the meditation program. According to Deepak Chopra, morning is the best time to do meditation, after a good night's rest.

Email—an Ideal Channel for Nurturing Education

Reminders were sent at periodic intervals to those who had not regularly logged in to participate in the twenty-one-day program. While a person was in the program website, they also had the option to browse other sections of the Chopra Center website and read information or purchase products which may have interested them.

The registrants were also given the option to continue to receive newsletters as well as promotional offers via email. For those who opted to receive newsletters and marketing offers, ongoing emails were sent on a regular basis. As registrants began to show interest in certain products or services of the Chopra Center, a sales team assisted them in obtaining various products and services.

The Implementation

To implement the email program for Chopra Center's 21-Day Meditation Challenge program, we worked through a number of interesting hurdles. First of all, another digital service provider performed the registration forms and data capture. With the provider's core technical staff located in Israel, support personnel in different parts of the United States, and the data itself hosted on an Internet cloud system on servers somewhere in United States, it presented some unique hurdles for EchoMail to overcome.

One of the challenges of this project required EchoMail to send out alert-type notifications based on specific activities taking place on the registration and program websites. Multiple emails needed to be sent when each person registered or attempted to log into the program. To implement this, data needed to be exchanged across servers hosting the program website and EchoMail servers. EchoMail presented several data exchange methods with due-thought process given to speed, security, and integrity of data. The digital service provider, considering their internal capabilities, decided to utilize one of the basic methods of data exchange. While not the best in terms of speed or security, this method was safe enough to implement and the teams moved forward with this option.

By the time EchoMail was invited to join the project, the start of the 21-Day Meditation Challenge was just a few weeks away and the time required to implement, test, and approve other more comprehensive methods of data exchange was just not available. The EchoMail development, infrastructure, and project management team worked round the clock to implement the specific requirements needed for the project. The alert-type notifications were sent based on a number of activities by the user: initial sign up, confirmation of user name and password, various emails to assist the registrant in situations such as forgotten password etc. Considering the situation, the teams did experience some difficulties at the initial launch of the campaign, but the EchoMail team recovered from these issues within hours and got the project back on track right away.

During the twenty-one-day program, timing of the activities was another interesting requirement. Each day, every registrant needed to receive a reminder email early in the morning. Considering the early risers in the east coast of the United States, it was decided that the emails should be sent before 4 AM EST. Therefore, data from all of the registrants needed to be compiled and sent to EchoMail for us to test, approve, and send on through the reminder email campaign. The Chopra Center wanted to include as many registrants as possible for the next day's reminder campaign. The EchoMail team had to consider the hurdles of exchanging large volumes of data securely, assessing the integrity of the content, and uploading the information for the email campaign in a timely manner. Thus, a certain cut-off time was decided each evening by which the data would be packaged by the digital service provider and sent to EchoMail, after which EchoMail would test the integrity of the data, confirm that with the provider, test the messaging one more time with the Chopra Center team, and finally initiate the campaign some time after midnight to ensure delivery before 4 AM EST.

The EchoMail team came together and performed an excellent job during every one of the twenty-one days, successfully completing the program. The brands of Oprah and Chopra used email to connect with millions across the globe, as never before, and got them to meditate by delivering an email-based curriculum. The "21-Day Meditation Challenge" had integrated Oprah's global reach on television with Chopra's incredible ability to communicate ancient wisdom.

PART THREE

EMAIL TAKEAWAYS

10 Reasons Why Email Is Here to Stay

"Email is here to stay for a long, long time. Myths of its demise are just that: myths."

Email is electronified paper mail, and it's here to stay as long as humans need to write a love letter, send a bill, or file a legal notice. Our journey through *The Email Revolution* has allowed us to understand what email is, its origin, differences relative to other media, and how major brands have used it in compelling ways. This journey should have acquainted you with the unique elements of email.

A Look Back

The organizations we've reviewed have discovered, in their own way, solutions to existing problems, as well as new opportunities, in their use of email. Each case was different. For Nike and JCPenney, email was powerful for managing crisis communications. The Clinton White House used the medium to feel the pulse of the public. Calvin Klein used email to connect with fans through a "soap opera" over three years. Senators like Kennedy and Frist demonstrated that email could lead to more transparency and accountability in government. Unilever used email to personalize relationship marketing. P&G learned about consumer behavior, neighbor to neighbor. The George W. Bush campaign for president gained a decisive advantage by integrating email with their grassroots efforts, door-to-door. QVC and Hilton chose to look at customer service complaints as a source of value instead of as an annoyance, saving money while creating value for both company and customers. Cookie Jar Entertainment looked at email as a way to communicate with a tech savvy youth in a way that protected their security. Finally, American Express and Allstate took email management to the next level with the development of a global and enterprise system that allowed them to monitor interactions across internal and external constituencies—thereby protecting their brand.

Remember the Properties of Email

As we have learned, email is *Asynchronous, Flexible, Targeted, Cost-Effective, Immediate, Costly to Manage,* and *Ubiquitous.* These features have been a running theme throughout this book. Email is not Phone. Different organizations have found these features to be both blessings and curses in their attempts to familiarize themselves and tap the potential of the medium. Email's asynchronicity gives one time to think but can also invite delay. The flexibility of email allows targeted communication on a large scale as well as the dissemination of useless or downright disruptive information. Email's immediacy reduces delays in communication, allowing businesses to run more smoothly. The cost effectiveness has led to its widespread use, and its pervasiveness has led most of us to take email for granted.

Email is a unique medium, and integrating email with other media opens opportunity for creative branding. The brands reviewed have shared their particular approaches. However, if we move beyond the confusion of email and the recurrent predictions of its death knells, the use of email in new and creative ways remains wide open. We have only scratched the surface.

REASONS FOR THE PERSISTENCE
OF EMAIL

1. Email Facilitates Engaging Communication

Email facilitates engaging and rich communication. It is not limited to a few hundred characters like the Text Message Systems. Content, presentation, and creativity make email a better-suited platform for expressing oneself or for marketing purposes.

2. Email Is Controllable

Email is ideal in situations which require control of information that is transmitted to recipients. The amount of information that is sent to each recipient can be controlled, unlike social media platforms where such controls are either not present or are unwieldy, requiring locked postings which need a password to open them. Furthermore, since email is asynchronous, you can control when you want to send and receive email, unlike social media or text messaging, which are more or less instant.

3. Email Can Be Personalized

Email can be personalized to the recipient or group that is being targeted. This is not possible with social media platforms, where everyone gets to read the same information, irrespective of his or her interest or outlook.

4. Email Is Legal

Since email is a written form of communication, courts have ruled that email is a legal and permissible document of record. On the other hand, social media postings and text messaging are not classified as legally permissible records.

5. Email Is Perfect for Permission-Based Reach

Email continues to be the only option where permission-based reach is required. It can be used both for single opt-in and double opt-in methods of subscription or news dissemination. Social media resources, by design, are not capable of this.

6. Email Is Familiar and Easy to Use

Since email has been around for some time, familiarity with the technology is very high and, due to the constant refinement of technology, has become very easy to use. Email passes the "Mom and Pop Usability Test" quite easily, unlike social media and messaging which are still not user friendly or are slow and unwieldy.

7. Email Is Elegant, Stable, and Reliable

As noted in reason 6 above, email has evolved over the years and is now extremely elegant, stable, and reliable when it comes to usage. Standards and technologies for email transmission and retrieval have become universal, and implementing email is easy compared with the complexity of XML- and RSS-based social media systems, which are still not standardized.

8. Email Is Accessible

Email is virtually accessible on any communications platform, right from the latest uber-tech gadgets and the newest smartphones to the relatively "dumb" feature phones.

9. Email Is Ideal as a Push Medium

Due to its very nature, email is ideal when it comes to pushing information or data or communication with people, unlike social media, which is more pull oriented. This is of great advantage when you have only one chance to grab someone's attention.

10. Email Will Live as Long as Businesses Will Live

Email is the communications tool of choice for businesses today and email will continue to be the tool of choice as there is no other medium that offers the flexibility offered by email. Social messaging and text messaging are alright for short, snappy exchanges, but they are of no use when it comes to business communication where typically a larger amount of data has to be moved, and incremental archiving and saving of communications for legal reasons are required.

50 Tips on Using Email

*"These 50 tips will serve as guideposts for
you to build your own best email practices."*

1. Read Your Email Before Sending

This is the most simple and basic rule one must follow before hitting that Send button. However, this is a rule that is often ignored. Take time to proofread your email and you will avoid errors and misunderstanding. You can correct any misspelled words or wrong grammar. More importantly, you can also delete any inappropriate comments that might have slipped in inadvertently, saving you a lot of grief later on.

2. Avoid All-Capital Words and Abbreviations

Capital letters should be reserved for the beginning of sentences and proper nouns. Capital letters are akin to shouting on the web. It is seen as an impolite thing to do, and certainly not professional. The same rule applies for abbreviations. They do not make for easy reading. Some abbreviations (like LOL for Laughing Out Loud) are considered juvenile and are not suitable at all for a professional environment—likewise, smileys and emoticons are best avoided in business use. You may, of course, use them when the recipient is someone you are close to.

3. Using High Priority and Reply to All

Do not abuse these functions in your email client or program. An email marked High Priority could have a feeling of being more aggressive than it actually is. Moreover, excessive use might actually end up with the recipient not looking at your email. Use Reply to All only if it is absolutely necessary for all the original recipients to receive your reply.

4. Respond to Email in a Timely Manner

People send you an email because they expect a quick response. The rule is to respond to an email within twenty-four hours and preferably the same day. If you can not immediately respond to a question, send an email saying that you have received their email and that you will respond as quickly as possible. Thus, the person knows that you will get back to them soon.

5. Structure Your Email

Reading on a screen is harder than reading a printed document. So be sure to structure your email. Use a clear layout. Short sentences and paragraphs make an email easier to read. If you are using a list, make sure to have bullets to delineate each point in the list.

6. Using the Cc: Field

Use the Cc: field only when you are absolutely sure that the information you are transmitting is important to those you CC. Remember, *do not overuse* the CC: feature. People might just start ignoring your email if they think whatever you send is not relevant to them.

7. Using the Bcc: Field

Use the Bcc: field when you do not want recipients to know who else you have sent the email to. The Bcc: field ensures privacy of your contacts since recipients cannot view this field. If you use the Bcc: field, be sure to leave the To: or Reply To: blank, or your email may be considered spam.

8. Anything You Send Could Be Used Against You!

As a medium for communication, email is not secure. Sure, email is fast and convenient. Suppose you have sent an email to a friend, which also contains personal information about yourself. Your friend could easily forward the email to someone you would never have sent your personal information to yourself. This could be inadvertent but the damage is done. There is no command to undo this! Therefore assume that everyone can read your email. Do not send confidential information via email. Offensive, racist, or discriminatory language also could get you in trouble, even if you meant just humor. Remember the bottom line: Anything You Send by Email Could Be Used Against You.

9. Forwarding a Chain of Email

When you forward a chain of email to someone, add a note of explanation before the series of forwarded messages. Do not expect them to burrow through your email and read every linked message if you just forward them without any explanation. Take the time to explain your reasoning or what you want them to focus on. It is then easier for the person to whom you are sending the email to respond to the question at hand rather than be puzzled about what exactly you require or expect.

10. Be Safe When Sending Sarcastic Email

Sending sarcastic email to people with whom you are not too familiar could create unpleasantness when the other person is offended by or misunderstands your sarcasm. In general, avoid sending such email to people you do not know very well. Use your address book. It is there for a reason. Create a group and add only people you know very well to this group. If you really have that urge to forward or send a sarcastic comment to a friend, just send them to this group alone.

11. Avoid Sending Unnecessary Attachments

Use attachments sparingly. If the recipient has no need to view the whole document or edit it anyway, just use the text of the document as part of your email body. Attachments can be very heavy and have the potential to send an email system crawling on its knees. Also make sure to have effective anti-virus software checking that the documents you send are not infected.

12. No Attachment Is the Best Attachment!

Attachments take time to download. The bigger the attachment, the longer it takes to download. If you mail a big attachment to many people, bandwidth could be clogged or wasted. It would also take up disk space on the recipient's computer. Some email attachments may not be necessary. Consider putting attachments on a site with hyperlinks so they don't increase the size of the message. This way your recipient can make a decision to download or not.

13. Using Filters to Sort Email

If you receive a lot of email and your Inbox is getting too cluttered to focus on the important email, it would be a good idea to use filters, with whatever email program you use, to sort incoming email automatically.

14. Identify Yourself

If you are the person initiating email contact with someone, do not forget to include your name, profession, or organization where you work, or any other important information to identify yourself. You could have this information in the first few sentences of your email as an introduction. If you are just following up on an earlier conversation or contact and are not sure whether the other person will remember you, drop a few casual hints or bring up a reference to the earlier conversation. If you are emailing someone outside your organization, it helps to have a signature line that includes your full name and, if you choose, your telephone number or a link to a blog or website.

15. Use a Meaningful Subject Line

A meaningful subject line is an important prerequisite of any email. The recipient most likely has many emails in his Inbox. He or she is going to scan the Subject line quickly to narrow down the list of email on which to take action or read. If you do not have a meaningful Subject line, the recipient may not read it, or worse, may even trash it without reading. Take a moment to see whether the Subject line conveys the essence of what is in the actual email body before hitting that Send button.

16. Do Not Send a Blank Subject

Do not send an email message with no subject as this will not give any idea as to your email's message content, and the reader will likely ignore it. This not only wastes the recipient's time but also, sometimes, can be annoying.

17. The Subject Line Is Your Message

The subject line is the most-read part of an email. Often, the email recipient decides whether to read your email or send it to trash based on the subject line.

Not adding a subject line or forgetting to put a subject line is even more of a guarantee that your email will not be read. Email marketing professionals live and die by subject lines. A good subject line will sum up what the message is all about, but will still entice someone to open the message, read it, and take action. For email marketing, personalizing a subject line with your company's name or the recipient's name or other information can also lead to higher message open rates. Various research studies have shown that including the company name in the subject line can increase open rates by more than 30 percent, over a subject line without branding.

18. Prioritize Your Email Content

If you have a lot of action points to discuss, try to spread them over a few separate emails. If it is a very long email, recipients may only read partway and hit Reply as soon as they have something to contribute. It is quite common for them to forget to keep reading. This is part of human nature. Spreading them over a few emails reduces that risk. Alternatively, you may first inform the recipient that there are a lot of action points and you need them to read through all the points before replying. You may also consider numbering them and presenting them in order of importance.

19. One Screen Fits All!

Remember to keep the length of your email within one screen. Long, drawn-out emails can be cumbersome to your reader. They also could result in your email being on multiple screens. This would result in your reader having to scroll up to reread your message. Making it difficult for your recipient to read your email is not effective email writing. Avoid long email messages. Avoiding long email messages is another way of stating that conciseness is important in effective email writing.

20. Email for Specific Audiences

Being aware of your audience means taking a moment to think about the perspective of the person who is receiving the email—also, focusing on the purpose of the email. It helps to consider whether the message is being sent to a family member, a friend, a potential employer, or someone else encountered in the course of business. An email message to a family member or close friend usually does not require the same level of formality that would be used in a business setting. If you know that the person receiving your email appreciates brevity over formal grammar then it might be appropriate to abbreviate or add things like smileys. However, make sure that email sent as part of a business message is brief and to the point. Avoid abbreviations in business email and make sure to check grammar for obvious errors.

21. Out of Office Notification

If you are leaving on vacation or will be away from the office for any reason, do not forget to redirect your email to another person who can deal with the email you receive. Further, leave an Out of Office notification that will be sent as a reply to the email sender with details on who will be dealing with your email and when you are expected back. You may also give out the email, the telephone number, or both, of the person handling your email. If there is no one you can forward your email to, just mention in your Out of Office notification that you are out on vacation or whatever the case is. Mention the date you are expected to return. Also, customers would feel reassured if you tell them that you will contact them as soon as you are back. Most importantly, do not neglect to *deactivate* the Out of Office notification as soon as you are back. People sure won't be impressed if they email you and receive a reply saying the recipient will return on a date that has already passed.

22. Avoiding Spam and Junk Email

Email has become ubiquitous as a communication tool today. With the rising usage of email comes the rising occurrence of spam. Here are some basic tips for avoiding or at least reducing spam in your Inbox:

1. Do not use your primary email address on message boards, online forums, etc. Use a second "disposable" email address for these websites.
2. Avoid opening email from someone you do not know or do not trust. These could contain software or script which might harm your computer.
3. Do not reply to a spam email. You are unknowingly just validating your email address as being currently live.
4. Use anti-spam and filtering software. However, even the best anti-spam software cannot stop all the spam and some may even mark legitimate email as spam.
5. Instruct your anti-virus software to scan incoming email.
6. Install a spyware/malware checker and run it once a week to detect and remove any spyware or Trojans.

23. Using a Signature File

You may attach a signature section to every outgoing message you send, usually containing contact details and other relevant information. If you are in business you should almost certainly use an email signature in your communications. It is a great way to draw attention to products or services you offer, and you are making yourself easier to contact as well. Other uses for an email signature include confidentiality statements, drawing attention to website addresses, promoting something, and adding other contact details such as telephone or fax number.

24. Resize Pictures to Handy Proportions

Do not send multimegapixel-sized images weighing in tens of megabytes as this will only lead to the email server getting overloaded. Try to keep images to sensible proportions. Email is not a high-resolution medium and you do not require anything more than 640 to 800 pixels width for an image to look good in email. If you do need to send high-resolution images (maybe for printing), compress them using ZIP or RAR formats to make them more portable and easy to handle. There are a lot of freeware tools to create ZIP or RAR archives from selected files.

25. Assume Nothing

Never assume that the recipient is familiar with the thinking behind the email at hand. Make sure that you let the person know the background and the issues. When following up, don't assume everyone remembers whatever you said earlier. If you are worried that an acronym, term, or reference is going to elicit confusion, it is better to explain it. Check before sending to make sure that you are not hiding anything from the recipient, even unintentionally.

26. Email and Efficiency

Email is a vital communication tool today. However, there is a possibility of spending too much time on email, thus reducing your work efficiency. To avoid wasting time, maintain an email log and record how frequently you check email. You can do this with a sheet of paper. Do it for about a week, and see how much time you are spending on email. Measure it against the average email received in your Inbox during that week. If you are checking your email so often that you do not receive any new email until your third or fourth check, you are certainly wasting too much time. Try a pattern for checking email based on when new email reaches your Inbox. If you discover that you receive most new email during lunchtime or just before closing time, alter your pattern accordingly. You will find yourself automatically becoming more efficient in a very short time.

27. Humor in Email

Email is a medium where communication is through words. This is not the best medium to express emotions or use humor, especially if you're unsure how the other person will receive it. The reason is because, unless done appropriately, it may not come across very well in an email. You can use emoticons and smileys to get over some of these shortcomings, but there's just no way to express tone or inflection unless you have a flair for poetry. Further, you will not be able to judge whether the recipient really understands that you are only joking. When you are having a conversation in person and happen to say something that the other person does not really appreciate, you can always say that you were only joking. This may not happen over email as you never get to see the recipient's reaction, unless he or she writes back to say so. In that case, you can try and limit the damage already done. So, the basic rule would be to avoid humor unless the recipient knows you well enough to understand that you're joking. It may not be worth the risk.

28. Anticipate

As email is a back-and-forth method of communicating, and it can take a day or more (in some cases) for a response, you may want to limit the number of times a message has to go back and forth. To do that, use "if . . . then" scenarios, anticipating the possible responses to your question. By anticipating the possible responses, and giving a desired action for each possible response in advance, you're cutting out a lot of wasted back-and-forth exchanges.

29. Make Relevant Changes to the Subject Line

It happens often that in an email thread, the order of correspondence, or the people to whom it is addressed, get changed. In such a situation, update the subject line to reflect the new topic of conversation.

30. Include Alternative Contact Information

There may be times when the recipient of your email might want to reply or to discuss something over the phone or some other medium. Make it a point to include any alternative way of reaching you in your signature.

31. Keep Email Folders Clean

Every time you check email, go through your Inbox, read messages, and either reply, delete, or transfer them to another folder. Have folders categorizing your emails for your various contacts or projects. When you finish an email session, follow the same process with messages in the Outbox and delete junk mail. You will find that you save a lot of time by keeping your Inbox empty and your messages organized.

32. To-Do Lists and Email

At first glance, they may seem unrelated, but To-Do Lists can greatly reduce your Inbox clutter. Oftentimes the reason an email is lingering in your Inbox is because there is an action required in order to process it. Instead of leaving it in your Inbox, and using the Inbox as a de facto to-do list, make a note of the task required by the email in your to-do list, notebook, planner, or whatever you use. The aim is to get the task out of your Inbox. Make a reference to the email if necessary. Then archive the email and be done with it. This will get rid of a lot of email in your Inbox very quickly. You still have to do the task, but at least it's now on a legitimate To-Do list and not keeping your Inbox full.

33. Using Multiple Email Accounts

Many people make the mistake of maintaining just one email account and use the same email account for personal messages, business messages, sign-up for subscriptions and other online services. The likelihood of a phishing attack or a hacker installing malicious files increases because the number of spam messages is greater when all email from various people and agencies land in the same email account. As a result, the user has to be on guard at all times. A simple way to address this problem is to use different email accounts for different purposes: personal, business, online mailing lists, and another for when you go shopping online. If you do not want too many email accounts, you should at least have an email account where you receive anything not related to work, friends, and family letters. Chances are that any spam you might receive will mostly be concentrated on this particular email account.

34. Proper Names Are the Proper Choice

While sending email, take an extra few seconds to type out the recipient's proper name. Research has shown that using just initials or abbreviations puts some people off. Chances are, they may not go ahead and read your email at all. Take a few more seconds to include a greeting like "Hi, Bob" or "Good Morning, Jim" and your email will be better received. It's simple, but effective.

35. Acknowledge Email—Avoid Misunderstandings

There are many times that you may not be in a position to respond immediately to an email. In such a situation, make sure that you send a short message acknowledging receipt of the email and informing the sender that you will respond soon. This way, the sender does not have to wonder whether their email has reached you or wonder why you have not responded to their email.

36. Short Paragraphs Make Big Sense

Always remember: Email as a medium is ideal for short and simple messages. Try not to have more than three lines in a paragraph and always leave a blank line between paragraphs. Otherwise, your email may tend to look cluttered.

37. Be Friendly When You Write Email

An email relationship is not much different from an offline relationship. It always pays to be friendly and personable. Take time to add something friendly in your email. You could remark on something relevant to the receiver or add a quick comment about their website or work. End your email with a friendly comment like "Have a relaxing weekend" or "Have a great day."

38. Short and Sweet Does It!

Use as few words as possible to convey the message. Your recipient may not have the time to go through a long, rambling email. No one really appreciates email that has to be read more than once to be understood.

39. Hoaxes—Stamp 'Em Out

We all at times can get a lot of hoaxes in our Inbox. It is easy to identify one. Any email which claims to offer you easy money or for that matter free money, or chain email (email that guarantees disaster if you do not forward it to all the people you know or care about) is most certainly a hoax. *Do not forward* these at any cost. Besides being terribly annoying and irritating, they make you look vulnerable and easy prey. Not good for your personal brand.

40. Message First, Recipient Next

If you are sending an important email, always compose the email message first. Proofread it thoroughly and *then* add the recipient's name and email address.

So remember: Message First, Recipient Next. This way, you will not be able to send your email without having proofread it, reducing the chances of any error or wrong information being sent out.

41. Who Sent You Email?

Quite often, you may find yourself sending email to someone you don't know or don't know too well. Identify yourself in the email clearly so that the recipient knows who you are without a doubt. It may be helpful to add details like how you found out about the recipient or any prior meetings or email exchanges if you think it would serve to jog the recipient's memory. You may also want to indicate what the email is about and what you need from the recipient. Ideally, these points should be communicated in the first one or two lines of your email. Otherwise, you may find that your email goes straight to the trash can.

42. More Meaningful Email Forwards

Forwarded email is a fact of life. I am sure all of us receive at least a couple of forwarded emails every day. It is one thing to receive meaningful and interesting email that is profitable and informs or educates us about something that we really did not know about. It is another matter when you receive stale, obscure jokes and links that are just plain annoying. If you are forwarding any email or links, make sure that you indicate why you are forwarding it to them and how you think that it could be of use to them. In an instant, the recipient knows that you care about their time and will appreciate the fact that you yourself took time to think about their requirements and interests.

43. Use Color Fonts for Emphasis

All modern email clients allow you to choose colors for your fonts. This comes in handy to emphasize something in your email. Use a different color for any particular text that you would like to be emphasized. Sometimes, people think using red color fonts in email is akin to shouting or using a louder voice in normal speech, but this is false. Using all CAPITALS is akin to shouting when it comes to email. So go ahead, do not be afraid to use color in your email. After all, the most important thing is to get your message across effectively and color can certainly help you do so.

44. Stop Viruses and Worms!

This may not seem to be directly related to email, but it is. Email worms and viruses are spreading via messages that could be sent from your computer without your knowledge. It is essential that you use current anti-virus software, update it frequently, and keep up to date with security fixes of your email software. Your email recipients will thank you for taking this precaution.

45. Sending Group Email

Group people, if you can, by categories, using group names. When you want to send an email to all the people in that category, simply send it to the Group. Only the Group name will be visible in the To: field. Individual recipient names are not revealed. This also provides a degree of privacy. Such grouping and targeting can be especially useful in email marketing, special offers, and messages to particular groups.

46. Avoiding Misinterpretation of "Date" in Email

Email allows you to communicate easily with your friends and associates, wherever they are in the world. Be aware that people from other countries may use a different format for Date. If you are American, you will most probably interpret 05/10 as May 10. No doubt about that. Or is it? In another area of the world, this may mean to be the 5th of October. That is why you should always check to ensure your settings are set, as best as you can control, to spell out the month (e.g., May 10 or 10 May or something similar instead of 05/10 or 05-10). This makes it clear what date you are referring to.

47. Don't Rely On Email Alone

Email is a great tool for efficient communication. It can be (and certainly has been) used for building relationships. However, don't rely on it exclusively. Set a goal to talk to people at least once for every ten email exchanges. Relationships are best built using a combination of media: in-person, phone calls, and the written word. Integrate them all fully if you really want relationships to grow.

48. Avoid Excessive Exclamations!

Some people have the idea that the more exclamation points they put in an email, the more likely the receiver will get their point. The exclamation symbol sends different sensory cues to different people. So use it wisely. If you use it too much, it will be hard for others to know what you are *really* excited about. We humans are exceptional at detecting unauthentic phrasings and remarks—even in email! Use the "!" when you really mean it.

49. Forwarding Nested Email Conversations

When you forward an email containing several nested email conversations to someone, add a note of explanation before the series of conversations. Do not expect the recipient to burrow through your email and read every linked message if you just forward them a thread without any explanation. Take the time to explain your reasoning or what you want them to focus on. That will make it easier for the person to whom you are you sending the email to respond to the question at hand rather than be puzzled about what exactly you require or expect.

50. Check Your Trash or Junk Folders Too

You may be looking forward to a response from someone you have had an email conversation with but have not received any response from. Before getting angry or frustrated, just check your Trash or Junk folders in case you had inadvertently deleted the response. We are all human! It is also possible that some filter might have directed that particular email to your Trash or Junk folder too.

AFTERWORD

"Email can save the US Postal Service, for if the USPS dies, we all lose—it will signal the loss of our most basic freedom: the right to communicate freely."

The United States Postal Service (USPS) was created during the birth of America. The postal mail system became a core part of America's connective democratic tissue, enabling each citizen to exercise their right to freely communicate: to send and receive postal mail, across even the most remote parts of the country—an amazing achievement! Over the years, that core part of our connective tissue has been under attack step by step. As a systems biologist, I know that the connective tissue of our body, the fascia and collagen, are critical to our existence. The connective tissue stands at the interface of mind and body. This important part of our anatomy ensures that we can convert what we sense in our environment into responsive action. Without it, we are nothing.

The USPS is a core part of our social connective tissue. Its destruction means that we as social organisms will cease to have essential and important functional elements for our sensing, movement, and responsiveness. Bit by bit, parts of the USPS have been gutted, the best parts of it privatized, and what remains are the spoils. And, as this catastrophe has taken place, the volume of email has grown explosively, overtaking postal mail starting in 1997. At that point in history, the USPS should have embraced email and provided the same infrastructure of postal mail services in electronic form and renewed itself and its deteriorating connective tissue. However, the management at USPS did not have the vision or the courage to do that. They were happy with making $50 billion a year on an old and dying business model.

Today, email is the medium of choice over postal letters. However, nearly all of our email is not private. Others, including individuals and private companies, can access it anytime. We have implicitly traded our rights for "free" email services that at any point can shut us down or be used to sell us out. Consider the Arab Spring revolution in Egypt. At one point the government was able to shut down all SMS and Text Messaging through collaborating with Vodaphone, a private company whose only accountability was to its shareholders. This is dangerous. The Declaration of Independence proclaimed that all citizens are free and that each has the right and duty to change the government if it no longer services the broader needs:

> That to secure these rights [of life, liberty, and the pursuit of happiness] Governments are instituted among men . . . that whenever any form of Government becomes destructive of these ends, it is the right of the people to alter or abolish it . . .

How can this happen if citizens cannot even organize themselves? The USPS mail system governed by a body of law, laid down by our Founding Fathers, ensures that our mail will not be tampered with. Email privacy can be invaded without concern for the private citizen.

I see only one choice for the USPS: embrace email. Offer email as a public service, like the highway and water systems. I am sure many Americans will be willing to pay some nominal fee, let's say $50 per year, to know that their email is not being read, is totally secure, and cannot be shut down, like Vodaphone did to those fighting for their freedom in Tahrir Square.

When I created email, I did it for the love of creation and science. At that time in 1978, there was never any intent to patent it or make money off it—it was an amazing sense of accomplishment to create the electronic version of the inter-office postal mail system, and to see its affect on the users. However, somewhere along the way, our email became no longer ours, and soon our postal mail will no longer be ours.

As the creator of email, my appeal is for American citizens now to boldly proclaim their rights to free and open communication and demand that the USPS get its priorities clear—that is to say, provide us with the public infrastructure for email that we all deserve.

APPENDIX

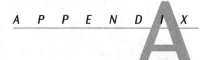

History of Email Infographic: 1978–2011

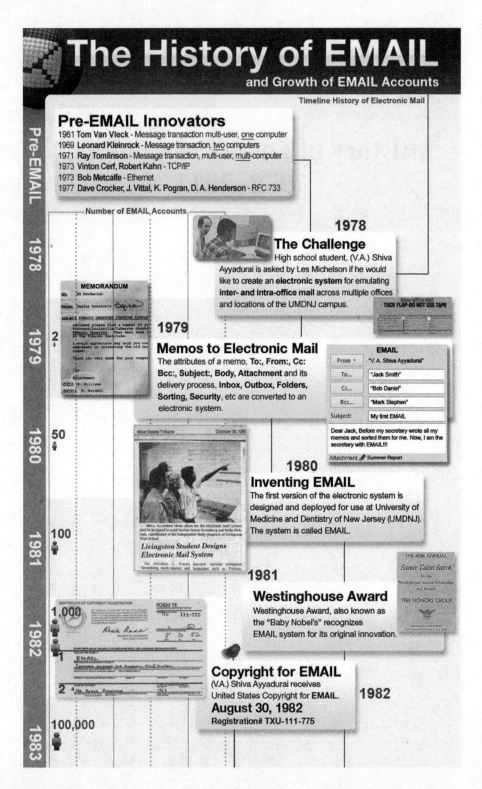

The History of EMAIL
and Growth of EMAIL Accounts

Timeline History of Electronic Mail

Pre-EMAIL Innovators

1961 **Tom Van Vleck** - Message transaction multi-user, <u>one</u> computer
1969 **Leonard Kleinrock** - Message transaction, <u>two</u> computers
1971 **Ray Tomlinson** - Message transaction, multi-user, <u>multi</u>-computer
1973 **Vinton Cerf, Robert Kahn** - TCP/IP
1973 **Bob Metcalfe** - Ethernet
1977 **Dave Crocker, J. Vittal, K. Pogran, D. A. Henderson** - RFC 733

Number of EMAIL Accounts

1978
The Challenge
High school student, (V.A.) Shiva Ayyadurai is asked by Les Michelson if he would like to create an **electronic system** for emulating **inter- and intra-office mail** across multiple offices and locations of the UMDNJ campus.

1979
Memos to Electronic Mail
The attributes of a memo, **To:, From:, Cc: Bcc:, Subject:, Body, Attachment** and its delivery process, **Inbox, Outbox, Folders, Sorting, Security**, etc are converted to an electronic system.

EMAIL	
From ▾	"V. A. Shiva Ayyadurai"
To...	"Jack Smith"
Cc...	"Bob Daniel"
Bcc...	"Mark Stephen"
Subject:	My first EMAIL

Dear Jack, Before my secretary wrote all my memos and sorted them for me. Now, I am the secretary with EMAIL!!!

Attachment: 📎 Summer Report

Livingston Student Designs Electronic Mail System

1980
Inventing EMAIL
The first version of the electronic system is designed and deployed for use at University of Medicine and Dentistry of New Jersey (UMDNJ). The system is called EMAIL.

1981
Westinghouse Award
Westinghouse Award, also known as the "Baby Nobel's" recognizes EMAIL system for its original innovation.

THE 40th ANNUAL
Science Talent Search
for the
Westinghouse Science Scholarships and Awards
1981 HONORS GROUP

Copyright for EMAIL
(V.A.) Shiva Ayyadurai receives United States Copyright for **EMAIL**.
August 30, 1982
Registration# TXU-111-775

1982

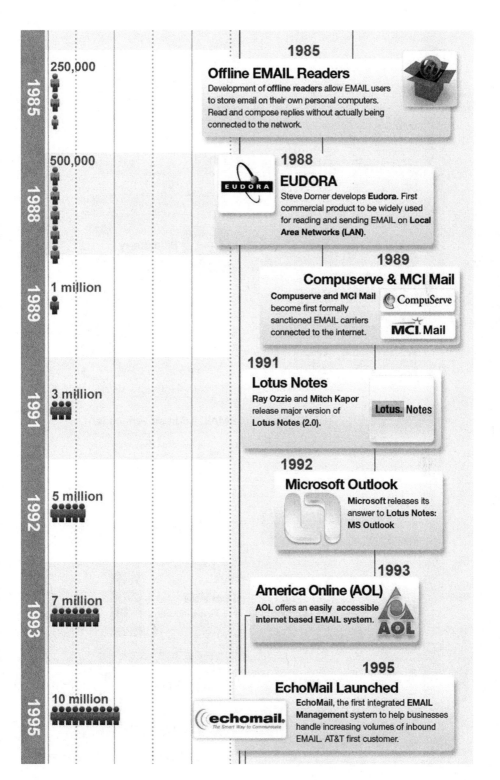

1985

Offline EMAIL Readers
Development of **offline readers** allow EMAIL users to store email on their own personal computers. Read and compose replies without actually being connected to the network.

250,000

1988

EUDORA
Steve Dorner develops **Eudora**. First commercial product to be widely used for reading and sending EMAIL on **Local Area Networks (LAN)**.

500,000

1989

Compuserve & MCI Mail
Compuserve and MCI Mail become first formally sanctioned EMAIL carriers connected to the internet.

1 million

1991

Lotus Notes
Ray Ozzie and **Mitch Kapor** release major version of Lotus Notes (2.0).

3 million

1992

Microsoft Outlook
Microsoft releases its answer to **Lotus Notes**: **MS Outlook**

5 million

1993

America Online (AOL)
AOL offers an easily accessible internet based **EMAIL** system.

7 million

1995

EchoMail Launched
EchoMail, the first integrated **EMAIL** Management system to help businesses handle increasing volumes of inbound EMAIL. AT&T first customer.

10 million

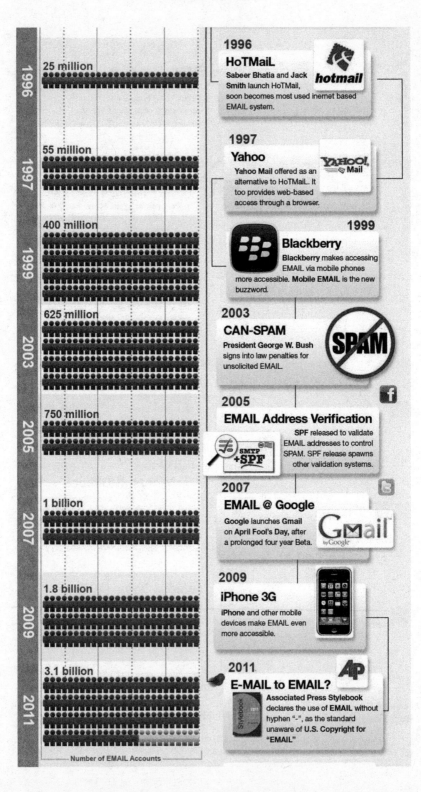

1996

25 million

1996

HoTMaiL

Sabeer Bhatia and Jack Smith launch HoTMail, soon becomes most used inernet based EMAIL system.

hotmail

1997

55 million

1997

Yahoo

Yahoo Mail offered as an alternative to HoTMaiL. It too provides web-based access through a browser.

YAHOO! Mail

1999

400 million

1999

Blackberry

Blackberry makes accessing EMAIL via mobile phones more accessible. **Mobile EMAIL** is the new buzzword.

2003

625 million

2003

CAN-SPAM

President George W. Bush signs into law penalties for unsolicited EMAIL.

SPAM

2005

750 million

2005

EMAIL Address Verification

SPF released to validate EMAIL addresses to control SPAM. SPF release spawns other validation systems.

SMTP +SPF

2007

1 billion

2007

EMAIL @ Google

Google launches Gmail on April Fool's Day, after a prolonged four year Beta.

Gmail by Google

2009

1.8 billion

2009

iPhone 3G

iPhone and other mobile devices make EMAIL even more accessible.

2011

3.1 billion

2011

E-MAIL to EMAIL?

Associated Press Stylebook declares the use of **EMAIL** without hyphen "-", as the standard unaware of U.S. Copyright for "EMAIL"

Stylebook

AP

— Number of EMAIL Accounts —

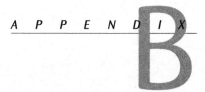

Computer Program for Electronic Mail System: 1978

```
11 C----------------------------------------------------------------------
12       PROGRAM EMAIL(3,98)
13       COMMON IBASE(7),IDCB(144),ICOM(48),ICLOS,MAIN,LU,JVAL(4),NODE,
14      1ILEN,MCBCRT,MCBSEC,MFLCRT,MFLSEC,ISTATE(2),KFILE(3),IDCBQ(144),
15      2IPRMT1,IWHER1,IPRMT2,IWHER2,IWHOM,IPARAM,IFINIS,INODE
16       COMMON/LABL/ IPL,ISL,LUH,IRWAIT,IPWAIT,ISCAN,ICREAT,IPRINT
17       COMMON/REQS/ KERR,IFNAM(3),IVAR1,IVAR2,MFILE(3),NFILE(3),IRND,
18      1ICODE,NABL,MABL,IFORMT,ISNAME(13),IGRP
19       COMMON/RECV/ ISBUF(12),LBUF(25),ICONT,MACCPT,ISRIAL
20       DIMENSION ISTAT(18),ITABL(11),ISEGS(3,9)
21       DATA ITABL/2H??,2HGM,2HTM,2HCM,2HEM,2HDN,2HDG,2HLM,2HDM,2HRD,2HEX/
22      1,IMODE1/1/
23       DATA ISEGS/2HRE,2HCE,2HV ,2HTR,2HAN,2HS ,2HCM,2HPO,2HS ,2HCM,2HPG,
24      12HS ,2HNA,2HME,2HS ,2HGR,2HOU,2HP ,2HME,2HMO,2HS ,2HDE,2HLE,2HT ,
25      22HRE,2HDS,2HT /
26 C----------------------------------------------------------------------
27 C
28 C*********************************************************************
29 C*
30 C*                   ELECTRONIC MAIL SYSTEM                          *
31 C*   THIS IS THE MAIL SYSTEM INTERFACE.  ALL COMMANDS ARE PROCESSED  *
32 C* HERE AND APPROPRIATE SEGMENTS ARE LOADED.  THE DATA BASE IS NOT   *
33 C* OPENED HERE BUT BY A STARTUP SEGMENT CALLED 'INITL'; HOWEVER, THE *
34 C* DATA BASE IS CLOSED HERE.  WHEN EMAIL IS INITIALLY INVOKED, A PARA-*
35 C* METER IS ACQUIRED FROM THE INITIAL COMMAND STRING.  IF THE PARAMETER*
36 C* IS NON-ZERO, THEN THE USER IS INFORMED WHETHER HE/SHE HAS MAIL.   *
37 C*********************************************************************
38 C
39 C
```

Email in the News: 1980

West Essex Tribune　　　　　　October 30, 1980

Shiva Ayyadurai shows plans for the electronic mail system that he designed to math teacher Irman Greenberg and Stella Oleksiak, coordinator of the Independent Study program at Livingston High School.

Livingston Student Designs Electronic Mail System

On October 7, Irman Greenberg, math teacher, and Stella Oleksiak, Independent Study coordinator, along with Shiva Ayyadurai and his father visited the Computer Center at the College of Medicine and Dentistry of New Jersey to observe the design and implementation of Ayyadurai's electronic mail system.

Ayyadurai, a senior at Livingston High School under the tutelage of Blair Krimmel, head of the math department and the Independent Study program, with the encouragement of Dr. Leslie Michelson, manager of the lab computer, created an electronic mail system with enough sophistication for immediate practical use at the college and commercial potential.

Since the eighth grade, Ayyadurai has proven that he could work mathematically far beyond the traditional classroom. During ninth grade he was bussed from Heritage to the high school where he passed the Algebra I and II tests while studying geometry at the same time.

During the summer of 1978, he was accepted for the computer science program at New York University where he learned various computer languages such as Fortran, Basic, Cobol and Snobol, and was graduated with honors. As a consequence of his math background and his computer training, he began his work at CMDNJ.

During the same year, he was accepted for the Atlantic Regional Math League and competed in the Essex County League and the Iron Hills Conference. As a veteran member of ARML, he and the team placed seventh out of the 43 teams.

While studying Ptolemy's Theorem, Ayyadurai observed an entirely new geometric relationship in the field of vector geometry. This finding was published in the journal "The Mathematics Teacher," Fall 1980 issue. In April 1980, he won individual first place in the advanced math competition in the Essex County Math League.

He is continuing his Independent Study Program under Krimmel in the area of statistics.

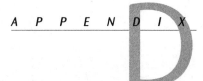
Westinghouse Science Award Notification: 1981

THE 40th ANNUAL

Science Talent Search®

for the

Westinghouse Science Scholarships

and Awards

1981 HONORS GROUP

Administered by SCIENCE SERVICE

1719 N Street N.W., Washington, D. C. 20036

FOR RELEASE: WEDNESDAY, JANUARY 21, 1981

The Science Talent Search was the pioneering endeavor to discover at the high school senior year level those who have the potential to become the research scientists and engineers of the future. It has fulfilled this function far beyond the hopes entertained when this educational project was conceived. Many millions of dollars in scholarships in colleges and universities throughout the nation, supplementing the Westinghouse Science Scholarships, have been given to those who have thus been discovered to have high science talent.

This selection of students with research ability in science and engineering has become an institution and tradition due to approval from the academic community and the creditable records of winners in colleges, universities and professional positions.

The participation of a great industrial organization in the financing of the annual Science Talent Search is a notable contribution to the advancement of science in America. This activity can be considered a support of "pure research" of importance equal to the fundamental researches in the Westinghouse Research Laboratories. Science and education are grateful for the financial support of the forty Science Talent Searches by the Westinghouse Electric Corporation and the Westinghouse Educational Foundation.

Science Service, engaged in the interpretation and public understanding of science on a broad front, is proud of administering the annual Science Talent Search. From the newspapers, educators, scientists and engineers of America, there has been enthusiastic cooperation in this annual activity that means so much to high school seniors interested in science and engineering.

DeGrandpre, Michael David 18 Capital H.S. 901 Garfield Ave. 59601
Comparision of Two Water Systems Through Quantitative and
Qualitative Chemical Analysis
Sawitke, James Arthur 17 Capital H.S. 1522 Flowerree 59601
Milling Stones of Indian Canyon-2 35WH13

NEBRAKSA

Omaha

Geppert, John Marion 18 Creighton Preparatory School 3282 S. 77th Ave.
68124   Solar "C" Collector, A Compound Parabolic Concentrator
Earl, Catherine Ann 17 Northwest H.S. 7809 Manderson 68134
A Determination in the Relations of Tonal Differentiation

NEW JERSEY

Fair Lawn

Rubenstein, Sidney Charles 17 Fair Lawn H.S. 3-01 Morlot Ave. 07410
Relationship Between Wing Damage and Flight Capability in the
Housefly, Musca domestica

Hillside

Simmons, Elizabeth Helen 17 The Pingry School 422 Wyoming Ave.,
Millburn 07041   Effects of a Drainage Culvert Upon the Fresh
Water Region of the Maidford Marsh

Livingston

Ayyadurai, Shiva 17 Livingston H.S. 7 Baker Rd. 07039   Software
Design Development and Implementation of a High Reliability,
Network-Wide, Electronic Mail System

Maplewood

Hsu, Anna Yee 18 Columbia H.S. 17 Ridgewood Terr. 07040
Pepsin and Its Formation of Inhibitor-Enzyme Complexes

Mendham

Fox, John Alan 17 West Morris Mendham H.S. Oak Knoll Rd. 07945
Levels of Chromium Pollution in the Upper Narragansett Bay and
Accumulation Found in Mercenaria mercenaria

Montvale

Wall, Michael Francis 18 Pascack Hills H.S. 90 Bedford Rd., Hillsdale
07642   ASTEROID: A Real-Time Graphic Game for the TRS-80
Microcomputer

Parsippany

Sohn, Regina Lee 17 Parsippany Hills H.S. Box 33, Mountain Lakes 07046
Genetic Linkage in the Metabolic Pathway for Aromatic Amino Acids
Through Transformation in Acinetobacter calcoaceticus

Waldwick

Leventhal, Ezekiel Michael 17 Waldwick H.S. 90 Lincoln Pl. 07463
A Uniformly Distributed Sequence and Its Generation of an
Infinite Sequence of Unit Fractions
Shoop, Daniel Ray 17 Waldwick H.S. 127 E. Prospect St. 07463
Investigation Into the Set of Pseudo-Squared Numbers

Wayne

Kriegman, Michelle Robin 17 Wayne Valley H.S. 33 Eleron Pl. 07470
Perceptual Developmental Changes Over Short Time Periods
in the Structure of Classifications in Adults
Lambert, Diana Cary 18 Wayne Valley H.S. 56 Greenrale Ave. 07470
Effects of Mycellia Filter Cake on Corn Plants

Westwood

Tarr, Jeffrey Richard 17 Westwood H.S. 1 Upland Dr., Rutland, VT
07675 Use of X-Ray Fluorescence Spectroscopy for the Determination
of the Areal Density of Particle Accelerator Target Foils

NEW MEXICO

Albuquerque

Wayland, Sarah Catherine 17 Eldorado H.S. 3809 Madrid Dr., N.E.
87111 Effects of ELF-EMF on Phaseolus lunatis, Phaseolus vulgaris
and Raphanus sativus

NEW YORK

Angola

Menzel, Lyle Jeremy 17 Lake Shore Central Sr. H.S. 7431 Erie Rd.,
Derby 14047   Effect of Fluorescent Light on Clam Mantle
Cells in Culture
Miggiani, Victor Alfred 17 Lake Shore Central Sr. H.S. 1404 Independence
Dr., Derby 14047   Trail-Laying in Ants

Baldwin

Bedrossian, Peter John 17 Baldwin Sr. H.S. 154 Delaware Ave.,
Freeport 11520   Synthesis of Some Potential Immunomodulating Agents
Drogin, Jack Paul 17 Baldwin Sr. H.S. 806 Vivian Ct. 11510   Effects
of Ammonia Uptake and Assimilation on Carbohydrate Excretion in
Dunaliella tertiolecta on a Diel Cycle
Gross, Mara Mae 18 Baldwin Sr. H.S. 3154 Grand Ave. 11510   Novel
Assay Procedure for Prunasin Hydrolase Activity
Ilivicky, Howard Jay 17 Baldwin Sr. H.S. 793 Allwyn St. 11510
Purification and Analysis of Antibodies to Pancreas Tumor Acid Protein
Kaplan, Todd Mitchell 18 Baldwin Sr. H.S. 3287 Bertha Dr. 11510
Inhibitory Effects of Glycerol Mono-Laurate and Sorbate on Ten
Commercially Important Fungi
Laxer, Michele 17 Baldwin Sr. H.S. 812 Marilyn Ln. 11510 Ground
State pKa Values of Beta-Adrenergic Blocking Agents

APPENDIX E

Westinghouse Science Award
Submission: 1981

SOFTWARE DESIGN DEVELOPMENT AND IMPLEMENTATION OF A HIGH-RELIABILITY

NETWORK-WIDE ELECTRONIC MAIL SYSTEM

The purpose of this project was to create a highly-reliable, network wide
electronic mail system for the transmission and retrieval of mail and to assess
the feasibility of such a system in an academic research environment. Researchers
at the College of Medicine and Dentistry of New Jersey (CMDNJ), where I have designed and implemented this system, use computers in their daily work. Many of
these researchers also have their terminals and/or computer equipment in their
labs. It was evident that some rapid means of communication, in an official memo
style format, with colleagues whom they frequently confer would prove to be quite
practical. This mail system, known as EMAIL (Electronic MAIL system), permits
messages to be created, edited, sent, tagged with the names of sender and receiver,
postmarked, and retrieved. EMAIL also makes extensive use of data base management
tools, is implemented in modular form, and has numerous "fail-soft" capabilities.
An effort has also been made to provide a "friendly" and understandable user interface for those unsophisticated in computer lore.

To exemplify the use of this system, consider the following situation. A
busy executive is hardpressed for time and needs to send an important document to
his business associate in Japan. Instead of using conventional means to send his
mail, he instructs his secretary to compose the document on their personal video
terminal which is connected to a computer network. The document is then transmitted
to his associate several thousands of miles away. His associate, in turn, is then
capable of receiving a hard copy of the document, on a similar terminal, in a matter
of minutes.

-2-

The above scenario does not take place at some time in the future; infact,
it illustrates a somewhat daily experience encountered by many researchers, secretaries, and administrators at CMDNJ. The original goal in developing EMAIL was to
have communication among the various departments and groups; however, this system
has proven to be quite dynamic in that throughout its two and a half years of
development, including school days, weekends, and summers, it has grown to the
point where it now services some several hundred users. Its built-in networking
capabilities, by which mail may be transmitted to users who are geographically
distributed, has also enabled its linking to the Rutgers Medical School (RMS) in
Piscataway, New Jersey some thirty miles away. This capability may be easily
expanded to many nodes (computer sites). The computer network to which EMAIL is
currently linked, is illustrated in Appendix I.

In developing this package, factors such as reliability, security, efficiency
and effectiveness, versatility, and expandability of the system were considered.
Primary importance was given to reliability. The notion of software and hardware
reliability, especially in the era of the 80's in which computers shall be used to
a great extent, will become a paramount issue. The consideration given in EMAIL's
development are reflected in many of its features. Since a great volume of mail
is constantly transmitted, the system was developed to insure that no mail is lost
or destroyed under almost any circumstance, whether human or mechanical. This was
achieved through a series of intricate updating features. The details of these
fail-soft techniques are shown in Appendix II. Thus, a user is assured that a memo
that he/she sends will reach the designated addressee(s). Security was insured by
allowing no user to tamper with or corrupt the "mailbox" of another user without
knowledge of the user's mailbox number. This "number" is actually a string of eight
characters which may contain printing as well as nonprinting (control) characters.

-3-

The versatility of EMAIL is reflected in the various modes that a user may send and receive mail. Appendix III shows the various modes that a user may issue. The scan option, for example, allows a user or "busy executive" to read priority or preferential mail on a certain subject or from certain individual(s). Another salient feature is that a user may send carbon copies and broadcast mail. This ability to transmit a memo to more than one receiver by merely entering the body once and then listing all the addressees is very convenient and reveals the enormous potential of EMAIL. A feature that the user is transparent of is that his mail is edited through a word processor. The aforementioned features reveal a few of the many options that EMAIL offers.

To implement EMAIL it was necessary to use HP/1000 running under the HP/RTE-IV B operating system. It was programmed using Fortran IV and other system available utilities. These included the DS/1000 Network Communications Manager, the IMAGE/1000 Data Base Manager, HP/1000 Editor, and Word Processor.

Various techniques were used in the development of EMAIL. The most significant characteristic is that it is constructed in modular form. The user interface, for example, is uncoupled from the actual task of mail set-up and transmission since a separate program called 'SENDR' actually processes, edits, and transmits mail. Thus, a user, is free to issue other commands while his mail is being processed; he may even compose another memo. Appendix IV shows the process what occurs when mail is sent. It also reveals the complex program-to-program communication that exists between the user interface and 'SENDR.' The importance of this modular form in developing EMAIL cannot be but over emphasized; it, in fact, has greatly contributed to its versatility. Improvements and new features, for example, may be easily implemented without upsetting the program logic or coding. This modular form is also apparent in the various message transmitting and retrieving components that exist in the user interface. These components are shown in Appendix V.

-4-

It is evident that though the concept of electronic mail may be trivial in
nature, the actual design and implementation of such a system is highly complexed.
The reason for its complexity is that numerous factors had to be considered in the
design and implementation of the system. These considerations have, in turn, resulted in a practical and extremely viable mailing system.

When Thomas Alva Edison invented the light bulb, he never perceived that his
invention would have such world-wide acceptance and acclaim; however, it has. The
light bulb is an integral part of our daily living. One day, electronic mail, like
Edison's bulb, may also permeate and pervade our daily lives. Its practical applications are unlimited. Not only is mail sent electronically, as many telexes and
teletypes are capable of doing, but it offers a computational service that automates
a secretary's or file clerk's work of writing a memorandum, document or letter,
editing, filing, and retrieving. If electronic mail systems become a reality,
they will surely create different patterns of communication, attitudes, and styles.
Volumes of written work, for example, shall become obsolete.

Acknowledgments

The author would like to thank Dr. Leslie Michelson for his encouragement and advice in the initiation of this project.

The College of Medicine and Dentistry of New Jersey (CMDNJ) for offering the use of their facilities.

Principal Allen Berlin of Livingston High School for permitting the author to travel to and from CMDNJ during school hours to continue work on the project.

-6-

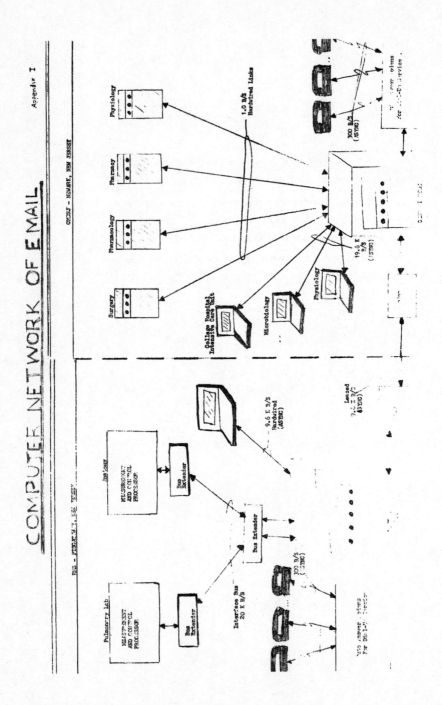

COMPUTER NETWORK OF E MAIL

Appendix I

Appendix   II

The following diagram illustrates the updating feature that occurs as
each individual(if there are more than one receiver of a memo) is being transmitted a copy of the memo.

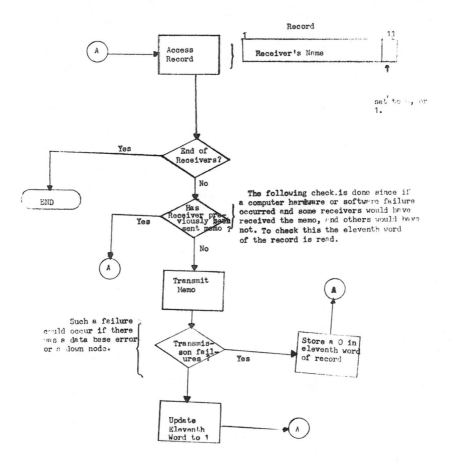

Record

Receiver's Name

set to 0, or
1.

The following check is done since if
a computer hardware or software failure
occurred and some receivers would have
received the memo, and others would have
not. To check this the eleventh word
of the record is read.

Such a failure
could occur if there
was a data base error
or a down node.

Appendix III

Command	Meaning	Purpose
??	Display Command Menu	To list all the commands a user may issue from this part of the user interface
SC	Scan Mail	Allows user to print only the top part of his memo, containing the receiver's name, date, and subject. After reading the header he has the option of continuing with the body of the memo.
GM	Get Mail	Retrieves all existing mail in user's mail box and user may either delete or save his mail as he reads.
ST	STop	To exit from the user interface.
SM	Send Mail	To put user in Send Mail Mode.

The following commands are those that the user may issue in the Send Mail Mode:

Command	Meaning	Purpose
??	Display Send Mail Menu	To list all commands that the user may issue from the Send Mail part of the user interface.
DN	Display Names of listed users	To display names of those receivers who have their names on the listed directory.
DG	Display Group(or department) Names(ie. Pharmacy, Surgery,etc.)	To display currently existing names of a department or group.
WM	Write Memo	To write a personalized memo to an individual with or without Carbon Copies to several other individuals.
BM	Broadcast a Memo	To send personalized memos to more than one individual.
MG	Memo to Group	To send a memo to each and every member of the designated group or department under that group's or department's title. This may also be sent with or without Carbon Copies to several other individuals who are not part of the group.

Appendix III

Command	Meaning	Purpose
EM	Edit Memo	To allow the user to edit the file containing the body of his memo. (The system editor is scheduled from the interface)
DN@ ↑ (nonprinting)	Display Names of users on the unlisted directory	To allow a user who has a high capability level(a number is designated to each user to designate the commands which he may or may not issue. As of now DN@ is the only such command) to display the names of those on the unlisted directory.
RT	Return To the first part of the user interface	To allow the user to return to the other part of the user interface.
ST	STop	To exit from user interface.

Appendix IV

Flowchart for Sending of Mail

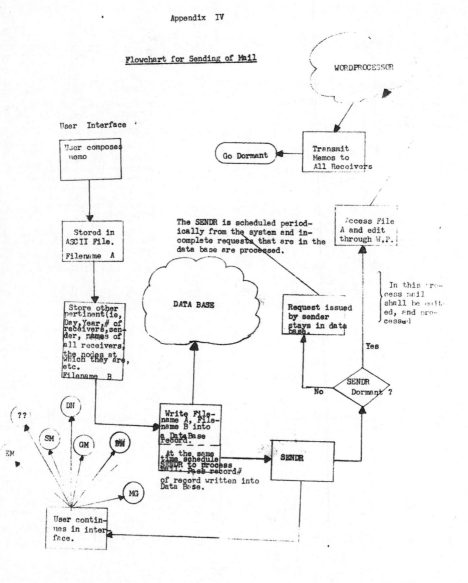

Appendix V

<u>Message</u> <u>Transmitting</u> <u>and</u> <u>Retrieving</u> <u>Components</u>

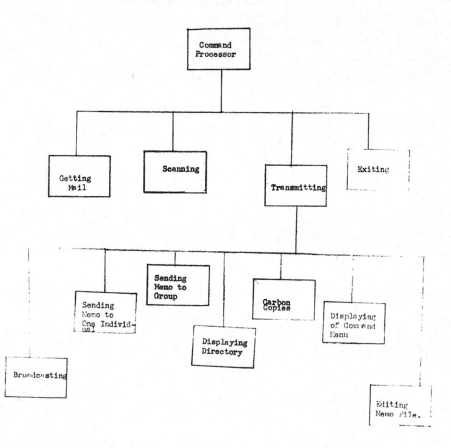

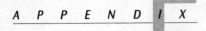

First US Copyright
for Email: 1982

CERTIFICATE OF COPYRIGHT REGISTRATION

This certificate, issued under the seal of the Copyright Office in accordance with the provisions of section 410(a) of title 17, United States Code, attests that copyright registration has been made for the work identified below. The information in this certificate has been made a part of the Copyright Office records.

Dhia Ladd

REGISTER OF COPYRIGHTS
United States of America

FORM TX
UNITED STATES COPYRIGHT OFFICE

REGISTRATION NUMBER

TXu   111-775

TX - - TXU

EFFECTIVE DATE OF REGISTRATION

8   30   82
Month   Day   Year

DO NOT WRITE ABOVE THIS LINE. IF YOU NEED MORE SPACE, USE A SEPARATE CONTINUATION SHEET.

1 TITLE OF THIS WORK ▼

EMAIL

PREVIOUS OR ALTERNATIVE TITLES ▼

COMPUTER PROGRAM FOR Electronic Mail System

PUBLICATION AS A CONTRIBUTION If this work was published as a contribution to a periodical, serial, or collection, give information about the collective work in which the contribution appeared.   Title of Collective Work ▼

If published in a periodical or serial give: Volume ▼   Number ▼   Issue Date ▼   On Pages ▼

2

a NAME OF AUTHOR ▼

MR. SHIVA AYYADURAI

DATES OF BIRTH AND DEATH
Year Born ▼   Year Died ▼
1963

Was this contribution to the work a "work made for hire"?
☐ Yes
☐ No

AUTHOR'S NATIONALITY OR DOMICILE
Name of Country
OR { Citizen of ▶
Domiciled in ▶ UNITED STATES

WAS THIS AUTHOR'S CONTRIBUTION TO THE WORK
Anonymous? ☐ Yes ☒ No
Pseudonymous? ☐ Yes ☒ No
If the answer to either of these questions is "Yes," see detailed instructions.

NATURE OF AUTHORSHIP Briefly describe nature of the material created by this author in which copyright is claimed. ▼

Created and Wrote entire text of the computer program.

NOTE
Under the law, the "author" of a "work made for hire" is generally the employer, not the employee (see instructions). For any part of this work that was "made for hire" check "Yes" in the space provided, give the employer (or other person for whom the work was prepared) as "Author" of that part, and leave the space for dates of birth and death blank.

b NAME OF AUTHOR ▼

DATES OF BIRTH AND DEATH
Year Born ▼   Year Died ▼

Was this contribution to the work a "work made for hire"?
☐ Yes
☐ No

AUTHOR'S NATIONALITY OR DOMICILE
Name of country
OR { Citizen of ▶
Domiciled in ▶

WAS THIS AUTHOR'S CONTRIBUTION TO THE WORK
Anonymous? ☐ Yes ☐ No
Pseudonymous? ☐ Yes ☐ No
If the answer to either of these questions is "Yes," see detailed instructions.

NATURE OF AUTHORSHIP Briefly describe nature of the material created by this author in which copyright is claimed. ▼

c NAME OF AUTHOR ▼

DATES OF BIRTH AND DEATH
Year Born ▼   Year Died ▼

Was this contribution to the work a "work made for hire"?
☐ Yes
☐ No

AUTHOR'S NATIONALITY OR DOMICILE
Name of Country
OR { Citizen of ▶
Domiciled in ▶

WAS THIS AUTHOR'S CONTRIBUTION TO THE WORK
Anonymous? ☐ Yes ☐ No
Pseudonymous? ☐ Yes ☐ No
If the answer to either of these questions is "Yes," see detailed instructions.

NATURE OF AUTHORSHIP Briefly describe nature of the material created by this author in which copyright is claimed. ▼

---

3 YEAR IN WHICH CREATION OF THIS WORK WAS COMPLETED This information must be given
1981 ◄ Year in all cases.

DATE AND NATION OF FIRST PUBLICATION OF THIS PARTICULAR WORK
Complete this information Month ▶   Day ▶   Year ▶   ◄ Nation
ONLY if this work has been published.

4 COPYRIGHT CLAIMANT(S) Name and address must be given even if the claimant is the same as the author given in space 2. ▼

MR. SHIVA AYYADURAI
7 BAKER ROAD
LIVINGSTON, NJ 07039

See instructions before completing this space.

TRANSFER If the claimant(s) named here in space 4 are different from the author(s) named in space 2, give a brief statement of how the claimant(s) obtained ownership of the copyright. ▼

NONE

APPLICATION RECEIVED
1 DEC 1982   8/30/82
ONE DEPOSIT RECEIVED   8/30/82
TWO DEPOSITS RECEIVED
REMITTANCE NUMBER AND DATE
353381- 8/30/82

DO NOT WRITE HERE
OFFICE USE ONLY

MORE ON BACK ▶

TXu   111-775

DO NOT WRITE ABOVE THIS LINE. IF YOU NEED MORE SPACE, USE A SEPARATE CONTINUATION SHEET.

PREVIOUS REGISTRATION Has registration for this work, or for an earlier version of this work, already been made in the Copyright Office?
☐ Yes ☒ No If your answer is "Yes," why is another registration being sought? (Check appropriate box) ▼
☐ This is the first published edition of a work previously registered in unpublished form.
☐ This is the first application submitted by this author as copyright claimant.
☐ This is a changed version of the work, as shown by space 6 on this application.
If your answer is "Yes," give: **Previous Registration Number** ▼   **Year of Registration** ▼

5

DERIVATIVE WORK OR COMPILATION Complete both space 6a & 6b for a derivative work; complete only 6b for a compilation.
a. **Preexisting Material** Identify any preexisting work or works that this work is based on or incorporates. ▼
No

b. **Material Added to This Work** Give a brief, general statement of the material that has been added to this work and in which copyright is claimed. ▼

6
See instructions
before completing
this space.

MANUFACTURERS AND LOCATIONS If this is a published work consisting preponderantly of nondramatic literary material in English, the law may require that the copies be manufactured in the United States or Canada for full protection. If so, the names of the manufacturers who performed certain processes, and the places where these processes were performed must be given. See instructions for details.
Names of Manufacturers ▼   **Places of Manufacture** ▼

7

REPRODUCTION FOR USE OF BLIND OR PHYSICALLY HANDICAPPED INDIVIDUALS A signature on this form at space 10, and a check in one of the boxes here in space 8, constitutes a non-exclusive grant of permission to the Library of Congress to reproduce and distribute solely for the blind and physically handicapped and under the conditions and limitations prescribed by the regulations of the Copyright Office: (1) copies of the work identified in space 1 of this application in Braille (or similar tactile symbols); or (2) phonorecords embodying a fixation of a reading of that work; or (3) both.

a ☐ Copies and Phonorecords   b ☐ Copies Only   c ☐ Phonorecords Only

8
See instructions.

DEPOSIT ACCOUNT If the registration fee is to be charged to a Deposit Account established in the Copyright Office, give name and number of Account.
Name ▼   **Account Number** ▼

CORRESPONDENCE Give name and address to which correspondence about this application should be sent. Name/Address/Apt/City/State/Zip ▼
SHIVA AYYADURAI / 97 BAY STATE Rd. / BOSTON / MA / 02215

Area Code & Telephone Number ▶ (617-247-8691)

9
Be sure to
give your
daytime phone
◀ number

CERTIFICATION* I, the undersigned, hereby certify that I am the
Check one ▶
☐ author
☐ other copyright claimant
☒ owner of exclusive right(s)
☐ authorized agent of

of the work identified in this application and that the statements made by me in this application are correct to the best of my knowledge.
Name of author or other copyright claimant, or owner of exclusive right(s) ▲

Typed or printed name and date ▼ If this is a published work, this date must be the same as or later than the date of publication given in space 3.
SHIVA AYYADURAI   date ▶ AUGUST 18, 1982

Handwritten signature (X) ▼
Shiva Ayyadurai

10

MAIL CERTIFI-CATE TO
Name ▼
SHIVA AYYADURAI
Number/Street/Apartment Number ▼
97 BAY STATE RD.
City/State/ZIP ▼
BOSTON, MA 02215

Have you:
• Completed all necessary spaces?
• Signed your application in space 10?
• Enclosed check or money order for $10 payable to Register of Copyrights?
• Enclosed your deposit material with the application and fee?
MAIL TO: Register of Copyrights, Library of Congress, Washington, D.C. 20559

11

Certificate will be mailed in window envelope

* 17 U.S.C. § 506(e): Any person who knowingly makes a false representation of a material fact in the application for copyright registration provided for by section 409, or in any written statement filed in connection with the application, shall be fined not more than $2,500.

G

Misuses of the Term "Email" and False Claims About Email

Sending text messages electronically could be said to date back to the Morse code telegraph of the mid- 1800s, or the 1939 World's Fair where IBM sent a message of congratulations from San Francisco to New York on an IBM radio-type, calling it a "high-speed substitute for mail service in the world of tomorrow." The original text message, electronic transfer of content or images, ARPANET messaging, and even the familiar "@" sign were used in primitive electronic communication systems. While the technology pioneers who created these systems should be heralded for their efforts and given credit for their specific accomplishments and contributions, these early computer programs were clearly not "email."

Historical accounts of the Internet are full of claims of certain individuals (and groups of individuals) in the ARPANET environment in the 1970s and 1980s "inventing email." These claims, based on the misuse of the term "email," have been compiled in the list below. For example, the "@" sign, early programs for sending and receiving messages, and technical specifications known as RFCs, have claimed to be "email." But as some claimants have admitted, none of these innovations were intended as a system of interlocking parts—Inbox, Memo, Outbox, Folders, Address Book—that comprise the email system of today and is used by more than 500 million people worldwide.

False Claim #1: Email was created on the ARPANET

The truth is that email was created at UMDNJ, *not* on the ARPANET. The following quote misuses the term "email": "Under ARPANET several major innovations occurred: email (or electronic mail), the ability to send simple messages to another person across the network."[6] The invention referenced here is command-line protocols for transferring text messages, not email as defined by a system of interlocking parts, like the platform created at UMDNJ in 1978, which was the full-scale emulation of the interoffice interorganizational paper mail system. As the related references show, early workers in the field of electronic messaging had no intention of creating a full-scale electronic version of an interoffice or interorganizational paper mail system (ref. 1.1, 1.2), and in fact were not even allowed to work on creating an electronic system to replicate "letters," or the interoffice memo (ref. 1.3).

Related references:

[1.1] "At this time, no attempt is being made to emulate a full-scale, interorganizational mail system."—Crocker, David. Framework and Function of the "MS" Personal Message System. Santa Monica, CA: RAND Corporation, December 1977.

[1.2] "The level of the MS project effort has also had a major effect upon the system's design. To construct a fully-detailed and monolithic message processing environment requires a much larger effort than has been possible with MS. In addition, the fact that the system is intended for use in various organizational contexts and by users of differing expertise makes it almost impossible to build a system which responds to all users' needs. Consequently, important segments of a full message environment have received little or no attention and decisions have been made with the expectation that other Unix capabilities will be used to augment MS."—Crocker, David. Framework and Function of the "MS" Personal Message System. Santa Monica, CA: RAND Corporation, December 1977.

[1.3] "The idea of sending 'letters' using [the Compatible Time-Sharing System] was resisted by management, as a waste of resources."—Van Vleck, Tom. "The History of Electronic Mail," http://web.archive.org/web/20110720215402/; http://www.multicians.org/thvv/mail-history.html

Note: Tom Van Vleck, after March 2012, revised his own history by inserting the word "initially" to the above sentence to read, "The idea of initially sending 'letters' . . ." to give the false impression that somehow later he was allowed to implement the letter, or interoffice memo.

False Claim #2: Ray Tomlinson "invented email"

Ray Tomlinson did not invent email. He modified SNDMSG for exchanging text messages across computers. This quote misuses the term "email": "Ray Tomlinson is credited with inventing email in 1972. Like many of the Internet inventors, Tomlinson worked for Bolt, Beranek and Newman as an ARPANET contractor."[7] The invention referenced is a program called SNDMSG, which was a set of highly technical computer codes that a sender had to type to transfer a message from one computer to another. Tomlinson updated an existing SNDMSG command program to transmit text strings over a network connection. SNDMSG was not a system of interlocking parts designed for laypersons to transmit routine office communications; thus it was not designed to replicate the interoffice paper mail system. As related references show, SNDMSG was not only not email but also just a very rudimentary form of text messaging.

What is more alarming is that Michael Padlipsky's reference in the standard "histories" has been removed. Padlipsky was one of Tomlinson's peers. He was present in the 1970s when "email" was *not* developed by Tomlinson.

Related references:

[2.1] "The very simple systems (SNDMSG, RD, and READMAIL) did not integrate the reading and creation functions, had different user interfaces, and did not provide sufficient functionality for simple message processing."—Vittal, John. MSG: A Simple Message System. Cambridge, MA: North-Holland Publishing Company, 1981.

[2.2] "I was making improvements to the local inter-user mail program called SNDMSG. The idea occurred to me that CPYNET could append material to a mailbox file just as readily as SNDMSG could. SNDMSG could easily incorporate the code from CPYNET and direct messages through a network connection to remote mailboxes in addition to appending messages to local mailbox files. The missing piece was that the experimental CPYNET protocol had no provision for appending to a file; it could just send and receive files. Adding the missing piece was a no-brainer—just a minor addition to the protocol."—Tomlinson, Ray. The First Network Email http://openmap.bbn.com/~tomlinso/ray/firstemailframe .html, April 7, 2012.

[2.3] "I don't believe Ray Tomlinson invented 'e-mail.' And not because of the quibble that we called it netmail originally, though that does offer an excuse to observe that I personally find the term 'e-mail' awfully cutesy, and references to 'sending an e-mail' syntactic slime. Nor because of the semi-quibble that 'mail' had been around intra-Host on several of the Host operating systems since well before anybody realized they were Hosts, though that one has a great deal of abstract 'historical' appeal. No, it's because I have a completely clear memory that Ray wasn't even at the FTP meeting where we decided to add mail to the protocol."—Padlipsky, M.A., (ARPANET contributor and author of more than twenty RFC specifications), "And they argued all night . . ."[8]

False Claim #3: The "@" symbol equals the invention of "email"

The "@" symbol separates the user name from the domain name. The following quote misuses the term "email": "When [Tomlinson] is remembered at all, it is as the man who picked @ as the locator symbol in electronic addresses. In truth though, he is the inventor of e-mail, the application that launched the digital information revolution. And yet the breakthrough he made was such a simple evolutionary step that hardly anyone noticed it till later."[9] The invention referenced is the use of the "@" symbol to distinguish two computers when sending a text message. The "@" symbol is not a necessary component of the system of interlocking parts, in some cases "-at" was used, or the "." symbol as in the first email system developed by Ayyadurai.

Some have mistakenly characterized the @ symbol as "underused" and novel. As a point of fact, the @ symbol was the line-kill character on Multics, another early timesharing system, and created a character conflict for those Multics users trying to use Tomlinson's SNDMSG. As Pogran noted, "Do folks remember that @ was the Multics line-kill character? We were opposed to Ray Tomlinson's famous (or is it infamous?) selection of @ as the character that separated the user name from the host name in email addresses. Early versions of ARPANET email specs allowed the use of space-a-t-space (i.e., "at") in place of the @ to accommodate Multics (and the mail composition software I wrote used the syntax -at on the command line)."[10]

The @ symbol was "underused" only to the extent that it interfered with some users' host environments.

Related references:

[3.1] "Because the @ was a line kill character in Multics, sending mail from Multics to other hosts used the control argument -at instead."—Van Vleck, Tom. History of Electronic Mail, www.multicians.org/thvv/mail-history.html, April 7, 2012.

[3.2] "Early versions of ARPANET email specs allowed the use of space-a-t-space (i.e., "at") in place of the @ to accommodate Multics and the mail composition software I wrote used the syntax -at on the command line to begin composing an email . . . "—Pogran, Kenneth, ARPANET.

False Claim #4: RFCs demonstrate "email" existed prior to 1978

Requests for Comments (RFCs) were simply written documentations, not an email computer program, nor an email system. This quote is a misuse of the term "email": ". . . email underpinnings were further cemented in 1977's RFC 733, a foundational document of what became the Internet itself."[11] Because the RFCs and RFC 733 were *written* documentation not a computer program or code or system, they are fundamentally different from email. Moreover, this quote and others like it are hyperbolic: "In 1977 these features and others went from best practices to a binding standard in RFC 733." RFC 733 was drafted in November 1977 and was an attempt at standardization of messaging protocols and interfaces; it should not be conflated as "email underpinnings" with the electronic system of interlocked parts defining the interoffice paper mail system. The RFCs by their own admission [ref. 4.1] did not even dictate which features of the interoffice mail process would be included, such as the basic components of user interfaces for message creation and reading.

RFC 733 was an attempted standard that was never fully accepted [ref. 4.3]. The very term "RFC" means "Request for Comments" [ref. 4.2]. It was merely a document and only proposed an interface for message format and transmission, but said little about feature sets of individual electronic messaging or mail systems. As the opening of RFC 733 states:

"This specification is intended strictly as a definition of what is to be passed between hosts on the ARPANET. It is not intended to dictate either features, which systems on the Network are expected to support, or user interfaces to message creating or reading programs."[12]

The authors of RFCs, by their own admission, clearly state this was not their intention. RFCs were the command-line terminology at best, but not email.

Related references:

[4.1] "This specification is intended strictly as a definition of what is to be passed between hosts on the ARPANET. It is not intended to dictate either features which systems on the Network are expected to support, or user interfaces to message creating or reading programs."—Crocker, DH, Vittal, JJ, Pogran, KT, Henderson, DA, STANDARD FOR THE FORMAT OF ARPA NETWORK TEXT MESSAGES http://www.rfc-editor.org/rfc/rfc733.txt

[4.2] "Prospective users, system designers, and service offering companies often compile lists of potential services [of electronic mail systems] . . . Nobody claims that these lists are complete, and most often it is admitted freely that these lists represent a first cut synthesis of services offered by other communication facilities. Unfortunately, these lists mostly convey just a number of buzz-words which everybody interprets in his own fashion."—Shicker, P. "Service Definitions in a Computer Based Mail Environment" Computer Message Systems. Ottawa, Canada: North-Holland Publishing Company, 1981. 159-171

[4.3] "Some of RFC #733's features failed to gain adequate acceptance."— Crocker, DH, Vittal, JJ, Pogran, KT, Henderson, DA, STANDARD FOR THE FORMAT OF ARPA NETWORK TEXT MESSAGES http://www.rfc-editor.org/rfc/rfc733.txt

False Claim #5: Programs for exchanging messages were "email"

The following quote is a misuse of the term "email," because programs like Hermes and Laurel were not systems of interlocking parts for emulating the interoffice paper mail system: "By the mid-1970s, other user-oriented e-mail programs arrived on the scene. Two of the more popular examples were 'Hermes' at Bolt, Beranek and Newman, now BBN—a wholly owned subsidiary of Raytheon— and 'Laurel,' which was in use at Xerox PARC."[13] Laurel was really only one component, a front-end for the independent, lower-level Grapevine messaging platform [ref. 5.1]. Though Laurel was beginning to incorporate some elements of the interlocked parts such as folders and the inbox, it was still like nearly all messaging systems of the period: heavily dependent on external system resources, and not designed as a true system of interlocking parts. Furthermore, internal Xerox documentation [ref. 5.1, p. 7] shows that independent Grapevine component was still being prototyped with five dedicated servers in 1981, well after Ayyadurai's invention of email had been in use for routine communications at UMDNJ for several years. No word of Laurel or Grapevine would be publicly available until 1982,[14] when the Xerox work would be published in the Communications of the ACM [ref. 5.1, 5.2].

Hermes was similar. It was not a system of interlocked parts and not something user-friendly that an ordinary office worker could use. Users had to learn about twenty commands to use it [ref. 5.3]. Another program, PLATO, which was an invention for computer-assisted instruction which some reference as "email," is one that Vallee's comments also help to place in context relative to Ayyadurai's invention [ref. 5.4]. In 1979, all known messaging systems were itemized in RFC

808 by the leading researchers who worked at the big universities, large companies and for the military [ref. 5.5]. Note, Laurel and PLATO do not appear on this list.

For a review of individual systems of the period, it is best to look at the 1979 RFC 808[15], which contains a listing of the names of all the computer mail systems anybody had ever heard of. The vast majority of the systems such as MSG, MS, SNDMSG, RD, and HERMES, all share a common ancestry, and inherit features (and deficiencies) from this heritage. John Vittal tried to distinguish the features and qualities of his MSG message system relative to its antecedents:

MSG started from a set of primitive message processing operations. Several of the commands listed above were not implemented in the initial version of MSG:

- o Creation: Answer and Forward
- o Motion: Move
- o File operations: Write
- o Marking: Mark and Unmark
- o User-interface and Profile: Koncise, Verbose, and Zap profile
- o Miscellaneous: Print date and Comment

It became clear, even before MSG was first publicly released, that the operations of Put and Delete were so commonly used together that a combining operation (Move) should be included in the functionality of the system. This was the first major modification.

COMPARISON WITH OTHER SYSTEMS

Many of the other CBMSs of the time have already been alluded to. The very simple systems (SNDMSG, RD AND READMAIL) did not integrate the reading and creation functions, had different user-interfaces, and did not provide sufficient functionality for simple message processing.

On the other hand, two systems came very close to MSG. BANANARD gained acceptance, but seemed to not have the right functionality. The user-interface seemed to be a little too verbose for experienced users. However, it is important to note that some users still prefer to use BANANARD. These tend to be users who view mail rather than respond to it.[16]

In his conclusion, he was careful to stress the limitations of MSG as a general communication tool:

However good MSG is, it is not perfect. Its major drawback is that it does not have a directly integrated message creation facility with the same style of user-interface as the rest of MSG. The result is that users are forced to use two separate interfaces for a single conceptual process—dealing with mail. In addition, the decision to use SNDMSG limits users because it has no way to edit various fields of the message after a specific field has been completely specified, especially address lists.

MSG was at best a rudimentary text-messaging client. It was a lightweight messaging system, designed to aid users of the TENEX operating system. It served its purpose well, but was crippled by a limited feature set.

Related references:

[5.1] "A client program of Grapevine generally obtains services through code... The primary clients of Grapevine are various mail interface programs, of which Laurel is most widely used."—Schroeder, Michael D., Andrew Birrell, and Roger Needham. "Experience with Grapevine: The Growth of a Distributed System." ACM Transactions on Computer Systems 2.1 (1984): 3-23.

[5.2] ". . . the Grapevine system was first made available to a limited number of clients during 1980."—Birrell, A., Grapevine: An Exercise in Distributed Computing, birrell.org/andrew/papers/Grapevine.pdf, p. 272.

[5.3] "In systems like SEND MESSAGE and its successors, such as HERMES, ON-TYME, and COMET, there is no provision for immediate response. A message is sent into a mailbox for later access by the recipient. No automatic filing is provided: any searching of message files requires users to write their own search programs, and to flag those messages they want to retain or erase. The burden is placed on users to manage their own files, and a fairly detailed understanding of programming and file structures is required. Both senders and receivers must learn about 20 commands, and if they misuse them they can jeopardize the entire data structure. Some messages may even be lost in the process."—Vallee, Jacques, (a principal investigator of ARPA and NSF messaging projects), Computer Message Systems. New York: McGraw-Hill, 1984.

[5.4] "The notes and memo systems are very similar to the ARPANET message systems, with the coordinators setting up access modes to define who gets in and at what level. A user can either respond to a note or create a new one. On the negative side, the system does not allow review of entries except in serial fashion. New messages generally cannot be sorted, filed, or ignored, although a sophisticated user can 'transport' various kinds of notes through buffers. Nor can it apply to them any facility to search for key words, to save information, or to recombine information. This implies a self-limiting feature—if the system were ever used heavily, users would spend all their time managing the flow of information. Clearly, this approach calls for powerful file management functions that had not yet appeared at the time of our survey of the system."—Vallee, Jacques, (a principal investigator of ARPA and NSF messaging projects), Computer Message Systems. New York: McGraw-Hill, 1984.

[5.5] "Dave Farber gave a bit of history of mail systems listing names of all the systems that anybody had ever heard of [see Appendix A]. . . . It was noted that most of the mail systems were not formal projects (in the sense of explicitly sponsored research), but things that 'just happened.'"—RFC 808, Meeting at BBN, January 10, 1979, http://tools.ietf.org/html/rfc808.

False Claim #6: MAIL on CTSS developed in 1960s was "email"

CTSS MAIL was an early text messaging system, not a version of email, as this quote would have you believe: "Electronic mail, or email, was introduced at MIT in 1965 and was widely discussed in the press during the 1970s. Tens of thousands of users were swapping messages by 1980." This refers to the MAIL command on MIT's CTSS timesharing system, and is a misuse of the term "email." The basic usage of MAIL, as documented in CTSS Programming Staff Note #39[17], is below:

```
The MAIL Command

    A new command should be written to allow a user to send
    a   private  message  to  another  user  which  may  be
    delivered at the receiver's convenience.  This will  be
    useful for the system to notify a user that some or all
    of his files have been backed-up.   It  will  also  be
    useful for users to send authors any criticisms.

            MAIL  LETTER  FILE  USER1  USER2  USER3 ....
            MAIL  'ME'

    LETTER FILE is the name of a BCD  file  which  contains
            the message to be sent.
    USERn  is the designation of the user who is to receive
            the message.  USERn may be a programmer's name  or
            programmer   number   or    the  problem-programmer
            number.  It may also be just the problem number if
            the message is to go to all  users  of  the  same
            problem number.

    MAIL ME is the command given by the  receiver  when  he
            wants the mail to be printed.  The files  will  be
            left in permanent mode and should  be  deleted  by
            the receiver at his convenience.

    The MAIL command will  create or append to the front  of
    a file called MAIL BOX.  System messages  to  the  user
    will be placed in a file called URGENT MAIL.  The LOGIN
    command will notify the user if he has either  kind  of
    mail.  MAIL ME will always print URGENT  MAIL     before
    MAIL BOX.
```

This invention, MAIL, was not a system of interlocked parts emulating the interoffice paper mail system. MAIL allowed a CTSS user to transmit a file, written in a third-party editor, and encoded in binary-decimal format (BCD), to other CTSS users. The delivered message would be appended to the front of a file in the recipient's directory that represented the aggregate of all received messages. This flat-file message storage placed strict constraints on the capacity of MAIL, and required users to traverse and review all messages one-by-one; search and sort mechanisms were not available. Corruption to the MAIL BOX file could result in the loss of a user's messages. From the CTSS Programmer's Guide[18] (Section AH.9.05):

```
BOX'.  Because of  the  appending  feature  of  the  MAILing
process, the command 'DELETE MAIL  BOX' should  be  issued
after a message has been PRINTed, to  avoid  having  to  run
through previous mesages to get to the latest one.)
```

The design choices in MAIL—lack of search and sort facilities, need for an external editor, dependence on CTSS-specific user IDs, and flat-file message storage—put strict constraints on the use and capacity of the command. It was well-suited to the low-volume transmission of informal (i.e. unformatted) messages. "The proposed uses [of MAIL]," wrote Tom Van Vleck, "were communication from 'the system' to users, informing them that files had been backed up, communication to the authors of commands with criticisms, and communication from command authors to the CTSS manual editor."[19]

The limited feature set of MAIL would be carried over to its progeny (*SNDMSG, MSG, HERMES*), creating headaches for even the most sophisticated technical staffers:[20]

> In systems like SEND MESSAGE and its successors, such as HERMES, ONTYME, and COMET, there is no provision for immediate response. A message is sent into a mailbox for later access by the recipient. No automatic filing is provided: Any searching of message files requires users to write their own search programs, and to flag those messages they want to retain or erase. The burden is placed on users to manage their own files, and a fairly detailed understanding of programming and file structures is required. Both senders and receivers must learn about 20 commands, and if they misuse them they can jeopardize the entire data structure. Some messages may even be lost in the process. These drawbacks are compensated for by the fact that the cost per message is very low.

Those who promoted MAIL as "email," even though the term "email" did not even exist in 1965, are attempting to redefine "email" as a command-driven program that transferred BCD-encoded text files, written in an external editor, among timesharing system users, to be reviewed serially in a flat-file.

One would be hard-pressed to draw a linear connection from MAIL to today's email systems. MAIL was not "email," but a text messaging command line system, at best.

False Claim #7: In 2013, the term "email" *now* needs to be defined

Email was defined precisely in 1978 as the electronic version of the interoffice mail system. Following news of Ayyadurai's invention of email, industry insiders have attempted to redefine the term "email" in order to take credit for earlier work in text messaging, which was clearly not email. For example, in an online statement in 2012, after news of the Smithsonian's acceptance of Ayyadurai's work, they stated:

" . . . we need a more specific definition that captures the essence of computer based electronic mail as it actually emerged. Here is one that was developed in discussion with email pioneers Ray Tomlinson, Tom Van Vleck and Dave Crocker:

'Electronic mail is a service provided by computer programs to send unstructured textual messages of about the same length as paper letters from the account of one user to recipients' personal electronic mailboxes, where they are stored for later retrieval.'" [ref. 7.1]

However, email was already clearly defined in 1978 as the electronic interoffice, interorganizational mail system, and formally in 1982 by Ayyadurai's US Copyright. Such a revisionist definition by industry insiders, in 2012, served one purpose, to allow them (Tomlinson, Van Vleck, and Crocker, who worked with the early messaging systems SNDMSG, MAIL and MS respectively) to retroactively choose a definition for electronic mail that ensured their primacy in the invention of "email," which they did not create and had no intention of creating.

The documentation of that period reveals that the term "email" did not exist prior to 1978 and the definition of "electronic mail," and a specification of its functions, was anything but clear-cut. It was Ayyadurai's work starting in 1978, and the formal copyright of 1982, which clearly defined "email" and "electronic mail" as a system of interlocked parts emulating the entire interoffice, inter-organizational paper-based mail system in an electronic format. Prior to Ayyadurai's invention, there was confusion even about the term "electronic mail."

As Gordon B. Thompson of Bell Northern Research wrote in 1981:[21]

Electronic Mail Systems give me some major concern. The use of the word "mail" brings with it a lot of baggage, and most certainly people are going to get some surprises because of this. A conventional letter always presents itself to the reader in the same format as it had when it left the writer. In the electronic situation, unless rigid controls are exercised over the terminals allowed on the system, there is no guarantee that the recipient will see the same lay out at all. Designers tell us that the way text is presented can significantly alter the attitude the reader has towards printed text. In electronic mail this variable is left wide open!

Peter Schicker wrote of similar concerns of messaging service and feature lists:

> Users of such computer based mail systems are less intrigued by the vari-
> ous internal mechanisms and resource allocation strategies but require
> exact definitions of the facilities and services that these systems offer.
> Prospective users, system designers, and service offering companies often
> compile lists of potential services . . . Nobody claims that these lists first
> cut synthesis of services offered by other communication facilities (e.g.,
> postal service, telephone, telegraph, telex, etc.). Unfortunately, these lists
> mostly convey just a number of buzz-words which everybody interprets
> in his own fashion.[22]

Even normally well-defined terms like "memo" and "conferencing" took
on confusing, often conflicting meanings, "Much confusion still exists about the
requirements for effective communications. One person calls "conferencing"
what another calls "mail."[23]

Or, as James Robinson wrote in the opening lines of his master's thesis on a
review of electronic mail, messaging systems:[24]

> 'Electronic Mail' is a term that means different things to different people. To
> one person, electronic mail may represent a technology as old as the tele-
> graph, while to another, it may mean high-powered computers that relay
> digitized information. Part of the confusion about what electronic mail
> really is can be traced to how the term is defined. Usually, electronic mail
> is defined as . . .

Email has had a clear definition since Ayyadurai's invention. There is no
reason in 2013 to redefine it, except to inappropriately assign "the inventor of
email" moniker to those who are not the inventors of email.

Related references:
[7.1] SIGCIS blog entry, April 17, 2012 www.sigcis.org

False Claim #8: Email is not an invention,
but VisiCalc is an invention

Like VisiCalc, email (Ayyadurai's invention of email) also created an electronic
metaphor for the interoffice paper mail system.

Some "historians," in collusion with industry insiders, who seek to discredit
Ayyadurai's invention of email, have gone to the extent of asserting that email is

not an invention, but that VisiCalc is. If they refer to "email" as a text message, then email is not an invention. However, in recognizing that email, the first email system created by Ayyadurai, is the electronic version of the interoffice paper mail system, then email, like VisiCalc, is an invention.

There is a clear analogy between the invention of email and the invention of VisiCalc. Bricklin's title as the "Father of the Modern Spreadsheet" belies significant contributions to the field of data processing completed prior to the release of VisiCalc. It was the subject of Iveron and Brooks's seminal book *Automatic Data Processing* and a major research topic for industry people and academia. What Bricklin did was to create an integrated system for data processing, complete with a consistent UI and strong metaphor, which was targeted toward end users. Bricklin's accomplishment wasn't that he invented data processing, but that he integrated it and increased accessibility.

In the same way that Bricklin's VisiCalc digitalized the system of paper spreadsheets, Ayyadurai's email digitalized the interoffice, interorganizational paper-based mail system. Both took well-defined social processes and gave them the power of computation, freeing users from the drudgery of manual recalculation in the former case, or the delivery of physical interoffice memos in the latter.

This puts both projects in stark contrast to the messaging systems of early timesharing architecture, which evolved to address the administrative and technical needs of mainframe users. As stated in RFC 808, most of these message systems "were not formal projects (in the sense of explicitly sponsored research), but things that 'just happened.'" Jacques Vallee wrote of these early systems:[25]

The human factors of communications are still largely ignored. As new companies get into the field, they hire the best programmers they can find to implement message systems. These programmers are often compiler writers or experts in operating systems and have had no experience in dealing with end users. They have operated in a completely different environment, where communications had a much narrower meaning. Some early successes have also had the unfortunate result of freezing the technical reality of the field for too long. Network mail on the ARPANET is a case in point. Introduced in the early 1970s, electronic mail systems have been very successful on the ARPANET, where they served a highly trained community of technical experts. When it came time to design new systems for wider communities, these same technical experts found it very difficult to be creative in ways that differed from what they had first learned.

One "historian," part of the industry insider clique, has falsely asserted, with reference to Ayyadurai's work that:

"The system will still be of interest to historians as a representative example of a low-budget, small scale electronic mail system constructed from off-the-shelf components, including the HP/1000's communications, word processing, and database programs."

This is a false statement. It reveals deliberate and reckless ignorance of the facts, which are accessible now at the Smithsonian. The first email system was designed as an integrated system—it included all its own facilities for message handling, distribution, composition, archiving, and user management. It was "small scale" only in the sense that it did not need the ARPANET, in contrast to systems like MAIL and MSG, which leveraged a host of facilities in the host environment. Email, the program and system, consisted of nearly 50,000 lines of FORTRAN IV code, unlike Van Vleck's MAIL command, which comprised less than 300 lines of MAD, a high-level language on the CTSS.[26]

Email was far from a "small-scale electronic mail system." Email was a full-scale emulation of the entire interoffice paper mail system, with all the features we now experience in modern email programs and many features which some email programs even in the late 1990s, did not have.

False Claim #9: DEC and Wang created email

Email systems were not available from DEC and Wang in 1980. By 1980, electronic mail systems aimed at the office environments were not "readily available from companies such as DEC, Wang, and IBM." Such statements are conflating the term "email" with all forms of electronic communication, from telegraph services, to Telex, or CBMS systems. This conflation is confusing, and a misuse of the term "email."

The offerings of electronic mail systems by private suppliers varied greatly, and were largely incompatible. Wang Laboratories, for example, had already been well established for its line of word processing equipment.[27] When network facilities became readily available, it bolted on file transfer facilities to its machines, creating a line of "communicating word processors."[28] This networking of word processors is *not* email.

In 1980, there was tremendous pressure to innovate in the "office automation sector." However, as addressed in James Robinson's 1984 thesis, An Overview of Electronic Mail Systems,[29] these offerings were part of a larger defensive strategy:

"[Computer-based message systems] are sold to users who have an interest in implementing electronic mail on their current equipment. Not surprising therefore, many of the vendors in this grouping tend to be minicomputer manufacturers such as Data General and Prime. The reason for this is not so much that minicomputer manufacturers have a real interest in electronic mail, but rather have devised messaging systems in an attempt to prevent other firms from selling a system that would run on their hardware. Thus, this type of electronic mail system has evolved as part of a defensive strategy by original equipment manufacturers (OEMs). An excellent example of a product by an OEM is Wang Laboratories Inc's Mailway."

The "electronic mail" offerings by private industry in 1980 were not the system of interlocked parts emulating the entire interoffice paper mail system. They were, at best, wildly unstable and inconsistent.

False Claim #10: Laurel was "email"

Laurel was a precursor to text messaging programs. The following quote misuses the term "email": ". . . the PARC email software, Laurel, ran on the user's local computer, was operated with a mouse, and pulled messages from the PARC server to a personal hard drive for storage and filing." The invention, Laurel, was a *mail user interface program* for the Xerox Alto. It was a graphical front-end to a series of messaging programs akin to *SNDMSG* and *MS*.[30] The use of mouse was an innovation of its host environment, Alto, not of Laurel itself.[31] Laurel was capable of basic message composition, scanning and flat-file storage (through the use of its *.mail* files). Like other flat-file approaches, mail management remained in the hands of users.[32]

The Laurel Manual, as it existed at Stanford in September 1980, provided a thorough explanation of what Laurel was and of its capabilities. Laurel was just a user interface, and not the system of interlocked parts to emulate the entire interoffice paper mail system.

Laurel was disconnected and relied on "Piping" other small programs which were loosely connected to each other.[33]

What is Laurel?

Laurel is an Alto-based, display-oriented, message manipulation system. It provides facilities that permit its users to display, forward, classify, file, and print messages, and to compose and transmit messages and replies. Laurel is an initial component of what will ultimately be a distributed message system. Although the distributed nature of this system has inherent technical interest, it is largely transparent to the users of the system, who see a collection of logical facilities resembling those provided by MSG on Maxc. Eventually, the services of Laurel will surpass those of MSG, but at present the two are largely equivalent in function. The important distinction for now is that Laurel executes on an Alto and uses the display in a fashion befitting Alto-based software. It also produces files that can be manipulated by other Alto subsystems.

Many initial users of Laurel will be familiar with MSG and will naturally be interested in the functional differences between MSG and Laurel. This manual, in addition to presenting the facilities of Laurel, points out some of the incompatibilities with MSG. *Prospective Laurel users with strong ties to MSG should read section 5 carefully before committing themselves to Laurel.* The Laurel team fully expects that some potential users will find the transition to Laurel too uncomfortable to undertake at present. Accordingly, we have provided a "free sample" of Laurel in the form of a tutorial (see section 2), which can be run without any commitment to further use of Laurel or danger to MSG files. We would much prefer that Laurel users "go in with their eyes open" and not be unpleasantly surprised when confronted with incompatibilities.

Mention of MSG in the official Laurel documentation refers to the same command program discussed earlier, created and critiqued by John Vittal, and listed in RFC 808 as running on a TENEX operating system. "Maxc" referred to a Xerox-produced machine that emulated the facilities of PDP-10 TENEX-based systems. Its operation is well documented.[34] It follows that Laurel, as it existed in 1979 and 1980, fundamentally depended on MSG and Maxc, for message transmission. It was an Alto-based front-end for a more pedestrian MSG program. Ironically, the revealing kinship of Laurel and MSG is well described in the 1979 Whole ALTO World Newsletter.[35] The sentence, "Eventually, the services of Laurel will surpass those of MSG, but at present, the two are roughly equivalent in function," should not be overlooked.

There are two message systems now in use: MSG, which is run from your Alto on MAXC and Laurel, which runs entirely on the Alto, using MAXC only to hold undelivered mail. MSG is a teletype oriented system with comparatively primitive editing facilities, though it does provide a wide set of message control operations. All messages, both intransit and received, and the MSG software reside on MAXC.

Laurel is now replacing MSG. The major differences are that it is oriented toward Alto-type operations, such as menu picking and Bravo-type editing, and resides entirely on the Alto disk. Undelivered messages are currently kept on the MAXC file server but they will soon be held on IVY. To receive messages from Laurel you must have a MAXC MSG account, though it does permit people without message accounts to send messages to registered users. MSG and Laurel are essentially compatible; users of each can send messages to the other.

The "distributed message system" mentioned in the Laurel Manual would eventually be realized in *Grapevine*, tested on a limited number of clients in 1980, and not publicly documented[36] until 1982, well after Ayyadurai's invention of email was well-established in a production environment. These points are corroborated by Larry Tesler, who was at Xerox throughout Laurel's development.[37]

A review of period documentation helps to put Laurel in perspective. As of 1979 and 1980, Laurel was an Alto-based graphical front-end for MSG. It stood on the foundations of the beautifully sophisticated Alto environment, and contributed Alto-specific operations like menu picking and Bravo-type editing, which were not available in other MSG environments. However, Laurel 2.0 provided only a small subset of the features available in Ayyadurai's email, lacking an attachment editor, relational database, administrator/postmaster functionality, prioritization and search tools, among others. The Alto was a brilliant machine, the precursor to the Apple machines, and Laurel would evolve to become a worthy Alto application. However, in 1980, Laurel was not state-of-the–art technology. Readers are encouraged to read the Laurel Manual for details.

False Claim #11: The term "email" belongs to CompuServe

As previously stated, V. A. Shiva Ayyadurai first coined the term "email" in 1978 at UMDNJ. Those five characters E-M-A-I-L were juxtaposed to name the main subroutine of the first email system. Ayyadurai coined the term email for the idiosyncratic reason that in 1978 FORTRAN IV only allowed for a six-character maximum variable and subroutine naming convention, and the RTE-IV operating system had a five-character limit for program names.

By 1980, Ayyadurai's email system was in production use at UMDNJ. Needless to say, email, the program, and its user manual were already in distribution around the UMDNJ campus. CompuServe has no clear claim to primacy here; a US Trademark database search shows the first commercial use of the term "email" in April, 1981. CompuServe applied for an email trademark on June 27, 1983, an effort that it abandoned in August 1984.

Email was a CompuServe trademark in 1983, but that remains a moot point for discussions of primacy. However, for the sake of clarity and transparency, two instances of CompuServe's 1983 email advertisements are included below:

This is called *interactive video* and is the future of the computer networks.

Both The Source and Compuserve (the two largest computer networks) are beginning to tap the wellspring of interactive video. Both began their services by offering electronic mail (called EMAIL on Compuserve and SMAIL on The Source), which meant you were no longer at the mercy of the Postal Service if your addressee was also hooked into the computer revolution.

Quick and easy-to-learn areas allow you to type in a message to anyone else on the network. And, your message is delivered in a few moments, or a couple of hours at most.

SIGs, or Special Interest Groups, is an area that has been pioneered by Compuserve, although The Source is now offering a "Participate" program that is similar. In a SIG, a person leaves a message about that group's interest. or he replies

Taken from the August 1983 edition of *Popular Mechanics* magazine page 107

It's important to note that CompuServe "popularized" the term "email" only to the extent that it triggered animosity and ridicule from system users; it was notoriously buggy and feature-light [ref. 11.1, ref. 11.2, ref. 11.3]. Interested readers are encouraged to explore the CompuServe Email documentation, as it existed for the Radio Shack TRS-80 in 1983, for details.

False Claim #12: "Email" has no single inventor

For nearly a decade, Raytheon's subsidiary, BBN, has been falsely promoting that it employs the "inventor of email," referring to Ray Tomlinson. The ceremony to honor Dr. Ayyadurai's accomplishment (50,000 lines of code, tapes, papers, and artifacts documenting his invention of email) by the Smithsonian Institution on February 16, 2012, appears to have caused great concern to BBN.

BBN has put a great deal of effort into their own branding as innovators, by claiming publicly that they are the "inventors of email." This branding involves juxtaposing the "@" symbol with the face of Ray Tomlinson as the "inventor of email." In fact, on BBN's home page the word "innovation" is visually juxtaposed to the @ logo, with Tomlinson's picture overlaid. Clearly, such a branding effort is to support BBN's sales efforts.

Before the recognition ceremony of Ayyadurai's invention, BBN sent press releases re-asserting that Tomlinson was the "inventor of email." Consistent with

LAST NIGHT WE EXCHANGED LETTERS WITH MOM, THEN HAD A PARTY FOR ELEVEN PEOPLE IN NINE DIFFERENT STATES AND ONLY HAD TO WASH ONE GLASS...

That's CompuServe, The Personal Communications Network For Every Computer Owner

And it doesn't matter what kind of computer you own. You'll use CompuServe's Electronic Mail system (we call it Email™) to compose, edit and send letters to friends or business associates. The system delivers any number of messages to other users anywhere in North America.

CompuServe's multi-channel CB simulator brings distant friends together and gets new friendships started. You can even use a scrambler if you have a secret you don't want to share. Special interest groups meet regularly to trade information on hardware, software and hobbies from photography to cooking and you can sell, swap and post personal notices on the bulletin board.

There's all this and much more on the CompuServe Information Service. All you need is a computer, a modem,

and CompuServe. CompuServe connects with almost any type or brand of personal computer or terminal and many communicating word processors. To receive an illustrated guide to CompuServe and learn how you can subscribe, contact or call:

CompuServe

Information Service Division, P.O. Box 20212
5000 Arlington Centre Blvd., Columbus, OH 43220

800-848-8990
In Ohio call 614-457-8650

An H&R Block Company

Taken from the January 1983 edition of *Byte* magazine

these efforts, industry insiders, supported by SIGCIS "historians," Ray Tomlinson, BBN supporters, and ex-BBN employees continued to perpetuate a false history of email by discrediting Ayyadurai's invention. They used revisionism and confusion to redefine and misuse the term email. Through these efforts, they redeclared Tomlinson, and thereby the BBN brand, as the singular "inventor of email," the "Godfather of email," and the "King of email," as reported in popular press releases between April 24–26, 2012.

In the midst of this self-promotion, they released hypocritical statements such as:

"Email has no single inventor. There are dozens, maybe hundreds, of people who contributed to significant incremental 'firsts' in the development of email as we know it today. Theirs was a collective accomplishment, and theirs is a quiet pride (or at least was until recent press coverage provoked them). Email pioneer Ray Tomlinson has said of email's invention that "Any single development is stepping on the heels of the previous one and is so closely followed by the next that most advances are obscured. I think that few individuals will be remembered."

This statement served to feign a false humility and "collaborative spirit," while isolating and dismissing Ayyadurai's singular and rightful position as the inventor of email. Ayyadurai did singularly create email, the system of interlocked parts emulating the entire interoffice paper mail system.

One ex-BBNer, Dave Walden, though part of the Tomlinson coterie acknowledged the following:

"Naturally this was discussed on the ex-BBN list. In my view, this "new guy" [Shiva Ayyadurai] has described something not quite like what the rest of us understand when we say 'email.'"[38]

Walden recognized the misuse of the term "email" as the transmission of text messages between terminals, as was the case with the early messaging systems such as MAIL. This text-message transmission can signify nearly all forms of digital communication—facsimiles, communicating word processors, online bulletin board systems, instant messaging clients, and formal communication.

However, email has a very clear meaning, as established by Ayyadurai in 1978: the electronic interoffice, interorganizational paper-based mail system. It includes all the features one expects from paper mail systems: memo composition, editing, drafts, sorting, archival, forwarding, reply, registered mail, return receipt, prioritization, security, delivery retries, undeliverable notifications, group lists, bulk distribution, and managerial/administrative functions. Like the interoffice mail system, it is meant to be an integrated system of parts, as accessible to a secretary as it is to a compiler writer. It has to be fault-tolerant, familiar, and universal. By this definition, Ayyadurai's invention is the only instance in which this level of integration was achieved, the same level we all experience now in products such as Gmail, Hotmail, and others.

Acknowledgments

It takes a lot to put together a book that spans nearly thirty-five years of history. The following people were extremely helpful in reviewing and providing important input as to the contents of this manuscript, including Sonu Matthew Abraham, Devon Sparks, and Tad Crawford and his team at Skyhorse Publishing. The stories in this document would not have been possible without those people in my early days at UMDNJ, including Leslie P. Michelson, Phil Goldstein, Bob Fields, David Ritacco, Marily Bodow, Marty Feuerman, my mom Meenakshi Ayyadurai, and Swamy Laxminaraynan. My high school teachers Stella Oleksiak and Gerald Walker and principal Alan Berlin were there to support and encourage me in my work, and they took a big chance on bending rules of the day so that I could travel to UMDNJ, to create email. And a special thanks to my sister Dr. Uma Dhanabalan, for being a good older sister and watching out for her young brother, while working at UMDNJ.

All the case studies in this book would not have been possible without the many people who came and went through the offices of EchoMail over those past twenty years: colleagues, friends, customers, and partners. Special love and blessings to Bruce Padmore, wherever you are. My dad, Vellayappa Ayyadurai, Dick Rosenblum, Ed Fredkin, Ted Johnson, G.M. O'Connell, Doug Ahlers, Tom Zawacki, and John Bradley, the angels who provided the right connections so I could build EchoMail. To the many others at EchoMail, over the years, including long-timers and those who believed and still do—Hariharan Subramanian, Ramachandran Subramanian, Kannan Arumugam, Subramanian Ramasubramanian, Manjula Balaji, and many others—I salute you for being with me as pioneers in an industry we literally helped to create and define.

Special thanks again to Martin Feuerman, my mom's colleague at UMDNJ, and another of God's angels, who told my mom about Professor Henry Mullish of New York University, and the special program at NYU that made it possible for a fourteen-year-old kid to learn computer programming in 1978.

Finally, my deepest thanks to my blood brothers and sisters, Leslie P. Michelson, John Contee, Lorraine Monetti, Devon Sparks, Eileen Cope, C. Forbes Dewey, Jr., Teddy Monetti, Matthew J. Labrador, Shekhar Shastri, Rocky Acosta, Richard Buckley, Renato Umeton, Laurie Cestnick, Usha Raghavan, Tom Zawacki, Noam Chomsky, Hauke Kite-Powell, Deepak Chopra, Deepa Rao, Todd Reily, Rob Wolff, Carole Kammen, Gene Deans, J. Paul Rickett, Neil Devine, (and those previously mentioned), who demonstrated through their actions the rare qualities of courage, friendship, and above all, love. They have stood strong against the "priesthood" of academia, "scholars," and the so-called "computer historians," to boldly defend and share a humble truth: a fourteen-year-old, brown-skinned, immigrant kid, working in Newark, New Jersey, invented email, in 1978—a fact that demonstrates a larger truth that innovation can take place anytime, anywhere, by anybody!

www.inventorofemail.com

About the Author

V. A. Shiva Ayyadurai is a scientist, technologist, entrepreneur, and educator. In 1978, while a fourteen-year-old high school student, he invented the world's first email system, which was the full-scale emulation of the inter-office paper-based mail system, for which he was awarded the first US Copyright for "email." He is a Fulbright Scholar, a Lemelson-MIT Awards Finalist, and a recipient of the Westinghouse Science Talent Honors Award. He holds four degrees from MIT.

Born in Bombay, India, V. A. Shiva moved to America in 1970 at the age of seven. He completed his secondary school education at Livingston High School. He pursued his bachelors, dual masters, and doctoral degrees at MIT, spanning the fields of electrical engineering and computer science, media arts and sciences, applied mechanics, and systems biology. V. A. Shiva's research on pattern recognition and large-scale systems development has resulted in multiple patents, numerous industry awards, new computational platforms such as CytoSolve, and commercial products such as EchoMail. He has also published works on topics involving science and industry.

Medicine has intrigued V. A. Shiva since the age of five when he would observe his grandmother, a farmer and healer, apply Siddha, one of India's most ancient forms of medicine, to heal and support local villagers near the small village of Muhavur in South India. Those early experiences drove him to pursue modern Western science and technology and Eastern medicine with the aim of becoming a scientist and healer. Over the last three decades, he has focused on formal Western research and study of developing new systems for pattern analysis across multiple disciplines. At the same time, he trained in many Eastern practices including various forms of yoga, meditation, and nutritional and herbal medicines, which he has learned from esteemed sages and masters through the oral tradition.

Today, he teaches a pioneering new course called Systems Visualization in the Department of Comparative Media Studies. He has also created Systems Health™, a revolutionary educational curriculum developed from his research in traditional medicines and systems biology, which is now being offered to major medical colleges and holistic healthcare centers. He is also the chairman & CEO of CytoSolve, Inc., and the executive director of the International Center for Integrative Systems located in Cambridge.

As an entrepreneur, he has started and successfully grown several start-up companies. In 1992 he created a program for the White House to automatically analyze and sort incoming emails from US citizens to President Bill Clinton, which was the foundation for his company EchoMail, Inc. EchoMail achieved a market valuation of nearly $200 million. He has appeared in several prominent publications including *MIT Technology Review, Wall Street Journal, New York Times, NBC News, USA Today*, as well as other major media platforms. The Improper Bostonian named Shiva among their "Top 40 Under 40." He has also authored books about the Internet and early social media, namely *Arts and the Internet* and *The Internet Publicity Guide*, respectively.

V. A. Shiva continues his passion for entrepreneurialism as managing director of General Interactive, a venture incubator that cultivates, mentors, and funds new start-ups in various areas including rural healthcare, media, biotechnology, and information technology, among others. He has launched Innovation Corps, which fuels innovation among teenagers worldwide. He serves as a consultant to CEOs and executive managers at Fortune 1000 companies, as well as government organizations such as the United States Postal Service, Office of Inspector General.

V. A. Shiva is a member of Sigma-Xi, Eta Kappa Nu, and Tau Beta Pi. He supports the Shanthi Foundation, which raises money to provide scholarships for the education of orphaned girls. He is also a supporter of various arts and nonprofit organizations including the Guggenheim Museum, Very Special Arts, National Public Radio, and the National Geographic Society. V. A. Shiva enjoys yoga, travel, tennis, animals, art, and architecture. He lives in Belmont, Massachusetts.

Endnotes

1. InnovationCorps (www.innovationcorps.org) is a project of the International Center for Integrative Systems, a 501 (c)(3) nonprofit organization.

2. This adage is an observation of Marshall McLuahn who was one of the 20th century's leading media theorists, also know for the comment, "the medium is the message."

3. Huffington Post "29th Anniverseary of Email," 2011, http://www.huffingtonpost.com/2011/08/30/email-turns-29-infographi_n_941699.html

4. Ayyadurai, V. A. S., 1978-1982 Papers and Notes of the University of Medicine and Dentistry of New Jersey (UMDNJ)'s interoffice, interorganizational paper-based mail system, submitted to the Smithsonian Institution on February 16, 2012. This table provides a detailed analysis of the system of interlocked parts.

5. Ayyadurai, V. A. S., FORTRAN IV Code Samples developed in 1978, submitted to US Copyright Office for "email," as a "Computer Program for Electronic Mail System," 1982; submitted to Smithsonian Institution, February 16, 2012. This table is derived from the core parts developed in the implementation of email.

6. http://inventors.about.com/od/estartinventions/a/email.htm

7. http://www.nethistory.info/History%20of%20the%20Internet/email.html

8. http://tinyurl.com/8373917, April 7, 2012.

9. http://socrates.berkeley.edu/~scotch/innovation/inventing_email.pdf

10. http://www.multicians.org/mx-net.html, April 2012.

11. http://gizmodo.com/5888702/corruption-lies-and-death-threats-the-crazy-story-of-the-man-who-pretended-to-invent-email, March 5, 2012.

12. http://tools.ietf.org/rfc/rfc733.txt

13. Article titled "A history of e-mail: Collaboration, innovation, and the birth of a system" http://www.washingtonpost.com/national/on-innovations/a-history-of-e-mail-collaboration-innovation-and-the-birth-of-a-system/2012/03/19/gIQAOeFEPS_story_3.html

14. See Larry Tesler's comments (who worked at Xerox, 1973-1980) on the internal development of Laurel: http://tinyurl.com/83nlq32. He acknowledges that he himself did not " . . . know what, if any, email systems based on unofficial Internet standards were implemented before 1979," but was aware that Laurel was still under development in 1979.

15. http://tools.ietf.org/html/rfc808

16. Vittal, John. MSG: A Simple Message System. Cambridge, MA: North-Holland Publishing Company, 1981.

17. See pg 4: http://www.multicians.org/thvv/psn-39.pdf

18. http://www.bitsavers.org/pdf/mit/ctss/CTSS_ProgrammersGuide_Dec69.pdf

19. http://www.multicians.org/thvv/mail-history.html, April 18th, 2012.

20. Vallee, Jacques. Computer Message Systems. New York: McGraw-Hill, 1984: 53-55.

21. Thompson, Gordon B. "What's the Message?" Computer Message Systems. Ottawa, Canada: North-Holland Publishing Company, 1981. Pages 1-6.

22. Schicker, Peter. "Computer-Based Mail Environments." Computer Networks 5 (1981): pages 435-443.

23. Vallee, Jacques. Computer Message Systems. New York: McGraw-Hill, 1984: xiii. Print.

24. Robinson, James G. "Introduction." An Overview of Electronic Mail Systems. Cambridge, MA: MIT, 1983. Page 4.

25. Vallee, Jacques. Computer Message Systems. New York: McGraw-Hill, 1984: page xiii.

26. See source listing.

27. See the July 1979 Wang Newsletter.

28. Trudell, Libby, Janet Bruman, and Dennis Oliver. "Distributed Electronic Mail Networks." Options for electronic mail. White Plains, N.Y.: Knowledge Industry Publications, 1984. Page 67.

29. Robinson, James G. "Computer-based Messaging Systems." An Overview of Electronic Mail Systems. Cambridge, MA: MIT, 1983. Page 32.

30. Schroeder, Michael D., Andrew Birrell, and Roger Needham. "Experience with Grapevine: The Growth of a Distributed System." ACM Transactions on Computer Systems 2.1 (1984): pages 3-23.

31. See the ALTO User Handbook for details.

32. This is well-demonstrated by Another Laurel Hack in the August 1979 Whole ALTO World Newsletter. Page 325.

33. Included as part of the Stanford Computer Science Department document Welcome to ALTO Land.

34. See MAXC Operation, May 1974.

35. See endnote 20 above, page 94.

36. As published in the April 1982 Communications of the ACM.

37. See his recent response to the acceptance of email into the Smithsonian.

38. From a February 22 SIGCIS-Members post.

Index

Books from Allworth Press

The Art of Digital Branding, Revised Edition
by Ian Cocoran (6 x 9, 272 pages, paperback, $19.95)

Brandjam: Humanizing Brands Through Emotional Design
by Marc Gobe (6 ¼ x 9 ¼, 352 pages, hardcover, $24.95)

Citizen Brand: 10 Commandments for Transforming Brand Culture in a Consumer Democracy
by Marc Gobe (6 ¼ x 9 ¼, 256 pages, hardcover, $24.95)

Emotional Branding, Revised Edition: The New Paradigm for Connecting Brands to People
by Marc Gobe (6 x 9, 344 pages, paperback, $19.95)

Building Design Strategy: Using Design to Achieve Key Business Objectives
by Thomas Lockwood (6 x 9, 272, paperback, $24.95)

Corporate Creativity: Developing an Innovative Organization
by Thomas Lockwood (6 x 9, 256, paperback, $24.95)

Design Thinking: Integrating Innovation, Customer Experience, and Brand Value
by Thomas Lockwood (6 x 9, 304, paperback, $24.95)

Brand Thinking and Other Noble Pursuits
by Debbie Millman (6 x 9, 336 pages, hardcover, $29.95)

Infectious: How to Connect Deeply and Unleash the Energetic Leader Within
by Achim Nowak (5 ½ x 8 ¼, 232 pages, hardcover, $24.95)

Power Speaking: The Art of the Exceptional Public Speaker
by Achim Nowak (6 x 9, 256 pages, paperback, $19.95)

The Pocket Legal Companion to Copyright: A User-Friendly Handbook for Profiting from Copyrights
by Lee Wilson (5 x 7½, 320 pages, paperback, $16.95)

To see our complete catalog or to order online, please visit *www.allworth.com*.